Against
Extraction

Against Extraction

Indigenous
Modernism
in the
Twin Cities

Matt Hooley

Duke University Press
Durham and London 2024

© 2024 Duke University Press
All rights reserved
Printed in the United States of America on acid-free paper ∞
Project Editor: Ihsan Taylor
Designed by Aimee C. Harrison
Typeset in Portrait Text by Westchester Publishing Services

Library of Congress Cataloging-in-Publication Data
Names: Hooley, Matt, [date] author.
Title: Against extraction : indigenous modernism in the Twin Cities /
Matt Hooley.
Description: Durham : Duke University Press, 2024. | Includes
bibliographical references and index.
Identifiers: LCCN 2023033081 (print)
LCCN 2023033082 (ebook)
ISBN 9781478030362 (paperback)
ISBN 9781478026129 (hardcover)
ISBN 9781478059363 (ebook)
Subjects: LCSH: Ojibwa Indians—Minnesota—Minneapolis
Metropolitan Area. | Ojibwa Indians—Minnesota—Saint Paul
Metropolitan Area. | Ojibwa Indians—Colonization—Minnesota. |
Ojibwa literature—History and criticism. | American literature—Indian
authors—History and criticism. | Ojibwa art—Minnesota. | Settler
colonialism. | Minnesota—Ethnic relations—Political aspects. | BISAC:
SOCIAL SCIENCE / Ethnic Studies / American / Native American Studies |
LITERARY CRITICISM / Indigenous Peoples in the Americas
Classification: LCC E99.C6 H66 2024 (print) | LCC E99.C6 (ebook) |
DDC 897/.333—dc23/eng/20231025
LC record available at https://lccn.loc.gov/2023033081
LC ebook record available at https://lccn.loc.gov/2023033082

Cover art: George Morrison (1919–2000), *Untitled (Dayton, Ohio)*,
1960. Brush and black ink on paper, 16 ½ × 13 ⅞ in. Courtesy of the
Estate of George Morrison / Briand Morrison.

Contents

Acknowledgments

Acknowledgments are an event and not a structure. And the fact that this book took me so long to write intensifies all the ordinary problems of the genre: how it depends on memory, and how difficult it is to describe the different ways that people have made it possible for me to write. What follows is so very far from a comprehensive appreciation of all of these people.

I began writing this book while on fellowship at the Institute of American Cultures and the American Indian Studies Center at the University of California, Los Angeles. Mishuana Goeman, Angela Riley, and all the extraordinary faculty and staff there gave me indispensable insight and space to reconceptualize this project. I have also received support from the Critical Ethnic Studies Summer Institute, the Center for the Humanities at Tufts, the Clemson Humanities Hub, and the Clemson University Office of Research Development. Elizabeth Ault is an expert and generous editor. I thank her for her knowledge of the fields this project speaks to, for the unwavering ethical commitment with which she works, and for sharing a loving determination to try to make sense of the strange and extraordinary place, the Twin Cities, this book is about. My thanks to Emily Shelton; Benjamin Kossak, Ihsan Taylor, and the staff at Duke University Press; my encouraging and insightful referees; and Sarah Osment for bringing the book into the world. Thank you, Jaida Grey Eagle, Emily Marsolek, the Minnesota Historical Society, the Minneapolis Institute of Art, the Weisman Art Museum, and Briand Morrison for making it possible to include the images reprinted in this book. I asked Craig Willse to help me think through basically every aspect of this book and basically every life decision I made while writing it. Unfortunately for him, I will never stop asking for his help. He is too wise an editor and far too dear a friend.

Sitting in on a seminar of Fred Moten's at the University of California, Riverside, I heard him reassure his students once that everyone has "to learn to want" to endure the often demoralizing work of reading and writing in the academy. There are so many people who taught me how to learn to want to write this book, including Kristin George-Bagdanov, Sherwin Bitsui, Rana Barakat, Orisanmi Burton, Jessica Cattelino, Sumita Chakraborty, Phil Deloria, Michael Elliott, Sarah Ensor, Maura Finkelstein, Santee Frazier, Tao Leigh Goffe, Christina Hanhardt, Angie Hume, Joan Naviyuk Kane, Eun Song Kim, Karen Kramer, Amy Lonetree, Layli Long Soldier, Mallory Lovice, Dana Luciano, Ted Martin, Annie McClanahan, Tiya Miles, Nancy Mithlo, Penelope Mitchell, Tyler Morgenstern, Michelle Niemann, Alyssa Mt. Pleasant, Margaret Noori, Gillian Osborne, Cody Reis, Margaret Ronda, Jen Shelton, Circe Sturm, Melanie Benson Taylor, Maggie Thompson, David Treuer, Jennifer Wenzel, Orlando White, and Will Wilson.

At Carleton College, I learned so much from Nancy Cho, Tom Church, Adriana Estill, Mary Hermes, Frank Morral, Bob Tisdale, and especially Michael McNally, who taught me how to recognize poetry in social practices. At the University of Wisconsin, I was fortunate to meet and work with Anna Andrzejewski, Ned Blackhawk, Russ Castronovo, Sarah Dimick, Jack Dudley, Travis Foster, Sebastian Frank, Josh Freker, Susan Stanford Friedman, Lenora Hanson, Doug Kiel, Jacques Lezra, Anne McClintock, Mario Ortiz-Robles, Omar Poler, Cyrena Pondrom, Theresa Schenck, Henry Turner, Aarthi Vadde, Rand Valentine, Skott Vigil, and Rebecca Walkowitz. Members of my dissertation committee—Lynn Keller, Rob Nixon, and Sean Teuton—have meant much more to me than that role would suggest. I came to Tufts feeling precarious and isolated, and many people contributed to an incomparably warm and generative intellectual community there (one that, I am relieved to have found, has extended well beyond the university's boundaries): Tom Abowd, Amahl Bishara, Heather Curtis, Kendra Field, Kareem Khubchandani, Nidhi Mahajan, Kris Manjapra, Mark Minch, Kamran Rastegar, Khury Petersen-Smith, Natalie Shapero, Christina Sharpe, and Adriana Zavala. It was also through Tufts that I met Lisa Lowe. There's no one more generous, committed, or brilliant I've ever met in the academy, and I am so grateful for her encouragement and her example.

I finished this book between jobs at Clemson and Dartmouth. Thank you to wonderful colleagues at both institutions: Desiree Bailey, Emily Boyter Hager, Colin Calloway, David Coombs, Matt Delmont, Bruce Duthu, Maziyar

Faridi, Laurie Furch, Jerad Green, Erin Goss, Mike LeMahieu, Brian McGrath, Lee Morrissey, Clare Mullany, Angela Naimou, Jami Powell, Elizabeth Rivlin, Will Stockton, Rhondda Thomas, M. Ty, Keri Crist Wagner, and Rachel Wagner. Students, too, have been essential to this book. With great patience, they have taught me about asking expansive questions, about trying to clarify the always-material stakes of study, and about always trying to write with bravery and belief. I know I have not finished with these lessons. Special thanks to Mina Brewer, Emma Brown, Eve Feldberg, Carissa Fleury, Morgan Freeman, Sophia Goodfriend, June Gordon, Joyce Harduvel, Raymond Henderson, Ben Kesslen, Brianna Moody, Jon Jon Moore, and Hannah Sparks.

In a really basic sense, writing is just a way to stay in and to try to know the world. Writing this book, I have learned that the only world I want is one with Kelsey Sheaffer. The care, creativity, and joy you bring to our life, every day, is the most extraordinary and humbling gift. Thank you for sharing all this with me, with Camper and Ham, and with our families.

Finally, the earliest inspiration for this book was probably my persistent inability to explain how the ready structures and language that we have to talk about kinship always fall so far short of describing the unlimited love, patience, and happiness given to me by my parents, Dan and Mary Hooley. It was my original lesson in the essential inextricability of love and the critique of the status quo. Thank you for this and for everything else. And however an impossibly insufficient gesture it is to say so, this book is for you.

P.1. George Morrison, *Collage IX: Landscape*, 1974, wood, 60 ⅛ × 168 ½ × 3 in. Minneapolis Institute of Art, the Francis E. Andrews Fund, 75.24. Reprinted courtesy of Briand Morrison.

Prologue

Collage: Landscape

In 1965, George Morrison started making landscapes out of driftwood. He gathered wood from Atlantic beaches near Provincetown, Massachusetts, where he rented a studio on breaks from teaching at the Rhode Island School of Design. He looked for scraps of wood grayed and weathered by the sea to the brink of abstraction, but that also bore some trace of human use or attachment ("bits of paint, half worn off," "rust stains or colors soaked in," "the top of an old scrub brush").[1] Morrison began each landscape, which he also called "wood collages" and "paintings in wood," by fitting together a few pieces in the bottom left corner of the frame that, along the broken lines of driftwood edges, gathered out into massive sweeps and rivulets of fragments to fill frames up to fourteen feet wide and five feet tall. Setting off the top quadrant of each collage, a single, twisted but unbroken line—a horizon line—is the only gesture spared from the turbulence of fracture and motion that characterizes the landscapes.

Morrison was born in 1919, in a house near the shore of Lake Superior, a member of the Grand Portage Band of Lake Superior Chippewa.[2] He was sent to a boarding school in Wisconsin, attended and graduated from the Minneapolis School of Art, and in 1944 moved to New York, where he made and showed work alongside Jackson Pollock, Willem de Kooning, Joan Mitchell, Robert Motherwell, Mark Rothko, and Franz Kline. During the years he lived on the East Coast, Morrison was excluded from exhibitions of "Indian art" that were coming into fashion in the US art market. In 1948, the Philbrook Art Center in Tulsa rejected his work, noting that it "was not painted in the traditional manner of your forefathers." And even when the Philbrook eventually did accept Morrison's work in 1964, the curator wrote to Morrison that she "was aware that [Morrison was]...not an artist in the 'Indian style.'"[3] Although this question of whether his work belonged in the category "Indian art" did not preoccupy Morrison, it is one that continues to dominate criticism of his work.[4] One reason, perhaps, is that Morrison began making driftwood landscapes just as he decided to move back to Minnesota in 1970 to join the faculty of the country's first American Indian studies program at the University of Minnesota, a move, he wrote, that was inspired by an "Indian connection...[and] the need to put certain Indian values into my work."[5] His move to the Twin Cities (Minneapolis/St. Paul), for which the driftwood landscapes became an avatar, is often interpreted as a pivot from an abstract period to a politically and ideologically situated one—a homecoming that structures a narrative of development in the life of a path-making Indigenous modernist.

Questions about the Indigenousness of art often displace questions about the Indigenousness of the places where that art is made and shown. It is a critical habit that has unfortunately structured much of the history of the interpretation of Morrison's work. Writing against that habit is one reason I wanted to write this book, to ask: How can we read art and place together under conditions of ongoing colonialism? Can practices of cultural interpretation denaturalize the coloniality of place and at the same time show how Indigenous art-making is always also Indigenous place-making? While these questions motivated this book, it is still important to me that the book not be mistaken as an attempt to resolve them. Therefore, before I turn to the central arguments and archives in the introduction, I want to use this prologue to stage these questions—not to answer them but to hold them open. This prologue is an experiment in writing the politics of art, Indigeneity, and land together that I hope will also function as an invitation for others to join in the urgent decolonial work of continually rewriting the entangled histories of place- and art-making to which each of us is connected.

Extraction and Cultural Interpretation

When Morrison returned in 1970, the Twin Cities seemed to be remaking itself. A city whose political and economic life had always centered the Mississippi and Minnesota rivers and the milling industries those rivers powered, was emptying itself into suburbs. Strategically devalued Black, Brown, and Indigenous neighborhoods were obliterated by a new interstate system as the manufacturing jobs on which those neighborhoods economically depended were replaced by the rise of a finance and retail economy increasingly situated in the suburbs. The Twin Cities' transformation is a familiar story of "urban crisis" in the United States, but one that hinged in more immediately identifiable ways than it did in other US cities on the unresolved contradiction of the social and jurisdictional form of the city that depends on the recurrent displacement and absorption of Indigenous people and land relations. In the 1960s and 1970s, the contradictions of Indigenous displacement and absorption was most famously manifest in the rise of the American Indian Movement.[6] Like other urban anti-racist and decolonization movements, AIM demanded equal access to employment, health care, safety, and education. What distinguished AIM's insurgency, from Alcatraz Island to the National Mall in Washington, DC, was the way it used occupation as a style of protest in order to denaturalize the settler city as a primary or coherent social and jurisdictional form. In one sense, the history of that denaturalization begins in the Twin Cities, where AIM started as a cop watch system, a street patrol, two Indigenous schools, and a local health care and legal support system before it became a national organization.

Only a few months after Morrison arrived in Minnesota, AIM occupied the Naval Air Station in Minneapolis: an unused military facility associated with Fort Snelling, the original colonial installation in Minnesota situated on a Dakota sacred site and adjacent to Wita Tanka, or "Pike Island," where thousands of Dakota people were held in a concentration camp in 1862. Like the concurrent occupation of Alcatraz, the Naval Air Station occupation was premised on a common provision of US treaties (in this case, the 1805 Treaty of St. Peter) that afforded for the return of unused federal land to Indigenous people. AIM demanded that the Naval Air Station be redeveloped as an Indigenous school, a demand that city and federal officials immediately rejected.[7] However the broader effect of AIM occupations like this one was to demonstrate the spatial and historical incoherence of the jurisdictional form of the settler city itself, to indicate its internal and irreparable broken edges, and to insist that those edges—never the spaces of vacancy or pathology the city made them out to be—were sites of abiding political motion.

As soon as Morrison arrived in the Twin Cities, he became an active member of AIM. At the same time, his driftwood landscapes were embraced by the cities' most powerful settler corporations and cultural institutions. He sold driftwood collages to the Minneapolis Institute of Art (MIA), General Mills, Honeywell, and Prudential—all organizations whose wealth depended on the seizure and extraction of Indigenous life and land.[8] He had a solo show at the Walker Art Center, a gallery named and funded by lumber baron T. H. Walker, and received public art commissions for a wood statue exhibited in a skyscraper named for the French explorer René-Robert Cavelier, Sieur de La Salle, and a granite collage built into a pedestrian mall named for Jean Nicolet, the French explorer sometimes credited with "discovering" the Great Lakes. How these corporations and institutions misread Morrison's work, and why they were interested in using that work to attach themselves to a narrative of the frontier past and neoliberal future of US colonialism, gets to questions at the heart of this book about how colonialism attempts and fails to control the meaning of art, about how colonial political and aesthetic forms are produced by the management of belonging, and about how we can clarify the always-material, always-ecological stakes of struggles around aesthetics and power, colonialism and decolonization. At a moment characterized both by insurgent assertions of urban Indigenous space and by systematic disinvestment from the cities' central Black and Indigenous neighborhoods, settler corporations and institutions leveraged a particular and violently constrained idea of the "Nativeness" of Morrison's art to facilitate a transformation of the spatial and economic order of the city. Here, Nativeness was not understood as a radical counterclaim to the operation of US colonialism but rather as a minority cultural aspect of it. I argue that, as such, colonial institutions misinterpreted Morrison's work and its relation to modern Indigeneity by obscuring the aesthetic and political invention to which that work was actively committed.

The first landscape Morrison sold after moving back to Minnesota is titled *Collage IX: Landscape*. The piece is made of driftwood that he brought from the Atlantic coast, and that he collected from the "alleys and backyards" of his neighborhood in St. Paul.[9] Like all of his collages, it is a study of material in social and historical relation. Morrison immersed himself in the process ("the chance element") of "taking driftwood or discarded wood and playing one piece against the other."[10] The patterns of "color, shape, and texture" that emerge are functions of Morrison's own manipulation and of the possibilities or limits of attachment manifest in each piece. Those patterns are ornate, massive, and mutating, and they express within the piece's huge frame a multidimensionality of motion beyond the vertical and horizontal, a coruscation of density, gesture, and reference. The complexity of this effect is intentional and has to do with how the wood pieces-in-pattern express a present of exposition and, like a shoreline, gather the residue of moving histories of growth, harvest, commodification, shipment, use, and disposal that mingle below and beyond that present. For Morrison, those histories were insistently environmental and social, and they generate an animating tension that never resolves into familiar postures of presence or absence, location or loss.

Collage, for Morrison, is both a response to the formal operation of colonial extraction and a practice of ecological invention. In a formal sense, Morrison's interest in collage is plainly unrecuperative. The pieces of driftwood he used are not joined to represent or restore what of them was lost to extraction, and in this sense *collage* does not refer to a total effect of fragments rearranged into pattern. In Morrison's work, collage is better understood as attention to the formal and affective generativity of wood worn—in odd angles and unnatural lightness, and in subtly incurvate or arching sanded surfaces—to extractive remains. It is a practice that collects both wood arrayed in a fluid pattern and the interstitial spaces between each piece, and thereby creates a formal tension between what, of each piece of driftwood, it is and is not possible to connect. Morrison remembered the history that preceded the wood's inclusion in the collage ("There was an interesting history in those pieces—who had touched them, where they had come from") and its eventual decay ("The wood won't last forever, I know that").[11] Thus we can read the gaps between driftwood pieces as a space not of loss but of organic exchange— where, within the collage, the pieces literally gather and decay together.

If, for Morrison, collage is a way of gathering with and among the absent, the other primary formal framework of the piece—landscape—is a rethinking of the sociality of setting. The term is one that Morrison hesitated around or qualified when he talked about the collages. "I think a respectful, knowl-edgeable person," he reflected, "would know that they're paintings in wood, landscapes."[12] Later, he added: "I imagine that people see the wood first. They don't look at it as a landscape painting, though it's subtitled *Landscape*. They may not even see the horizon line at first. The initial appeal comes from the wood itself, from the tactile surface."[13] In a colonial context, as W. J. T. Mitchell notes, landscape is "a medium" and a making, an enclosure fantasy. Landscape is the imagination of space primally unclaimed but through whose mixing of proximity and spaciousness property is remade as an effect of see-ing, "'the dreamwork' of imperialism."[14] In Morrison's collage, these dynam-ics are referenced and actively thwarted. For Morrison, landscape is also a medium and is concerned with how art participates in the politics of space. But whereas imperial landscape derives a rhetoric of control out of a con-struction of spatial ideality ("the antithesis of 'land'"), Morrison's landscape problematizes interpretive control by revealing the generative indistinction between space and land. As he points out, the experience of observing the collage is one that frustrates the acquisitive choreography of spectacle: "They don't look at it as a landscape." Rather, the force of the collage is affective. The piece draws the observer to it, to touch it, in "an appeal," as Morrison points out, that "comes from the wood itself." The effect, then, is not the abstraction of or from an idea of land but a feeling of being overcome by the materiality of land, even in the moment of observing the collage in the gallery. Morrison's landscape makes land and, as such, resets the terms of its encounter beyond interpretation, closer, perhaps, to something like the terms of relation.

The MIA purchased *Collage IX: Landscape* in 1975, the year after it completed a massive, $30 million expansion to its main building. Designed by the renowned Japanese architect Kenzo Tange, the addition was intended to modernize and expand the museum's founding democratic concept: a public exhibition space joined to an art school and a theater. As a part of that expansion, the museum updated its curatorial scheme, adding the department first called Primitive Art before it was renamed Art of Africa and the Americas, in which *Collage IX: Landscape* would be exhibited. The MIA is situated in a neighborhood that became the vibrant center of Indigenous life and organizing in Minneapolis in the aftermath of postwar white disinvestment. Originally, it was land seized from Dakota people in the mid-nineteenth century by settler John T. Blaisdell.[15] Blaisdell sold the lumber and eventually some of the land itself to Dorilus Morrison, a man who started the city's first industrial sawmill and eventually became Minneapolis's first mayor. Dorilus Morrison made a fortune milling lumber harvested from all over the state, including from thousands of acres of pine forest he bought himself—land that had been acquired through a treaty with Ojibwe leaders in 1837 whose terms (e.g., the provision of Ojibwe hunting and fishing rights) were never upheld by the United States.[16] In 1911, Dorilus Morrison's son, Clinton, donated the land the family bought from Blaisdell to Minneapolis for the construction of a museum whose founding principle, characteristic of early twentieth-century progressivism, was (in the words of its first director, Joseph Breck) to liberate the museum from the model of "'the storehouse' [or] . . . 'prison of arts'" and to "extend no less cordial a welcome to the humbler amateurs than . . . to 'carriage folk.'"[17]

Like the other corporations and institutions that acquired George Morrison's collage landscapes in the early 1970s, the MIA is an effect and a technology of extraction. Here and throughout this book, extraction is a cultural and an ecological concept; it signals both how forms of colonial belonging proliferate around Indigenous land dispossession and how those forms remake themselves through the management of ecological meaning. Thinking about the MIA through the lens of extraction is less about singling out that institution—or even the institutional form of the museum—than it is about showing how colonial cultural forms that organize the politics of belonging function as thresholds of the constant transformations of land, capital, and power on which the broader operation of US colonialism depends. For instance, the museum's self-concept as a public institution is only possible through a recurrence of Indigenous alienation: of the land under the museum, of the trees and water through which Dorilus Morrison made a fortune, of the civic investment that city officials directed to a colonial museum in an Indigenous neighborhood instead of the Indigenous school that AIM asked to be installed on the abandoned naval air station. And each such recurrence elaborates its publicness in a particular way, as a derivative of what Dene scholar Glen Coulthard calls "persistent" colonial accumulation, as a primal symbol of colonial occupation (what Jean O'Brien calls "firsting"), and as a threshold from or into which Indigenous life can be categorically excluded or assimilated.[18] Thus the museum, like other colonial institutions, transforms multiple spatial, economic, and political operations of extraction into a differential experience of access. For those it reproduces as subjects of extraction, it makes access (to land, to capital, to the public, to knowledge of what is excluded from the public) available and ideologically defining. For the people and the ecological relations it reproduces as objects of extraction, it makes being available to access ontologically defining.

The MIA's acquisition of *Collage IX: Landscape* helped define Morrison as an Indigenous modernist for the art world and for the Twin Cities in part by exhibiting the piece in the Primitive Art and then Art of Africa and the Americas department. By curating the work in this way, the MIA used Morrison to institutionalize a relationship between modernity and Indigeneity that erases the specificity of Indigenous claims to land. In the shift from Primitive Art to Art of Africa and the Americas, the MIA replaced a violent temporal (anachronizing) universalization of Indigeneity with a spatial (globalizing) one—a tactic Joanne Barker terms the "racialization of the Indian," in which "the notion that indigenous peoples are members of sovereign political collectivities is made incomprehensible ... [by] collaps[ing] indigenous peoples into minority groups that make up the rainbow of multicultural difference."[19] The fact that Morrison was a member of a tribal community whose expropriated land was the economic precondition for the MIA (itself also physically built on seized Dakota land) is transformed by a curatorial gesture that locates the museum in a global landscape of difference rather than evince the political contradictions of its spatial and temporal location. For Barker, "racialization" means replacing the treaty relationship between tribes and other nations with a political minority status, theorized in the Marshall Trilogy as a condition of "wardship."[20] And as she and other Indigenous studies scholars have pointed out, that erasure is not singular but recurrent. It recurs whenever colonial structures are thrown into crisis, expand, or remake themselves, what Patrick Wolfe defines as the "structure not ... event" of settler colonialism.[21] Barker's use of "racialization" in this context is comparative—in which Indigeneity stripped of its sovereign claim to land seems to make it comparable to positions of political minority already naturalized within US racial capitalism as landless and nonsovereign. However, the way colonial institutions used Morrison's collages at this moment of urban transformation invites an elaboration of this theory of racialization to understand how the colonial construction of modern Indigeneity as landless also served the intrinsically anti-Black discourse of civic revitalization.

In the aftermath of suburbanization, civic and business leaders invested in sites like the MIA and Nicollet Mall as spaces to return public interest to the downtown. In such spaces, Morrison's collage landscapes—works whose aesthetic interest in fragment and pattern were misconstrued as thematizing political unity from individual difference—were exhibited as avatars of a new urban, multicultural public life.[22] Here I am interested in how a discourse of the public "life" Morrison's collages were used to ornament operated in the city both metaphorically and literally on the level of biology and ecology. As in other gentrifying cities, Twin Cities officials relied heavily on metaphors of health (lifeblood, vitality, and growth) and damage (blight, disease, decay) to advertise and fundraise for investments like the MIA expansion and the Nicollet Mall renovation. As in other cities, that rhetoric was deployed on behalf of a revitalization that produced new forms and distributions of environmental violence outside of revalued urban spaces. Because expressed interest in renewed urban spaces was economic, revitalization in the Twin Cities depended on a classic neoliberal model of financing and governance. Remaking retail and cultural spaces "to bring life back to the street" depended on tax incentives and regulatory easements that concentrated profit around a few corporations and redistributed environmental vulnerability to poor and rural communities around the state and city.[23] Today the catastrophic toxification of the state's soil and water as a result of manufacturing, mining, and toxic dumping by companies like 3M and Honeywell—who directly invested in and benefited from the cities' revitalization—are only beginning to be understood.[24]

Within the cities themselves, the ecological logic of urban revitalization also depended on the "dysselection" of Black life as the governing concept of public life.[25] That dysselection was literalized when white federal, state, and city officials routed the new interstate connecting Minneapolis and St. Paul (I-94) through the Rondo neighborhood—the largest and most cherished Black neighborhood in St. Paul.[26] The destruction of 650 Black homes and over 100 Black-owned businesses in the name of heightened cultural and economic exchange between Minneapolis and St. Paul concretized the necropolitical logic of the cities' public life. In the aftermath of the police murder of Philando Castile in 2016, anti-racist protesters trenchantly marked the legacy of this concept of public life by stopping traffic on I-94, exactly at the site where the Rondo neighborhood once stood.[27]

Writing against Resolution

This prologue is an attempt to think about a work of art and a city together, to track the ways they are connected by genealogies of life and space in motion. At the same time, it is an effort to avoid repeating the reduction of both art and the city to and by colonial practices of interpretation, valuation, and recovery—the way the meaning of Morrison's life, his work, and Indigenous people in Minnesota, for instance, have been managed through the cultural economies of extraction that I have outlined. In this sense, to think about art and place together is primarily an incitement to reading and writing differently. How do we think and write about—which is to say around or among— forms linked by moving histories of colonialism and decolonization, seizure and endurance, domination and repair?

In this book, I try to hold open the question of how to write about art and place together by attending to convergences of culture and power that do not resolve to ready formations of identity, jurisdiction, or discipline. I bookmark these convergences with the word *against*: an ambivalent term that signals the trenchant opposition to US colonialisms that characterizes all the texts I write about, and the inescapable sense of proximity—the spatial, ideological, and social friction—that is a condition of production of decolonial art and organizing. It is also a term that expresses key methodological features of Morrison's collages, including their attention to generative possibilities of the meager, fraught, and collapsing spaces where ideas and materials in proximity are transformed but never resolved.

Writing-against as a mode of collaboration with difference is also important to me, a non-Indigenous person writing about Indigenous land and art. In one sense, it marks a familiar, and perhaps facile, aspiration to conditional alignment: that my writing can join the writing and organizing I describe in this book in opposing the legal, cultural, environmental, and political extraction that drives US colonialisms. But perhaps harder and more useful is the sense that this book is a challenge to account for the spatial, economic, and political proximity between the ideas and histories that have made me and the Indigenous land, people, and texts I consider here—a proximity uninvited by Ojibwe and Dakota people, and one structurally predisposed, as a function of colonialism, to my benefit. One reason to write this book is to ask if that proximity can mean something other than extraction, and that is also something other than resolution: if what can be made in that proximity can have meaning that does not just accrue to non-Indigenous people, and if what can be unmade are inherited ideological and disciplinary dispositions that understand proximity as something to be claimed or defended against.

Introduction

Where Extraction Takes Place

W hen the City of Minneapolis was officially recognized by the Minnesota Territorial Legislature in 1856, Franklin Avenue marked its southern border. Stretching east from a lake, Wíta Tópa, across the city to Haha Wakpa, the Mississippi River, it was a thoroughfare made to set the new settler city off from the surround.[1] Franklin Avenue was an infrastructure of colonial transit in both an economic and a phenomenological sense: a threshold that gave the city shape by managing the flow of people and capital along and across it. Within a few decades, as new industries and communities grew around it, Franklin Avenue, like Minneapolis's other oldest streets, no longer marked the city's outer limit. The city's edges became the grid of its central neighborhoods. But unlike those other old streets, Franklin Avenue never stopped being a borderland.

I.1. (above) George Morrison, *Untitled*, 1975. Minneapolis American Indian Center. Photograph: Jaida Grey Eagle. Reprinted courtesy of Jaida Grey Eagle.

Today, Franklin Avenue runs like a seam between communities that, anywhere else in the Twin Cities, would be more strictly segregated. Wealthy white and middle-class neighborhoods press against established queer, Indigenous, and Black neighborhoods, all shored against the southern edge of the city's financial district. For a century and half, it has been a street where immigrants, laborers, racialized and relocated people have lived and refused to become absorbed into the homogenizing cultural economy of the settler Midwest. Along or near Franklin Avenue, the city's most powerful engines of cultural assimilation—the Minneapolis Institute of Art, the Walker Arts Center, the University of Minnesota—stand in dissonant proximity to remarkable formations of anti-assimilatory community organizing like the United States' only urban housing project with an Indigenous preference, Little Earth, the largest Somali American community nicknamed "Little Mogadishu," and, for a while, the majority-Indigenous Franklin/Hiawatha houseless encampment. As a place where people have so steadfastly refused to reduce their lives to the meager fantasies of settler racial and economic incorporation, Franklin Avenue has always vexed and still yet vexes the cadastral fantasy of the stable form of the Twin Cities itself.

In 1975, Franklin Avenue also became the site of George Morrison's largest wood landscape, an 18-by-99-foot mural on the exterior of the newly built Minneapolis American Indian Center (MAIC). In many ways, the funding and production of the mural were part of federal and local governmental efforts to assimilate the vibrant urban Indigenous community of the Twin Cities into a regime that Jodi Melamed calls "liberal multiculturalism."[2] In the aftermath of relocation, and amid the rise of Indigenous decolonial radical movements like the American Indian Movement (AIM), funding for the MAIC came from sources including the 1964 Economic Opportunity Act, which sought to redirect community organizing efforts against the violences of capitalism and systematic land seizure via the promise of benevolent inclusion into colonial economic and cultural modernity.[3] On a local level, the MAIC was part of the development of what Minneapolis calls the "American Indian Cultural Corridor" along Franklin Avenue, which includes offices for the Native American Community Development Institute and the American Indian Industrial Opportunities Center. From the standpoint of federal and local colonial officials, transforming the street on which AIM started into a "corridor" for inclusion into capitalism and multiculturalism was both about executing what Melamed calls the "counterinsurgency against the robustly material anti-racisms of the 1960s and 1970s" and about closing down the social and jurisdictional opening those revolutionary movements opened within the form of the city itself.[4]

However, neither this political economic context nor even the concurrent academic institutionalization of Native American and Indigenous studies (NAIS), which also motivated the production of Morrison's mural, comprehensively encompasses the social or aesthetic meaning of the piece. I argue that the mural—an example of the approach to Indigenous modernism I theorize in this introduction—antagonizes colonial fantasies of cultural inclusion and political coherence at the same time it generatively remembers the continuities of Indigenous life and land those orders obscure. The mural holds open the space of unsanctioned gathering, organizing, and invention that is characteristic of the borderland history of Franklin Avenue that the form of the colonial city constantly works to disavow or forget. Made of stained cedar boards, the piece is distinguished by five clusters of intersecting chevrons joined to each other by fields of further, emanating chevrons. The mural overflows with movement and pattern, yet it also reflects itself exactly across both horizontal and vertical axes. The wood's variegated color produces a sense of depth and softness that contrasts the stern glass and concrete surfaces of the building that frames it. Morrison did not officially title the piece, but he later wrote that he wished it were called *Turning the Feather Around*—a reference both to a feather's barb and rachis structure that inspires the chevron formations and to the way the assemblage creates "the illusion" that the "chevrons are turning around."[5] Like his driftwood landscapes, the sense of motion that animates the MAIC mural is not progressive but rather a function of how the piece holds and circulates vectors of pattern in tension, never resolving them. The mural seems constantly to be turning into itself: a fractal dimensionalization of space and an opening of and out of the rudiments of surface. In aesthetic terms, the MAIC mural offers a theory of irresolution that defies totalizing concepts of composition or scale, a kind of spatial surrealism that abrades the logics of inclusion and multicultural belonging with which the Twin Cities tries to enclose it.

In 1975, when Morrison's mural was finished, the Twin Cities were thick with political change and contradiction. As I described in the prologue, what brought Morrison back to Minneapolis and St. Paul was the rise of new forms of Indigenous organizing, including AIM, the creation of the Native American studies program at the University of Minnesota, and educational and community-building organizations like the MAIC and the Survival Schools.[6] At the same time, like many other American cities, the Twin Cities were in the midst of a devastating physical and economic reinvention under the terms of neoliberalism, including new forms of public investment in infrastructures of white indemnity (e.g., mass incarceration, the interstate system, and the suburbs) and the privatization of health care, education, and housing. In this context, Morrison's mural is a work of Indigenous cultural production that exists in unsettled relation with the Twin Cities; with the land and life the Twin Cities extracts in order to exist; with enduring and shifting constructions of Indigeneity; and with the Indigenous people who came to the MAIC looking for sociality, for work, and for care. Precisely because the mural refuses the racializing and institutionalizing sequestrations of Indigeneity enunciated by colonial disciplinarity or jurisdictionality, it is a piece whose meaning the Twin Cities does not control—a piece that, at the center of a colonial city, marks the kinetic and proliferating limits of colonial spatial and political coherence.

This book centers works of Indigenous cultural production that, like Morrison's *Turning the Feather Around*, refuse and deconstruct the promises of belonging, peace, immunity, and protection associated with incorporation into modern colonial formations and cultural practices. These are works that antagonize the formal, affective, and historical coherence of forms like the colonial city from positions that can appear at first politically ambivalent, compromised, or undetermined. Ultimately, however, they are works that theorize and intensify the failures of colonial political and cultural systems with rigor and inventiveness even when it seems that affirming those structures is the only alternative to unabating conquest. In this book, I use the term *Indigenous modernism* to index these works, the expansive traditions of tribal cultural production of which they are a part, and their shared investment in holding Indigenous space and thought out against US colonialisms in ways that are analytically and socially generative.

As I elaborate in this introduction, I understand the critical significance of this term, Indigenous modernism, in two senses. First, I argue that these texts theorize their own relationship to colonial modernity and specifically to the always environmental and social operation of power in the US context. These are texts that create new ways to read and understand the violence of colonial political and cultural worlds, including how fictions of development, social belonging, spatial expansion, and historical progress are created through the processes I bookmark as extraction and the infrastructural distribution of interiority. These processes animate a fundamental quality of US colonial structures, which is that they do not produce anything other than the conditions for their own violent reproduction. Extraction is not just the precondition for colonial worlds; it is its governing logic and only outcome. The structures and even the ideas colonialism seems to make anew are never anything other than the infrastructural redistribution of seized life and land under the rubric of interiority. Put differently, the texts I associate with the term *Indigenous modernism* show where—which is to say, under what conditions—extraction takes place.[7] Here, I use *where* as a nominal relative to describe the conditions in which colonial formations seem to occur, or take place, as historically and materially coherent even as they are only ever the effects of the seizure and the illusion of succession (the taking, displacement, or replacement) of Indigenous life and land.

The second critical contribution these texts make is a generative challenge for disciplinary frameworks of cultural and historical analysis that are themselves the effects of extraction.[8] The works I center in this book all bear a real and ongoing relation to land and to the Indigenous communities that the modern formation "the Twin Cities" extracts to exist. Even as we might be given to describe these texts therefore as "from" or "about" that colonial jurisdictional fantasy "the Twin Cities," as occurring within constructions of temporality defined by US historiography, or as expressing a stylistic or political disposition resonant with certain versions of US or global modernisms, they also always vex and exceed these frameworks. They sustain continuities of spatial, historical, and aesthetic meaning that the premises of colonial jurisdiction and discipline are designed to foreclose, and, as such, they participate in a critical (re)generativity, a remembering of where, with what land, extraction takes place.

Of the colonial constructs against which these texts are composed, the form of the city in particular complicates the task of situating the relation of these texts to land within colonialism studies, environmental humanities, and NAIS. Within colonialism studies and the environmental humanities, my attention to the archival relation to place and power indicated by the formation "the Twin Cities" prompts questions about whether it might be mistaken as a city too remote or too small to stage a general critique of colonial extraction.[9] Here the mistake would be to assume that the impression of its provinciality is either unintentional or real. The texts I consider in the chapters that follow all demonstrate how the illusion of being inapposite to colonial power is itself a colonial tactic and an effect of the cities' repression of global political antagonisms. In other words, these texts show that what has made the Twin Cities seem forgettable within critical or historical accounts of global power is precisely how the formation operationalizes the forgetting of both what it displaces and its own mechanisms of displacement. This illusion of obscurity, this mendacity of settlement, is one way that archival power organizes colonial worlds generally.[10] And it is one way that the form of the Twin Cities is in fact intimately connected to histories of colonialism that, via the formal politics of liberal humanism, unfold in supposedly unremarkable places everywhere.[11]

That this illusory provincialism marks an integration of the Twin Cities into global power also presents a considerable analytical challenge. How do we attend to the actual political and cultural histories of this place without inverting that provincialism into a new historiographical exceptionalism? Here, at the same time that it generates a critique of global power, the Indigenous modernist disposition *against* colonialism also illuminates histories of decolonial cultural production that are incommensurable and materially specific to the land the Twin Cities extracts.[12] That is, while these texts reveal the Twin Cities to be a formal replication of colonial power, they bear a relation to the Twin Cities as elaborations of decolonial traditions whose political and social horizons are more specific and more expansive than global, comparative analytics can register. As they antagonize settlement, these texts open space for organizing with land itself, thereby joining histories of decolonization from the Dakota Uprising to AIM to the uprisings following the murders of Jamar Clark, Philando Castile, George Floyd, Daunte Wright, and Amir Locke, among others. Thus, the critical disposition *against* resonates with what Leanne Betasamosake Simpson and Glen Coulthard call "grounded normativity," where opposition and proximity are always both expansively social (a "fierce and loving mobilization" of decolonial organizing) and specifically grounded (an "intimate relation to place").[13]

That Indigenous modernist texts ground a critique of abstract colonial cultural and jurisdictional formations with material and generative relations with land is one way they engage what Raymond Williams calls the "problem of perspective" inherent to the colonial city form: the way the city produces the sense of its coherence and discreteness via a false antonymy to land (or "country"), and that this antonymy is itself an effect of extraction.[14] That is to say, the texts at the center of this book respond to this problem by showing how the city and Indigenous art produced there *are* land. That they are made of and make land means that literary historical assessments of their political or spatial belonging are qualified in ways that are always more material and more expansive than colonial disciplines or jurisdictions can express.[15] Thus, rather than understanding these texts' relation to the Twin Cities as their participation in a cosmopolitan, nationalist, or global modernism, we might more accurately think of them in terms of a modernism, among other things, of the prairie, of rivers and of the convergence of the Wakpa Mnisota and Haha Wakpa rivers in particular, and of the Indigenous people and living intellectual traditions that sustain and are sustained by that land.

Positioning these texts' intervention within colonialism studies and NAIS, however, this critical rematerialization of the city risks overstabilizing the relation between Indigeneity, art, and land in the context of extraction. While the form of the Twin Cities occupies Dakota land specifically, its extractive operation is not geographically or historically limited. Because Indigenous people from everywhere make life and art in the Twin Cities, their cultural production contributes to remaking land everywhere they are from. The formal and jurisdictional expression of occupation ("the city") is not identical to the scope of extraction or of Indigenous modernist (re)generativity, and thus the seemingly straightforward archival conceit that organizes this book—Indigenous texts produced in or about the Twin Cities—also refers to ongoing histories of extraction and (re)generation that unfold in the United States and all over the world.

Therefore, rather than attempting anything like a comprehensive account of Indigenous modernism in the Twin Cities, this book focuses on a single arc of texts composed by Anishinaabe writers and artists in or about—which is to say, against—that formation. This is, on one hand, an archival delimitation symptomatic of my own training, and one that should not be read as the suggestion that these texts could stand in for Indigenous modernist cultural production in the Twin Cities generally or for the relation between Isáŋyathi Dakota art and organizing and the land the Twin Cities occupies specifically. On another hand, it is a choice meant to underscore the expansiveness of Indigenous creativity that challenges how colonial jurisdictional limits structure cultural archival conventions. For Ojibwe writers and artists displaced to a colonial city, built on Dakota land, making and interpreting art elaborates what Robert Warrior calls "intellectual sovereignty" as a materially salient and politically and spatially creative practice. Reflecting on Vine Deloria's *Custer Died for Your Sins*, Warrior describes the politics of Indigenous cultural and critical production as inextricable from histories of struggle against colonialism: "Contemporary American Indian politics would have to grapple, [Deloria] argued, with a situation that made demands that required the creation of new categories of existence and experience."[16] Warrior continues, "what is now critical for American Indian intellectuals committed to sovereignty is to realize that we, too, must struggle for sovereignty, *intellectual sovereignty*, and allow the definition and articulation of what that means to emerge as we critically reflect on that struggle."[17] Although I elaborate the relation between Indigenous modernism and sovereignty below, Warrior's account usefully stresses the way intellectual sovereignty is necessarily responsive to the historical contingencies of struggle and is intrinsically inventive rather than normative. These axioms should also extend to the ways we interpret modern Indigenous texts and prompt us toward analytical postures sensitive to multiplicity and heterogeny of art practices whose intellectual, political, and material generativity exceeds the spatial and imaginative delimitations implied by the colonial city form.

The remarkable critical force of the work of the five Anishinaabe literary and visual modernists I consider in this book is a function of how they are ambivalently positioned against colonial formations, like the Twin Cities, that normalize extraction. The material and political conditions for the production of their work is neither reducible to nor extricable from the histories of colonial jurisdiction, discipline, and culture through which we are given to interpret urban Indigenous cultural production. This is an ambivalence that I read not as a failure of these texts to have achieved a stable separatism from colonial formations, but as a demonstration and intensification of the failure of those formations to realize their totalizing extractive project. Within Indigenous literary studies, one way of theorizing this kind of critical force, born in the blur of opposition and proximity to colonial power, is via Scott Lyons's formulation of the "x-mark."[18] In strictly historical terms, Lyons's term references the way some Indigenous people signed treaties: by signing Xs in the space those treaties gave them to attach their names to documents that, for instance, often enacted the dispossession of their land and communities. Lyons argues that in the ambivalence and obliqueness of that gesture, "a contaminated and coerced sign of consent made under conditions that are not of one's making," Indigenous signatories developed a generatively nontransparent modality of political and social intention against the colonial terms and demands "signing" supposedly consents to.[19]

X-marks are not, or not only, signatures in a colonial jurisprudential sense because they refuse the reduction of politics to the form of the individual subject that treaties as genres require. X-marks are rhetorical enactments of Indigenous world-making that, Lyons argues, are predicated on practices of human and epistemic motion, the production of difference, and continuities of relation that are durable and irreducible to colonial law. On the page of the treaty, x-marks are aporias. They are demarcations of acknowledgment of the impossible and incoherent terms of colonial agreement—namely, the violent fantasy that the question of land might be decided according to liberal distributions of interiority (e.g., the subject, the jurisdiction, the resource, the protected or unprotected noncitizen, the cultural artifact). X-marks refer to and throw into relief the impossible conditions of their production. They are signs that irrepressibly shimmer between word and visual art and that point out but never agree to the theatricality of the colonial bargain as a political document or to colonial belonging as a political outcome.

More than a work we might situate in the history of the Twin Cities or in the history of a given disciplinary canon, I read Morrison's mural on the exterior wall of the MAIC as an x-mark. It is a piece that directly acknowledges the political and disciplinary terms of its production but refuses to reconcile or reduce its meaning to those terms. In doing so, it holds open a living and unsettled space of Indigenous social and intellectual production on Franklin Avenue, a gesture that holds in irresolution the geopolitical meaning of the cities that surround it because the aesthetic and political coherence of the colonial city in general always depends on the closure, the extraction, of the meaning of Indigenous life and land. In his autobiography, Morrison thinks back on and worries about the piece, how it will last and how it will be kept. He specifically worries about how its meaning might be kept from collapsing into the MAIC and the economy of political interest of which it, as an aspect of the city's material and cultural infrastructure, is necessarily linked: "Now the mural needs refurbishing. People don't seem to care about the Indian center. They probably just think the mural is the side of the building. They don't understand that it originated as a work of art.... I'd like to put in spotlights and have a plaque made for the mural that states it is an original work of art. It would be nice to call it Turning the Feather Around. A mural for the Indian."[20] What "art" means for Morrison here is the way the piece is irreducible to and yet inextricable from the building, the cities, the capricious and devastating shifts of interest intrinsic to the politics of liberal multiculturalism, and even—held in that loving but oblique prepositional intention "for"—discourses of Indigeneity mobilized within academic and insurgent organizational contexts like AIM. Like the x-marks Lyons understands as gestures of Indigenous world-making that is never settled, Morrison's mural is a site of unfinished relation as long as it is held open by and to Indigenous interpretation.

US Cultures of Extraction

As an analytic, Indigenous modernism is concerned with ordinary colonial formations. In other words, it is concerned with the forms and structures integral to the specific political project of colonialism but that also seem to host the temporal, spatial, and social experience of everyday life in the United States. Formations like the city, or the Twin Cities, seem to answer ordinary questions including where or when we came to be here, and how we came to be together; they are formations whose limits and whose histories give shape to our experiences, even when we disavow or disidentify with them. One premise of this book is that such formations are never stable or autonomous, as they advertise themselves to be. The jurisdictional boundedness of the Twin Cities, the way its carceral, cultural, and economic power gives it shape, is never fixed because it always depends on the ever-intensifying extraction of Indigenous land and life. In the chapters that follow, I account for this quality of colonial formations by approaching them as systems of distribution, as infrastructures that move and manage people and land as the conditions of production of the illusion of colonial state and cultural coherence. Colonial infrastructures are protean; they obtain through transit and constantly reinvent and reproduce themselves in order to secure the steady expansion of state power. When thinking about the colonial formation "Minnesota" (as in the first chapter's consideration of William Warren's life and work), it is useful to recall that the systems that distribute political, cultural, and carceral power—the capitol, the university, and the state prison—were established prior to the state itself. This is not because these structures enacted a singular, originating distribution of power, but because they function as infrastructures through which the state, by defining and managing distributions of power, culture, and violence, can constantly reinvent itself.

In the course of writing or analyzing the history of formations like "Minnesota," one risk is that history itself becomes an infrastructure that administrates distributions of cultural meaning such that colonial extraction is normalized or obscured. This is a risk that Michel-Rolph Trouillot underscores when he argues that historical narratives that fail to attend to the "conditions of [their] production" render history an instrument for making historical "silences."[21] "Any historical narrative is a particular bundle of silences," he writes, "the result of a unique process, and the operation required to deconstruct these silences will vary accordingly."[22] To the question of how to write about Indigenous literary history in particular, most of the disciplinarily conventional formations around which we narrate history (the nation, the city, the period, the racializing economics of authorship and commodity intrinsic to the book market) actively obscure the systems of resource extraction that are their precondition and terms of production. In this context, one aim of this book is to indicate what kinds of "bundles of silences" colonial temporal, jurisdictional, and discursive formations are and, in the course of their unbundling, invite other relations among narrative, history, and power. To do so, I use two methodological concepts to help expose the conditions of production of the colonial and cultural formations against which Indigenous modernist texts are written and read: *extraction history* and *distributions of interiority*. In the chapters that follow, each of these concepts contributes to the way I demonstrate how Indigenous texts antagonize and exceed the administrative control of ordinary colonial infrastructures, including narrative conventions of cultural history writing integral to environmental humanities, modernist studies, and, to some extent, NAIS.

What I mean by *extraction history* differs in two ways from environmental history in how it understands what historical narratives of human and ecological interaction explain and what kinds of relations they make possible. First, extraction histories describe how the production of history is environmental. Where environmental histories leverage in/distinctions between humans and nonhumans (as subjects or objects of historical processes) toward analyses of political or ecological change, extraction histories ask what material processes produce the categorical distinctions through which history, power, and the environment are enacted. Broadly, *extraction* refers to removal, seizure, and separation as acts of interpellation into systems of resource management, including those dedicated to energy and commodity development, political domination (war, enslavement, incarceration), and social control (cultural institutions, health and social services). Rather than understanding extraction as a secondary process or an aspect of colonialism, a premise of this book is that extraction is the way that colonial worlds and the hierarchies of power on which they depend are created. Extraction is not something humans do to resources; it is how the categories "human" and "resource" are made and managed.

In this sense, extraction marks a disciplinary convergence between Black, Indigenous, and colonialism studies' analyses of colonial forms as effects of the seizure of life and land. Extraction histories attend to what Sylvia Wynter calls the "negative aspect of the dialectical process" of colonial constructions of the human, whereby what Zakiyyah Iman Jackson describes as "the violent imposition and appropriation... of black(ened) humanity" is necessary to sustain the form's illusory political coherence.[23] Similarly, my approach to extraction history is shaped by scholarship that challenges the coherence of settlement as a spatial form. Instead of tracking colonial expansion via the production of territorial forms, I look to work that reads those forms as nothing other than the conditions for further land seizure—what Glen Coulthard calls "dispossession," and Edward Said calls "possession."[24] And because extraction histories assume the instability both of colonial forms and their relation to power, they do not identify a particular form (territory or the human) as an explanatory point of origin.[25] That anything can be extracted indicates the volatility of colonial orders but not anything about the grounded and/or embodied relations extraction targets.

Attention to this convergence does not generate an encompassing theory of power. Extraction history is a method, a way of deconstructing categories through which colonialism regulates human and other-than-human relation. It is a method informed by materialist critiques of what Elizabeth Povinelli calls the binary of "Life and Nonlife" as well as of the conditions of analytical access that binary implies.[26] As scholars like Povinelli, Jane Bennett, and Donna Haraway rethink how "vitality" and matter are organized, they also reimagine the terms and outcomes of environmental scholarship—what Haraway indexes with the multivalent concept of "trouble"; what Bennett stages in a pivot from "demystification" to the critical disposition of "being caught up in" the world; and what Povinelli marks via three "figures . . . who exist in between two worlds of late settler liberalism": the Desert, the Animist, and the Virus.[27] Unlike materialisms that establish rigidly noumenal ontological schemes, these thinkers cultivate responsive methods that understand relational and analytical processes as coevolving.[28]

At the same time, as Kim TallBear points out, new and speculative materialist revisions of what Mel Chen calls "hierarchies of animacy" tend to overwrite Indigenous approaches to ontology and relation.[29] Doing so has particular stakes for Indigenous, literary, and environmental criticism in that it creates a dilemma in which "the relationless depth of objects" becomes "incommensurable with" deconstruction.[30] This is a dilemma irrelevant in Ojibwe theoretical traditions that understand texts as coextensive with but not reducible to human liveliness. What Ojibwe people call *aadizookanag*, sometimes translated as "sacred stories," are texts grammatically marked as animate (e.g., as opposed to *dibaajimowinan*). As Margaret Huettl writes, aadizookanag derive from and are "enacted through" human relations with land.[31] What English imperfectly names "sacred" indexes their ontological inextricability and irreducibility to the world of human elaborated meaning. That aadizookanag antecede and are reproduced with difference by Anishinaabe people is not a contradiction but a threshold of relational generativity that can also guide materialist analyses beyond a real/discursive binary.[32]

The extraction histories that organize this book's chapters understand the making and interpretation of Indigenous texts as integral to the making and interpretation of Indigenous land. Here, deconstruction and materialism are still essential tools for demonstrating the instability and violence of abstractions like the human, territory, and resource. However, because extraction histories center the relations between Indigenous texts and land, Indigeneity rather than species, object, or epoch organizes the book's contribution to the environmental humanities. As a consequence, extraction histories produce analyses that are not meant to be evenly accessible or redeeming—an interpretive horizon that poses an alternative to political universalizations that sometimes structure disciplinary justifications of environmental humanities as the principal disciplinary form with which to organize analyses of human and other-than-human worlds.

The second distinction between what I call extraction histories and canonical environmental histories is that extraction histories expose how, under US occupation, extraction is cultural. By centering the fluid and enduring relationship between extraction and culture, I want to reframe the question of what it is US colonialism destroys and what it produces. What Patrick Wolfe calls "the logic of elimination" offers a widely accepted answer to this question: "The logic of elimination not only refers to the summary liquidation of Indigenous people, though it includes that. In common with genocide... settler colonialism has both negative and positive dimensions. Negatively it strives for the dissolution of native societies. Positively, it erects a new colonial society on the expropriated land base... settler colonizers come to stay: invasion is a structure not an event."[33]

Although usefully clear as a diagramming of US domination, "the logic of elimination" conceptualizes colonial violence and production through binaries that it never deconstructs. As a theory of what is destroyed, it depends on a stable ontological opposition between "people" and "land base" that prefigures a sequencing of invasion. Indigenous people are eliminated before settlers "access... territory," before those settlers erect "a new colonial society on expropriated land."[34] As a concept of what is produced, the "logic of elimination" naturalizes the colonial fantasy that settlement is stable, permanent, and successive. I am not proposing here that Wolfe argues that what he describes as the binarizing internal "logic" of settler colonialism is real but rather that, even in the name of analytical description, the premise of any colonial interiority (epistemic, social, spatial) is specious. As Jean O'Brien observes, it is also for this reason that the logic of elimination provides no useful basis for the "historici[zing] of Indigenous resistance and survival."[35] Thus, rather than frame US colonialism as elimination succeeded by "colonial society," my interest in extraction draws attention to the volatile and contradictory relation between destruction and production: not a binary or any "structure," but an unstable threshold that colonialism administrates to obtain. In this sense, in shifting from elimination to extraction, I want to draw attention to the fact that although production is always the stated justification for colonial destruction, what is actually produced is nothing other than systems for the distribution of further destruction. Nothing succeeds extraction.

In social, political, and economic terms, systems that distribute and manage colonial destruction are called *whiteness, power,* and *capital.* But it remains an ongoing challenge for scholars of colonial power to describe how we experience or participate in colonial destruction in cultural terms. What this book calls *US cultures of extraction* joins scholarship that attends to thresholds of human and ecological destruction as sites that determine how knowledge and aesthetics work in the US context and that reproduce through colonial disciplinary traditions including literary history, ethnography, and environmental history. By identifying culture as the structure that distributes and manages colonial destruction in epistemic and aesthetic terms, I invoke it both as "a thing in itself" and as an imperial methodology.[36] Culture in the US context is an enactment of extraction and a way of turning extraction into knowledge, and in both senses it resolves contradictory colonial demands for unceasing destruction and unequivocal belonging. Thus, the primary distinction between the analytic I am calling *US cultures of extraction* and the logic of elimination is a refusal to naturalize the politics of survey intrinsic to colonial culture. This requires stressing both the fallacy of Indigenous political vacancy and the instability and fictiveness of colonial cultural forms that cannot exist without the reproduction and administration of that vacancy. Those forms that extraction constitutes are effects of seizure and of subject- and object-making, effects of what Jodi Byrd calls "transit," where "U.S. empire orients and replicates itself by transforming those to be colonized . . . through continual reiterations of pioneer logics."[37] In order to attend to the violent transit that characterizes colonial forms and the transit they enact (their transitoriness and transitivity), I examine them here and throughout this book not as forms as such, but as tenuous and volatile *distributions of interiority* whose apparent stability ought to be understood as a recurrent effect of vast networks of seizure.

Each of the chapters of this book offers an extraction history of a colonial formation—removal, the domestic, ruin, rights—whose conditions of production are the extraction of Indigenous land and life. Those formations (only) reproduce extraction, which means that they seize and distribute land and they sustain and distribute ontological and spatial orders that make extractive formations seem cultural—which is to say, like sites of social and epistemic creativity and attachment. I use the term *interiority* to index this inverse fetishization, in which (to corrupt Marx's famous formulation) material relations of extraction assume, in the eyes of colonial subjects, the fantastic form of a relation between people.[38] Here, the term *interiority* has an ambivalent genealogy, rooted equally in colonial theories of ideology and space.

In one sense, interiority is the principal constituent of forms that order colonial ideology under liberalism: what John Stuart Mill calls "inward domain of consciousness," in order to distinguish free subjects from "savages" and "slaves."[39] For Mill, interiority is also a problem of colonial governance. His basic formulation of liberty—that free subjects should be regulated only to the extent that they harm other free subjects—cannot be simply extended in the context of colonialism because rulers and colonized people "are not part of the same public."[40] In this sense, interiority is also the political association of free subjects or of "dependencies . . . of similar civilization," an association he describes as "a smaller community sinking its individuality . . . in the greater individuality of a wide and powerful empire."[41] Interiority characterizes free subjects and their "sinking" into a "greater" political order. Lisa Lowe describes this aspect of liberalism as a formalism that enables "expansion" at the level of the subject and polity.[42] Through what she calls "an economy of affirmation and forgetting," principles like liberty attempt to reconcile contradictions of status and governance by "accommodat[ing] existing forms of plantation slavery and colonial occupation, while providing rationales for the innovation of new forms of imperial sovereignty."[43] Liberalism takes shape with colonial expansion by incorporating subjects "capable" of interiority and by defining interiority as the capacity for incorporation.

Interiority is also how the United States makes territorial forms and administers their expansion. In her history of the Department of the Interior, Megan Black argues that the interior was never a simple territorial demarcation of national belonging but a method of expansion: a way "to wrest domestic meaning from foreign space" and "to domesticate the nation's settler expansion."[44] Like liberty for Mill, the US interior is a form that reconciles contradictions intrinsic to colonialism, including the contradictory relationship between the foreign and domestic that the apparent autonomy of the territorial US obscures. The Department of the Interior was established in the aftermath of the Indigenous land seizures of the Indian Removal Act and the Mexican-American War in order to produce a spatial sense of the national "public domain" by managing that land and the Indigenous people displaced from it. The interior marked the threshold of uncertain and imminent national belonging, where foreign became domestic through extraction. A "natural resource bureaucracy," the department developed territorial surveys to facilitate settler access to Indigenous land and people in addition to a system of agencies to regularize that access: the Forest Service, the Bureau of Mines, the National Park Service, the Bureau of Indian Affairs, the Bureau of Indian Education, and the Indian Health Service.[45] As Black observes, the department used these same mechanisms of conceptual and administrative expansion to make and manage global "mineral frontiers" throughout the twentieth century and into the present.

Interiority recurs when colonial structures attempt to reconcile contradictions of belonging via incorporation and expansion. In the context of US political philosophy and geography, interiority is a formalism that is always material, an effect and a precondition of colonial distributions of life and land. For cultural history, the same is true, and tracking the material, extractive conditions of production that colonial forms obscure is one of two principal aims of each of the chapters that follow. But Indigenous modernist texts are not only interested in the critique of colonial worlds; they are also, as I describe in the next section, gestures of creativity and remembering that work beyond the categorical delimitations of interiority and with relation to pasts and futures undefined by extraction. In other words, in addition to asking how colonial worlds reproduce extraction, these texts ask: If we refuse to allow analyses of Indigenous cultural production to aggregate to and stabilize colonial disciplinary, temporal, and jurisdictional formations, what other histories does it become possible to tell? What modalities of spatial and social being can we make room for when our cultural histories begin by deconstructing the categorical and infrastructural distribution of interiority that sustains extraction? Can such cultural histories help restore a socially and epistemically generative indistinction between art and land around which we might imagine new practices of decolonial interpretation? Can interpreting text and land beyond the formal protocols of colonial seizure cultivate a politically generative indistinction between reading and decolonial organizing?

Indigenous Modernism

In this book, *Indigenous modernism* refers to practices of critical and creative attention that Indigenous texts turn toward situated social and material histories shaped by US colonialism. Rather than another modernist canon, Indigenous modernism bookmarks the many ways such texts expose the conditions of production of colonial modernity while sustaining creative continuities of land and life irreducible to modernity's defining terms and methods. My aim is to open up the kind of interpretive relations that might be signaled by the juxtaposition of these two words: refusing both the ideas that *Indigenous* indicates a qualification or subset of modernism, or (via an analytical reversal qua settler colonial studies) that modernism would only be centered or stabilized as an object of critique. Instead, Indigenous modernism signals a contradiction that colonial modernity incites but never resolves because the disciplinary and jurisdictional formations through which it would try to do so always already bear a relation to Indigenous land and life as effects of extraction. Remembering those relations is the creative work of the texts I read, work that extends beyond the extractive mandates of form- and object-making.

Following scholars in Indigenous and colonialism studies, I understand the work of Indigenous modernism to be at once deconstructive and generative. Deconstructive in the sense that tracking histories of extraction through which land and life are refashioned into distributions of jurisdictional and disciplinary interiority throws into relief the fictiveness and volatility of colonial orders—the way those orders are effects of the occlusion, the "unknowing," and the dispossession of the lifeworlds they destroy in order to take form.[46] For literary studies—and particularly for readers interested in attending to the coloniality of disciplinary forms as they read—attending to the formal and cultural operation of colonial extraction invites a useful set of questions that we can turn to texts and interpretive methods. Rather than asking, for instance, where or when modernism is or what it includes, we might ask what land and life are the political, economic, and cultural forms to which modernism responds made out of; what trajectories of seizure are sustained by the disciplinary forms we use to organize texts as modernist; and what histories of material and epistemic confusion are normalized by accepting such forms as stable, accumulating, or coherent?

In another sense, Indigenous modernism indexes a generativity that jurisdictional and disciplinary forms fail to reconcile to colonial orders of power or meaning. Despite the dematerializing, extractive, and occluding formalisms of US colonialisms, Indigenous land remains and is creatively cultivated through the production and interpretation of Indigenous texts, an idea Mishuana Goeman's study of the aesthetics and politics of gendered Indigenous geographies conceptualizes as "(re)mapping." Goeman's parenthetical prefix suggests that the material generativity of Indigenous art does not need to depend on fantasies of separatism but is a matter of attending to relations proximate but not reducible to colonial forms—"geographies that sit along-side" colonial space and time "and engage with them at every scale."[47] For Goeman, Indigenous texts remember and recover spatial relations in spite of the constraints of colonial formalisms. They "produce wider realities," articulate transgenerational continuities of care, and "map our future."[48] The (re) in (re)mapping suggests the recursivity of "storied" relations both in a material sense of the worlds Indigenous stories make and in an epistemic sense: the way Indigenous analyses of US colonialisms are never fixed, are always growing more complex and more precise. As Indigenous people respond to that unstable array of colonial expressions of power, they remake and renew relations with each other, with others in solidarity, and with the land itself through analysis.[49]

Among George Morrison's late works, I am particularly drawn to his 1975 MAIC mural for precisely the ways it seems to look back at, problematize, and generate alternatives to many of the ready disciplinary rubrics through which we are given to read it. It is a piece whose analysis chafes against modernist and even certain Indigenous studies' approaches to situate or explain it, and that seems in some ways unwilling to be an object of analysis at all. That it is a mural, a piece that blurs the distinction between a work of art and a building, contributes to its opacity. The mural works less like a simple, interpretable plane than it does as a gesture of interpretation. Its design takes in and reorganizes the world around it—the building's shape, the movement of people and traffic on the street, and the shifting weight of sunlight across its face—and all in such a way that questions what is otherwise given as the concreteness of that world. The way its design rearranges space can feel, for someone walking or driving along Franklin Avenue, like a challenge to rethink the ordinary terms of their own presence there, where exactly they find themselves, and where it takes them to be caught up in chevrons' motion.

To read the piece within conventional modernist frameworks, even those expansively conceived, would be to stabilize formations that the mural, and Morrison's work in general, specifically unsettles.[50] For instance, although the movement in which Morrison matured as an artist, abstract expressionism, is fundamentally transnational (the resurfacing in New York of a European art scene in exile), it would underestimate the mural to understand it as connecting or constellating the Twin Cities into that cosmopolitanism. *Turning the Feather Around* points out the limitation and the extraction dependence of the political concept of the colonial city as it applies to the Twin Cities, as well as any other colonial place or arrangement of places. Similarly, to read the mural into modernism as a function of composition would reinforce a problematic and ultimately ethnographic distribution of interiority. That is, to understand the work using modernist comparative frameworks, to read it as a product of cultural exchange (the hybridization of Indigenous art or the "Indigenization" of US or European art), would jurisdictionalize techniques that were never proper to colonial cultural canons in the first place.[51]

All the formations through which theories and histories of modernism are articulated—the city, global systems of capital and culture, and even disciplinary or aesthetic concepts of expansion, newness, and experimentation—always already bear a relation to Indigeneity. One thing that makes them modern is that they are thresholds of the absorption or obliteration of Indigenous people and place that generate the distributions of interiority on which colonial worlds depend.[52] Thus, Indigenous modernism cannot be figured as a subaltern or minor modernism, or even one among an array of modernisms, because the criteria that would describe its inclusion, marginalization, or seriality are themselves effects of Indigenous extraction.[53] The construction *Indigenous modernism* marks an irresolution—a site of the explanatory failure of colonial categories and of the elaboration of Indigenous relation—that should not be settled via disciplinary comparison. Like Lyons's theory of the x-mark, Indigenous modernism signals "an interactable multiplicity" of space and relation against formations that require the simplification and stabilization of relation.[54] Unlike a countermodernist tradition that, following Foucault, might "imagine" the world "otherwise than it is," Indigenous modernist work turns to the challenge of imagining the world as it actually is in its relational possibility and complexity, and in excess of the political fictions that reify and reproduce extraction.[55]

Throughout his career, when Morrison was asked to position himself within US art canons or with relation to Indigenous cultural practices, he almost always responded by returning attention to the materiality of his work. In the case of *Turning the Feather Around*, he consistently underscored the strictly physical inspiration for the piece; "the pattern," he wrote in his autobiography, "was taken from a feather."[56] The mural, for Morrison, was the elaboration of a generative formal problem irreducible to technique or symbol. His interest in the materiality of the feather perhaps had more to do with its particular plasticity, the way it is not an object at all but a kind of vector of physical transformation, a form for converting mass and air into movement. The mural "form[s] something that is almost three-dimensional," Morrison wrote. "You can't explain it."[57] Here, although Morrison was always careful not to police the interpretation of his work, it is possible to read a little sharpness or specificity to the word *you*. As a work of public art in a colonial city, the mural, he knew, would be accessible to interpreters eager to incorporate its meaning into the cultural frameworks that naturalize or protect their own ideological positions. Given this, one way we might read the piece's interest in creating aesthetic or interpretive movement beyond what can easily be reconciled to a theory of cultural exchange is as a kind of "ethnographic refusal," in Audra Simpson's terms, as an expression of "an ethnographic calculus of what you need to know and what I refuse to write... [that] acknowledges the asymmetrical power relations that inform the research and writing about native lives and politics."[58] In this sense, spatially, historically, and stylistically, Morrison's mural might be read as against, rather than as an aspect of, modernism. That is to say that both its nonidentity and proximity to the concepts that organize modernist comparison and genealogy occasion the reconsideration of the extractive operations, the distributions of cultural and geographic interiority, that those concepts reproduce.

Sovereignty and Indefinite Space

In May 1975, the mural and the MAIC were unveiled at a public ceremony that included members of the National Congress of American Indians, the All Tribes Indian Church, cultural producers including Gerald Vizenor, and the Indigenous community in general. The gathering ended with an intertribal dance on the grounds of the MAIC, a celebration that now occurs there every year. The night before the event, Morrison dreamed that he walked onto the MAIC grounds to find a field completely filled with feathers—an image that directly invokes the central material logic of the mural itself and that also seems preoccupied with larger questions about the social, political, and artistic transformation of space. What is striking to me about his dream image is how it suggests spatial saturation and an incalculable scope of elaboration, whether the feathers read as melancholic traces of bodies or embodied gestures past, or as potential or latent forms for producing as-yet-unimagined motion. Aesthetically, the image recalls Morrison's ink drawings, which had been exhibited at the Walker Arts Center the year before. When asked if the expansive, shifting geometries of those drawings were "figurative or referential," Morrison replied that the drawings were "remote and hidden. Only an organic element remains. The abstract context takes over... into an effect of shallow cubist depth... and a sense of indefinite space extending outward from all sides."[59] A theory of "indefinite space" that refuses to be reconciled to figure or reference is useful for extrapolating from Morrison's strange dream to broader questions about how he understood the opening of the MAIC and the mural to be transformative of the colonial space in which it is situated.

Given the timing and disciplinary context of the mural's production, we might expect Morrison to think about these questions in terms of a disciplinarily conservative or nationalist concept of sovereignty. In the decades after the inauguration of NAIS at the University of Minnesota, *sovereignty* became a primary and contested term through which the field consolidated itself through a rhetoric of disciplinary interiority. For literary studies scholars like Jace Weaver and Craig Womack, sovereignty as an organizing logic of the institutionalization of NAIS means conceiving of the field as an explicitly nationalist or separatist project: a way to assert control over the interpretation of Indigenous texts and traditions. In *American Indian Literary Nationalism*, they, along with Robert Warrior, observe that "American Indian Literary Nationalism . . . is a defense of Native literatures against . . . co-optation and incorporation" and an assertion of "the ability of Natives and their communities to be self-determining," in part through an investment in the political discreteness of Indigenous cultural production. "Native literature," they write, "is a separate national/local literature from that produced by immigrants."[60] Using a nationalist concept of sovereignty as a keystone for the institutionalization of NAIS has the advantages of articulating the political stakes of the work of interpretation ("what is at stake is nothing less than Native identity") and distinguishing NAIS from the other ethnic studies formations it emerged alongside by referencing the treaty relationships that tribes negotiated with the United States prior to 1871.[61]

Despite his participation in nationalist movements like AIM and the formation of NAIS at Minnesota, Morrison's practice as an artist, a teacher, and a scholar bears little trace of what Elizabeth Cook-Lynn calls the "endogenous" or intramural disciplinary project of nationalist sovereignty.[62] Rather than a guarded space within institutions like the university or the community center, Morrison's career in the Twin Cities was dedicated to creating spaces for his students to gather outside institutional settings, including in the home in St. Paul he shared with Hazel Belvo. The MAIC dream is also an extension of this impulse toward the possibility of something like an extramural iteration of sovereignty, in which the generative work of remembering and reorganizing life and land might be elaborated anywhere, without regard for the authorization or the boundaries of colonial institutional or jurisdictional formations.

In the context of the Twin Cities, theorizing Indigenous organizing in these expansive, more-than-institutional, and more-than-defensive terms also corrects a major limitation of nationalist concepts of sovereignty, namely that in defining itself only in terms of the antagonism between Indigenous critical production and settler colonialism, it does not offer a theory of the complex, necessary, and generative intersections among tribal citizens, descendants, Black and African diasporic people, and other migrant and diasporic people that contribute to Indigenous intellectual production in the Twin Cities. The nationalist assessment that Indigenous art is defined as "separate from that produced by immigrants," in the context of the Twin Cities for instance, is one that would arguably ignore or misclassify the cities' Latinx and Hmong communities, non-Dakota Indigenous people like Ojibwe people (who came to Dakota land as a part of prophetic migration), and Black people (including the Twin Cities' vibrant Somali community) whose political status within colonial orders is irreducible and antecedent to a sovereign or immigrant binary. These are limitations that, broadly speaking, have already been examined by Indigenous and Black studies scholars who argue that sovereignty tends to resituate decolonial struggle on the terms of colonial power.[63] At the same time, because sovereignty is never extricable from intrinsically volatile colonial terms and systems, even critiques of sovereignty that stabilize it or stabilize positions outside it can reproduce its binaries and essentializations.[64]

Although debates about literary nationalism specifically are no longer central to NAIS, sovereignty remains a problem for interpretation in and beyond the field, particularly when scholars naturalize the illusion that it is a conceptually stable expression of power. The texts I read in this book approach sovereignty as the political effect of the interpretive foreclosure of land, typically executed via distributions of interiority including the jurisdiction, the person, and the resource. Rather than call for the recuperation or the abolition of sovereignty, these texts hold open the interpretation of spaces and histories that gathers alongside and despite sovereign forms, and, in so doing, they also indicate and intensify the intrinsic instability of colonial power. Here, by *hold open*, I mean that these texts pose questions about the interpretation of land and do so without recourse to final or comprehensive answers. One set of questions is historiographical, about how to give narrative shape to histories of land that has staged extraordinary and terrible enactments of colonial sovereignty without either stabilizing forms that convey sovereignty or erasing the ways that land always means more than those forms can reconcile. A second set of questions has to do with how to express the generative indistinction between art and land, and between art-making and place-making, that animates Indigenous modernist work in the midst of and against the interpretive foreclosures of the jurisdiction, the person, and the resource.

Against the common critical supposition that such foreclosures can be ranked or isolated, this book's attention to histories of sovereignty in the Twin Cities emphasizes how seemingly discrete sovereign forms are almost always articulated in order to qualify crises in other, formations of sovereignty. The 1856 *Dred Scott v. Sandford* case, for instance, considered whether the enslavement of Dred and Harriet Scott at Fort Snelling was actually grounds for their emancipation, because slavery was illegal in what was then called Wisconsin Territory. Justice Taney's decision in this case, delivered the same year Minneapolis became a city, uses an anti-Black construction of personhood to reconcile the inherently contradictory proposition that a colonial territory (which economically depended on the slavery it disavowed) could, as a sovereign spatial formation, convey freedom.[65] Only six years after *Dred Scott v. Sandford*, however, the qualifying relation between the sovereign forms of person and territory was inverted. The Dakota Uprising in 1862 was a crisis in the social construction of sovereignty, specifically in the treaty-sanctioned, biopolitical construction of Indigeneity as signifying contingent access of life-sustaining food, space, health care, and housing. Further emphasizing the fact that colonial officials perceived the uprising as a social rather than a territorial crisis, the state was not satisfied with the defeat of Dakota forces or the mass execution of thirty-eight insurgents. To settle the uprising, Minnesota created one of the world's first modern concentration camps at the convergence of the Minnesota and Mississippi Rivers, just below Fort Snelling, where it held Dakota families for two years. Here, the territorial form of the camp (what Agamben would call, in a very different context, the "nomos" of modern sovereign power) and its placement at the Bdote (a site of Dakota emergence and the center of the world) was meant to permanently constrain the meaning of Indigeneity within the state's social construction of sovereignty.[66]

These histories remind us both that intrinsically unstable sovereign forms are articulated in order to stabilize each other and that these brutal enactments of colonial sovereignty trace back to the very same place, the Bdote, the land occupied by Fort Snelling. To understand what meaning these sovereign forms attempt to foreclose, we have to look beyond the historiographical categories those forms inspire. The Bdote, like the places Tiffany King writes about in *The Black Shoals*, is a place where water and land mix and gather in excess of a single or mappable sense of land. It is a space of emergence in both Dakota social-historical and physical terms—the site, as Waziyatawin powerfully observes, of geographic juncture and human creation; the very "Center of the Earth."[67] As such, as King suggests of the shoal, the Bdote is irreducible to colonial investments in presence or interiority, a place where interpretive methods are slowed, chafed, and rearranged.[68] It is precisely the unguarded and unlimited social, spatial, and historical production of which the Bdote is an enactment and a symbol that colonial sovereign forms attempt to foreclose and obscure. Against the histories of these forms, the Bdote is a space of remembered and anticipated motion that is continually becoming an Indigenous place.

The Bdote is an example of what Morrison calls "an indefinite space": a space that gathers social meaning and that becomes more and differently Indigenous as more and different Indigenous people gather there.[69] Sustaining such spaces against colonial power requires organizing beyond ideological, analytical, or territorial singularities, a project central to the politics of the art-making that I index as Indigenous modernism. It is entirely possible that these politics might also be indexed as an iteration of sovereignty to the extent that Indigenous modernism is dedicated to reframing the formal and spatial borders of power as sites, in Leanne Betasamosake Simpson's terms, of "increased diplomacy, ceremony, and sharing," particularly insofar as "increased" indicates the possibility of an unlimited accrual, an unlimited increasing of "diplomacy, ceremony, and sharing."[70] Such a politics also blurs the distinction between Indigenous art-making and political world-building. The deconstructive and generative politics of Indigenous modernism evident in pieces like Morrison's *Turning the Feather Around* also animate actions that are often coded as activism—for example, the AIM occupation of the Naval Air Station near Fort Snelling in 1971, the Indigenous houseless encampment along Franklin Avenue, the occupation of I-94 at the site of the Rondo neighborhood, and the burning of the Minneapolis Police Third Precinct and the Midtown Corner Condominiums during the George Floyd Uprising. More than a defensive or space-claiming gesture, each of these is an emergent, artistic, and place-making enactment of the extramural theory of sovereignty Simpson develops. Each is a way of holding open the Twin Cities as a space of indefinite Indigenous interpretation and elaboration.

Writing against Extraction

Less than fifty years after Minneapolis was officially recognized as a city, my great-great-grandfather Thomas Wright sat on a recently lumbered white pine tree with five other settler men. Working fifty miles north of the Twin Cities on the bank of the St. Croix River, Wright was a cook for a logging

I.2. Sargent, photograph of Taylors Falls. John Runk Historical Collection, 1397, Minnesota Historical Society.

company, and, when the photograph was taken, that company was in the midst of deforesting land that had been seized from Ojibwe communities by the Allotment Act, designated as "surplus land," and opened to private settler and governmental resource extraction.

Thomas Wright's daughter, Alva Hooley, was my great-grandmother: someone I knew and loved, and someone I think about when I think about where and who I am from. At the same time, it is precisely through formulations like "being from" a place that is stolen that fantasies of colonial belonging are naturalized through the language of social attachment.

The history of property-making in and around the Twin Cities is coextensive with the history of settler sociality, and thus the language with which I am given to describe what it means to be from my great-grandmother Alva or from Minnesota is a language that is produced by and therefore reproduces structures of conquest.[71] Among the many reasons to critique and dismantle those structures and the discourses that secure them, the most important is the restitution of all Indigenous land now called the United States and the creation of a world without anti-Blackness. But there is also a lot at stake in decolonization for colonizers. For instance, while colonialism endures, there is no language extricable from colonial belonging with which I might describe what it means to be from somewhere or someone, to describe what it means to have known and to remember Alva and the rest of my family. For settlers, the language of extraction takes the place of language with which we might otherwise describe and make mutual relations with the world and with each other.

In the winters, when weather and infrastructure limited the work logging companies could do, Thomas Wright cooked at the prison in Stillwater, Minnesota. That prison is part of the oldest infrastructure of the state of Minnesota; along with the state capitol and the university, it is an infrastructure five years older than the state itself. When we try to spatialize and historicize colonialism in the US context, our language too easily naturalizes the terms through which it is reproduced, including by using spatial and temporal markers like *Stillwater* and *Minnesota*, and by presuming the relation those markers bear to supposedly distinct modalities of colonial violence (land seizure, genocide, anti-Blackness). In this book, I refuse the supposition that such modalities ever operate discretely, a supposition on which the easy deployment of *settler colonialism* as a catch-all analytic of colonial violence in the United States depends. Instead, I use the term *US colonialisms* to signal the always protean and plural quality of colonial power: the way that power draws on and can shift among a repertoire of brutalities even when, in a given place or circumstance, the violence of its articulation might seem singular. Every place colonialism makes refers to and reproduces the entire (racializing, orientalizing, un/gendering, settlement-making) repertoire of colonial violence, in both new and old arrangements of force, aesthetics, and ideology. Thomas Wright's two jobs (cooking for loggers and the prison) are useful in that they are a reminder of how Indigenous dispossession and anti-Blackness always occur together as the precondition and sustaining logics of the colonial state. In the history of Minnesota, the collusion of these logics reasserts itself every time the state form shifts or expands—a recurrent and restless threshold of conquest.

I begin this section with this photograph to consider the ways the social and material politics of colonial extraction shape me. My relation to Thomas Wright, to the Twin Cities, to the disciplines of literary and cultural studies, to Indigenous land, and to the Indigenous cultural production I write about in this book become, under the terms of colonialism, aspects of epistemic, ontological, and economic belonging. In other words, they are subjects and objects whose surpluses of meaning I am given to leverage to preserve a coherent sense of my own belonging. One goal of this book is to refuse those politics by deconstructing the cultural and material infrastructures that naturalize extraction. But doing so means trying to write cultural histories differently. In this sense, the chapters that follow ask basic methodological questions as well as literary and historical ones. For instance: How can we hold out against the grammars of cultural analysis that stabilize colonial periodization, jurisdiction, and canon? Can we generatively confuse those grammars that position archives as objects, as inherently untheoretical, and that render silent the material conditions of the production of theory? And how can we produce new languages for cultural analysis that, rather than staging interpretation as a scene of access or discovery, invite relations among texts, readers, and their worlds that can also restore and remember what structures of colonialism have sought to destroy or forget? For Trouillot, questions like these always have multiple answers. "Power," he writes, "does not enter the story once and for all, but at different times and from different angles. It precedes the narrative proper, contributes to its creation and to its interpretation. . . . In history, power begins at the source."[72] For this reason, although this book's chapters maintain several of the same methodological premises, patterns, and aims, they do not try to produce a single new way to read or write cultural history against extraction. Instead, each chapter is its own minor experiment in interpreting cultural history, and as such is ever only the start of an answer to these questions, never the end of them.

What is consistent across this book's chapters is the methodological practice I am calling *extraction history* through which I direct attention to the unstable material and historical production and distributive operation of those colonial formations that produce the fiction that colonial political and cultural worlds are coherent, settled, and permanent. Thus, the first chapter considers *removal* as a precursory environmental, political, and cultural condition to territorial formation in Minnesota. The second chapter frames *the domestic* as the repressive sociality that structures the forms of the allotment and the reserve through which land seizure is naturalized as a premise of colonial life. The third chapter develops a concept of *ruin* as the precondition and response to simultaneous colonial crises of economy and climate. And the last chapter's consideration of *rights* illuminates the troubling history of manoomin/wild rice extraction in and by Minnesota. Because each chapter's extraction history demonstrates the contingency and explanatory limitations of the political and disciplinary formations through which we are given to produce cultural analysis, I do not understand these histories as contextualizing the stories of the Indigenous texts I tell alongside or against them. That this book's central archive comprises Indigenous texts does not signal that its principal intervention is necessarily in NAIS, but that analyses animated by

Indigenous texts are relevant to all disciplines, including those to which this book speaks most directly: colonialism studies, American literary studies, and the environmental humanities. Thus, I understand the Indigenous texts at the center of each chapter to be part of the theoretical apparatus that unsettles and exceeds colonial formations, and, as such, my own critical relation to those texts is less to explain or illuminate them than it is to join with them in their deconstructive and generative work.

The first chapter's extraction history of removal centers a strange and brilliant work of nineteenth-century ethnography, the first authored by an Ojibwe person. William Warren's *The History of the Ojibways*, was written during the removal of Anishinaabe communities from their traditional and seasonal homelands in which Warren himself participated both as a colonial officer and as a removed tribal member. The chapter reads Warren's text as laying bare the cultural and political function of removal for the colonial state, specifically the way it inflects recurrent cycles of colonial war and aid. At the same time, I attend to the subtle and unpredictable ways that the text, and the conditions of its making, directly contravened removal—the way it manifested and made space for Indigenous narrative collaboration, multigenerational remembering, and imaginative invention.

The second chapter reads two novels by the contemporary Turtle Mountain Ojibwe writer Louise Erdrich, set in the period that followed removal: the allotment and reservation era. Allotment was both the most massive colonial land seizure in US history and the imposition of an array of repressive social affects that I bookmark with the term *the domestic*. This chapter's extraction history of the domestic tracks the social and psychic operations of haunting and what I call *social vacancy* imposed and interrupted via the attempted incorporation of Indigenous women into colonial reproduction. Against the violence and repression of the domestic, I read Erdrich's novels and their protagonist, Fleur, as developing a theory of return, of the taking and making of land back from the social vacancy of colonial domestic life.

The third chapter offers an extraction history of ruin. Here, ruin is the discursive premise and material outcome of US colonialisms, but it is also what colonial states displace because it is what they cannot bear. Ruin is the discourse that justified the policies of termination and relocation in which Leech Lake Ojibwe writer David Treuer's novel *The Hiawatha* is set. The chapter reads the novel's depiction of relocated Indigenous communities in the Twin Cities as exposing and refusing to repeat the colonial logic of racializing immunity from ruin through the dangerous and ultimately beautiful work of imagining social and environmental repair amid ruin.

The last chapter reads an essay by White Earth Ojibwe writer and theorist Gerald Vizenor toward an extraction history of rights, an avatar of what I call, more broadly, *the colonial politics of protection*. At the center of this history are the United States' and the state of Minnesota's efforts to control, financialize, and also protect the sacred Anishinaabe and Dakota food relation manoomin/wild rice. Against this, I attend to Vizenor's and the White Earth Band's efforts to reframe manoomin, beyond the colonial forms of protectable public and person, as a gift, a gathering, and an occasion to think beyond the colonial mandates of protection.

What shifts across these chapters is how Indigenous modernist texts antagonize and deconstruct colonial political and cultural formations and how they exceed them. The chapters' engagement with Federal Indian Law is an example of this. In one sense, the book's chapters seem to follow a rough chronology organized by changes in Federal Indian Law and policy, from William Whipple Warren's direct intervention in the removal era of the mid-nineteenth century, through Louise Erdrich's writing about the reservation and allotment eras at the turn and early decades of the twentieth century, to David Treuer's and Gerald Vizenor's engagements with relocation and rights eras of the second half of the twentieth century. At the same time, far from understanding such shifts in Federal Indian Law to amount to a stable political history, the chapters specifically challenge the judicial and disciplinary commonplace assumption that the history of Federal Indian Law and policy amounts to a neat chronology of political development. Instead, I understand Federal Indian Law and policy as targets of Indigenous critique, as institutions that do not operate in terms of temporal or political progress at all but are shifting and recursive thresholds of extraction. The shifts we have come to identify as "eras" primarily mark changes in the style or intensity with which colonial extraction is endeavored. Thus, the temporal scope of each chapter is designed to betray and exceed the fictions of coherence and development that colonial jurisdictional and historical taxonomies encode. Because, as I show, the changes in colonial law that we are given to call *policy eras* are always actually reactive and improvised, each chapter reveals colonial legal formations to be unstable in different ways.

The first two chapters' analyses of the Marshall Trilogy, for instance, demonstrate opposite formal relations between colonial power and Indigenous life and land. In the case of the first chapter, the political and territorial contradictions prompted by removal policy were resolved by the colonial judiciary by permanently linking ostensibly distinct concepts US and Indigenous sovereignty through the logic of aid. In the second chapter, in the context of allotment policy, the Marshall court developed a concept of the domestic that fundamentally distinguishes colonial political and social worlds by repressing Indigenous kinship and relation systems. The last two chapters take up legal projects of colonial reform in which relocation and rights policies were designed to remediate environmental crises set in motion by colonial extraction. Here, too, reading Indigenous modernist texts against these policy histories throws into relief the chaos and contradictoriness of colonial responses to the administrating environmental harm. Reading relocation policy in the context of climate change allows me to trace a genealogy of the discourse of immunity that derives from the inability of colonial worlds to endure the ruin they invariably produce. In contrast, the last chapter's analysis of manoomin law suggests that, in many cases, the political contradictions colonial states cannot resolve derive from their own legal reform projects. In this case, the contradiction I bookmark as *the colonial politics of protection* opens a space for Ojibwe writers and organizers to turn the political logic of rights back against the viability of colonial state itself.

Another, final way that I think about these chapters as experiments in cultural history writing returns me to the question of my own relation to the texts and the place, the Twin Cities, at the center of this book. When I describe my critical relation to Indigenous modernisms as "joining" its critical project, as gathering with these texts against histories of extraction, it is important to clarify that this does not mean that the texts' intervention become my own, and that thereby I become marked as innocent or as a "critical academic," in Fred Moten and Stefano Harney's terms.[73] Instead, I think about the personal stakes of this critical work in terms of specific questions about how settlers might practice remembering, describing, and elaborating the nonextractive relations that also constitute our social and aesthetic experience. These are questions that always occur in particular historical and geographic contexts—in my case, the modern Twin Cities. The book is not about these questions in a straightforward way, but it is how I have begun to answer them, by dwelling on the particular kinds of interventions the Indigenous modernist texts I read here make: Warren's theory of ethnographic interruption, the way Erdrich's character Fleur performs return with loss, the histories of living with ruin Treuer elaborates in *The Hiawatha*, and the possibility Vizenor's work provokes for organizing life outside of the conscripts of protection. These are interventions that are not "for" me, but they are, nonetheless, frameworks through which to begin to remember and restore complexities of relation that the formations of extractive sociality are designed to obscure or foreclose.[74] I find that these interventions do not lead me to the perhaps more clear-cut political demonstrations I might have imagined when I started working on this book—dramatic gestures of social disavowal, or a new commitment to a kind of pure anticoloniality. Rather, they suggest a more modest, ambiguous, and fraught set of prompting questions: What new languages, beyond the conscripts of extraction, can we invent as we answer ordinary questions like where are we, and how did we come to be together? Can that language also inspire practices of care or repair that do not convey belonging, protection, or redemption? And what relations might be possible if we trade the politically securing language of *being from* for a language that starts with *being with*—being with what remains, what is lost, and what might yet be?

Cultures
of
Removal

The history of US colonialisms is often narrated in terms of "eras" of Federal Indian Law, of which *removal* is a primary and politically explanatory point of origin. Removal is understood as the precondition of the progressive development of settlement, a discrete series of political events, a violent emptying of the land that sets the stage for modern US history, and a political moment perhaps regretted but never undone. The fantasies of US territorial, political, and historical coherence depend on the idea that Indigenous life and claims to land could be and were removed.

One aim of this chapter is to ask what political and cultural fictions conventional accounts of historically singular "Indian removal" secure. As Anishinaabe historian Jean O'Brien has observed, narratives of Indigenous vacancy are elemental to colonial practices of history- and place-making. The way US monuments, policy, and cultural texts commemorate colonial *firsts* (the first colonial explorer, the first colonial institution) and Indigenous *lasts* (the last tribal village, the last Native descendant) makes the transition from Indigenous to colonial occupation of North America seem singular and historically stable.[1] Crucially, O'Brien describes the relationship between the currency of colonial formations and narratives of Indigenous absence or extinction using the gerunds *firsting* and *lasting*. In this way, she underscores how any notion of the historical singularity of removal is always contradicted by the demand for its rhetorical rearticulation in colonial spaces and narratives. In this chapter, I build on this aspect of O'Brien's work to argue that removal is never a discrete aspect of colonial history but, rather, the constantly restated premise of a historically and spatially coherent colonial present. Removal never only happens once, and neither are the kinds of violence it indexes specific to a single era of US history. The massive evictions, the catastrophic assaults on tribal knowledge traditions, and the seizure of Indigenous life and land into racial capitalism are all constantly repeated or reinvented as the United States finds new ways to stabilize its political economy via the dispossession and commodification it calls growth. The periodization of removal as a discrete and singular era obscures removal's constant recurrence and sustains fantasies of stable colonial space and history. Another way to put this is that removal is an inaugurating gesture of extraction, which is itself a condition for the production of the political and narrative structures through which colonial history is articulated. In this chapter, I show how removal produces colonial history by analyzing removal, first as a political structure that aligns sovereignty with the politics of aid, and second as premise of the survey genre through which that alignment is historically narrated.

Of these two parts of this chapter's extraction history of removal, understanding removal as a generic method and an outcome of survey perhaps requires more explanation. The decades conventionally associated with US removal policy (the eviction of Cherokee people from the southeast in the 1830s to the "closing of the frontier" in the 1890s) are also the decades in which the cultural survey became a principal form through which anthropology, literary studies, and photography were institutionalized and nationalized. From Henry Rowe Schoolcraft's and John Wesley Powell's ethnographic surveys to the rise of the photographic survey of the American West by photographers including Carleton Watkins and Timothy O'Sullivan to the rise of the literary survey as keystone of university training in the 1840s, the survey as an example of what Anne McClintock calls "panoptical time" became a colonial nationalist form at the same time Indigenous eviction was an explicit and primary US federal policy.[2] Across disciplines, the survey is a hallmark of "firsting and lasting" insofar as it secures the fiction of Indigenous vanishing as a foundational principle of colonial cultural interpretation and archives. But removal and survey are linked by more than historical coincidence; through both small and systematic practices of erasure, the genre of the survey authorizes, organizes, and nationalizes distributions of cultural subjects and objects through disciplinary interpretation. Edward Curtis, perhaps most notoriously, removed items like clocks and European clothing from portraits of Indigenous people in his survey *The North American Indian*. Funded by J. P. Morgan, the mission of *The North American Indian* was to document and archive "a vanishing race"—that is, to create an aesthetic that periodized Indigeneity as past and an archive with which to confirm the colonial present. The conditions for vanishing to become a colonial cultural aesthetic—what makes the photographs archivable, and what makes the archive interpretable—is removal on the scale of the photographic frame. Like land surveys in which the erasure and displacement of Indigenous geographies is the precondition for rendering colonial jurisdiction, and like literature surveys in which the erasure of Indigenous texts (or their displacement into racializing subcategories) is the precondition for the categorization of colonial cultural periods, removal as an aesthetic practice in *The North American Indian* links colonial culture and colonial history through the terms, disciplines, and institutions it makes possible.

That removal is not a discrete era but the political and generic conditions of production of colonial history complicates the task of narrating Indigenous eviction and displacement in historical terms. How do writers interpret removal without naturalizing the United States as a temporally and jurisdictionally coherent form? How do writers narrate removal while still asserting Indigenous presence and claims to land that have been rewritten as historical by US cultural institutions, and, moreover, how do they do so without recourse to colonial methods of history writing? How do writers throw into relief the fiction of removal's singularity, and how do they record the ways it recurs every time the United States pursues political or economic growth? A third aim of this chapter is to argue that one point of origin of the modern Indigenous literary history of the Twin Cities is a text principally characterized by the strange and imaginative way it grapples with these questions.

History against Removal

This chapter situates William Whipple Warren's *History of the Ojibway People* at the convergence of multiple vectors of colonial removal. Written between 1846 and 1853, it is arguably the first and perhaps only ethnography of Ojibwe people written by an Ojibwe person. Under closer scrutiny, however, almost every aspect of that claim blurs. Although the text was deeply enmeshed in the emergent US anthropological establishment, and the book frequently tries on ethnographic stylistic postures, *History of the Ojibway People* is not a cultural survey in colonial scientific terms. If the ethnographic survey is the cultural application of what McClintock calls "the imperial science of the surface"—that is, the reduction of human and more-than-human worlds to the totalizing and mappable coordinates of colonial space and time—Warren's text performs the unusual trick of turning ethnography against its own colonial purposes. In its rendering of the rich and heterogeneous worlds of Ojibwe people, it muddles and thwarts ethnography's generic impulse to make Indigenous people mappable and knowable within the frameworks of colonial territory and history.[3] This is not to suggest that because Warren troubles the protocols and outcomes of survey that the genre of ethnography is irrelevant to reading *History of the Ojibway People*. Instead, one way to read the book is as an exposition of the limits of the genre of ethnographic survey—the fallacy of its objectivity and the illusion of transparency it offers readers. *History of the Ojibway People* is an investigation of ethnography itself, one that highlights the authority and access the genre demands without delivering either.

Beyond the generic question of ethnography, *History of the Ojibway People* also invites questions about its author and the Indigenous people it seems to position as its objects of inquiry. Warren was born in 1825 to an American trader (Lyman Warren) and a French Ojibwe woman named Marie Cadotte. He was taught his first language, Ojibwemowin, by his maternal grandmother and her brother, Tug wag aune, an elder and a tribal leader.[4] Even though many tribal leaders claimed Warren as a relative throughout his life, he never announces himself in his text as either an Anishinaabe tribal member or as a settler—a surprising posture at a moment when access to food, safety, land, and political autonomy was granted or withheld by the United States, based on those binarized identity positions. In his *History of the Ojibway People*, Warren's ideological exception expresses itself in incommensurable gestures of rhetorical intimacy and alienation. He constantly underscores his proximity to Ojibwe people, even calling them relatives, at the same time that he shares with his explicitly colonial readership patronizing rhetorical gestures of non-identity with tribal people, something he performs early in the book's preface:

> The writer of the following pages was born, and has passed his lifetime, among the Ojibways of Lake Superior and the Upper Mississippi. His ancestors on the maternal side, have been in close connection with this tribe for the past one hundred and fifty years. Speaking their language perfectly, and connected with them through strong ties of blood, he has ever felt a

deep interest in their welfare and fate, and has deemed it a duty to save their traditions from oblivion, and to collect every fact concerning them, which the advantages he possesses have enabled him to procure.[5]

Even as he invokes his relation to Indigeneity, here and elsewhere in *History of the Ojibway People*, Warren links himself to his colonial readership through the rhetorical and affective gesture of cultural salvage and distances himself from his Ojibwe relations by referring to them with a third-person pronoun, a convention he applies elsewhere in the book to settlers and also in this quotation to himself.

There are many plausible readings of the unusual way Warren ideologically positions himself in this moment and throughout the text. One possibility is that he is attempting to thwart the constraints of English grammar through an allusion to the system of linguistic personhood in Ojibwemowin, which accommodates modalities of personhood (including third and fourth persons) untranslatable to English. More immediately relevant to this chapter, however, is the sense that Warren's careful and opaque ideological positioning points to broader problematics of Indigenous authorship in the context of removal. For Warren—and perhaps any Indigenous writer working in a colonial book market—authorship demands interpellation into the distribution of interiority that cultural institutions naturalize as the relation between objects of analysis and their interpreters. The terms of that demand are explicitly heightened for writers who are directly engaged in ethnography, like Warren. However, they are also broadly relevant to the spoken and unspoken demands placed on all Indigenous writers working against colonialism. As Warren makes clear, Indigenous authorship against the conditions of removal is powerfully shaped by the politics of salvage—or, in his more precise terms, the politics of saving.

The beginning of Indigenous authorship in the modern US book market is historically and politically inflected by the institutionalization of anthropology. Consequently, the politics of saving for Warren were simultaneously archival and sentimental. In his preface, he leverages that ambivalence on behalf of an argument for the book's currency—at once a technology of cultural preservation and an appeal to liberal white middle-class sympathy: "Under the present condition of the red race, there is no time to lose. Whole tribes are daily disappearing, or are being so changed in character through a close contact with an evil white population, that their history will forever be a blank . . . a change is so rapidly taking place, caused by a close contact with the white race, that ten years hence it will be too late to save the traditions of their forefathers from total oblivion."[6] We do not have to read Warren as cynical or pandering to appreciate his awareness of the book's participation in the politics of colonial domination in which "sav[ing]" Indigenous people from "oblivion" is not about stopping or undoing colonialism, but about rendering living worlds as artifacts for colonial storage and analysis. Warren is not an uncompromising decolonial thinker here or elsewhere in *History of the Ojibway People*. However, this does not diminish the usefulness of his rigorous attention to the link between authorship and expropriation and between what Glen Coulthard calls recognition (the incorporation of Indigenous people into colonial subjectivity) and dispossession (the reproduction of colonial power via the reduction of Indigenous life and land to resource).[7]

Although Warren himself poses questions of his ideological positioning in *History of the Ojibway People*, we do not have to read his emphasis on this link as a disavowal of Indigeneity or an alignment with whiteness. Rather, we can read him as pointing to and challenging the ideological demands and political costs of colonial recognition broadly and the disciplinary construction of culture specifically. In his study of Dakota writers during the allotment and assimilation eras, Dakota scholar Christopher Pexa provides a powerful analytical framework for reading Indigenous writers grappling, as Warren does in *History of the Ojibway People*, with what he calls "settler colonial regimes of legibility."[8] Against the colonial representational logics that demand Indigenous erasure or incorporation, Pexa tracks how Dakota writers strike postures of strategic ambivalence that subtly but powerfully demonstrate the vital and material presence Indigenous intellectual and political and community.[9] Pexa applies the rubric the "unheroic decolonizer" to writers who use rhetorical "multiplicity, a representational shiftiness, to remain part of their own social frameworks while negotiating the possibilities and violences of what up to that point had been settler framing, ideologies and social forms."[10] This is a rubric that eloquently describes Warren's significance and the complexity and nuance he brought to the work of grappling with the generic, disciplinary, and ideologically loaded questions about authorship and authority that, for him, made the politics of removal always both material and textual. Warren understood that ethnography promises to save objects, not subjects, of analysis, and that ethnography, which always occurs in the context of colonialism, makes objects of analysis out of living human worlds. Thus, the strange discursive alienation that characterizes Warren's preface—in which Ojibwe people as a collective, settlers, and Warren himself are often evacuated of grammatical subjectivity and personal interiority—can be read as an assessment of the politics of ethnography as a cultural aspect of colonial removal.

At the same time that removal was a condition of textual production for Warren, it was a matter of immediate and personal concern. At the age of twenty-five, Warren was already a renowned interpreter. Moreover, he was about to be elected the first Indigenous territorial legislator of Minnesota in 1850 when he was asked to help administrate the removal of Ojibwe communities east of the Mississippi to unceded tribal land in Minnesota. For US officials, removing those communities was both about opening land to logging and copper mining and consolidating displaced Ojibwe people in the greatest possible numbers around the fewest possible "Indian agencies." With a larger group of tribal people made dependent on it, a given agency was positioned to profit from increased trading and the opportunity to embezzle treaty-guaranteed rations. Removal in this sense is both about natural resource extraction and about producing a human population whose manufactured precarity can be administrated, profited from, and scaled into mass death simply by withholding promised care. Warren struggled with the politics and consequences of removal but nevertheless decided, in 1851, to lead five tribal communities away from their homelands to the agency at Sandy Lake. Warren knew that doing so directly imperiled Anishinaabe communities, only a year after 350 Anishinaabe people died of cold and starvation during another removal attempt. It is clear, though, that Warren considered removing communities a better choice than facing the direct military intervention he expected if they refused. He also aspired to use the opportunity of the tribes' gathering at Sandy Lake to reorganize them into a single, more powerful, political organization.[11]

In the end, none of Warren's direct efforts to save tribes from colonial incursion succeeded. He did not unite displaced Ojibwe communities into a single, collective political unit; his advice to capitulate to removal did not soften US military, economic, or environmental assaults on tribes; and he was not able to publish History of the Ojibway People or complete the ethnographic trilogy he planned before he died of tuberculosis in 1853, at the age of twenty-eight. Published by the Minnesota Historical Society thirty-two years after his death, Warren's text provides a record of what it means to struggle with and against removal as a recurrent and multivalent colonial logic. One of the goals of this chapter is to understand how the book's strangeness and unfinishedness as well as its trenchant analysis of removal are functions of the way it grapples with the emergent narrative and institutional production of anthropology alongside the material and territorial removal of Ojibwe people from their homelands. The multiplicity and recurrence of removal are the conditions of production of History of the Ojibway People and the object of its political intervention. Further, Warren's text exposes a paradox at the heart of the colonial politics of saving generally: because genres and institutions of colonial archiving reproduce the fantasy that colonial history occurs where there once was not any, they necessarily demand and enact removal, at both territorial and epistemic levels, of the very Indigenous people and epistemic systems they claim to preserve.

This chapter is organized into four further sections. The first two examine removal as an aspect of colonial politics and genre, respectively. In the first, I identify removal as the point of inflection between the complementary and recurrent political logics of war and aid; in the second, I attend to survey as the generic structure that makes the politics of removal historically narratable. Warren's text points to these political and cultural functions of removal in the strange moments it seems to erase or second-guess its own living relation to Indigeneity. Whether it is in the way Warren reconciles his own identity position with the colonial survey's generic investment in authenticity or the moments he struggles to reassert a mode of analytical agency denied to him by ethnographic comparison, the text pointedly deconstructs where colonial demands for Indigenous erasure and preservation intersect. The chapter's final two sections turn to *History of the Ojibway People* to ask how it thwarts and exceeds the cooperating structures of removal, aid, and salvage. Because his text is, broadly speaking, composed to conform to the generic protocols of ethnography and colonial history, I attend to the unusual moments when Warren names and then vexes anthropological investments in Indigenous originality. In such moments, Warren interrupts himself as an ethnographer and, in so doing, indicates the tenuousness of colonial structures of culture- and history-making. Here, I pay particular attention to moments in which Warren invites into the main fabric of his text details that might seem, in a historical or social scientific context, banal, sentimental, or minor—details that derail or confuse the sense of the book as comprehensively or systematically explanatory. Against the generic expectations of the panoptical cultural survey, Warren commits to the richness of Ojibwe worlds in ways that cannot be reduced to the terms of savable, cultural evidence. As he notes, "The writer has confined himself altogether to history . . . as obtained from the lips of their old men and chiefs who are the repositories of the traditions of the tribe"; in other words, these are moments that come directly from the years Warren spent talking with tribal relatives, sometimes in the midst of state efforts to remove them.[12] More than just example, such moments ultimately articulate a theory of interruption as the refusal to remove.

Rather than attempting to position *History of the Ojibway People* as a model of decoloniality or to resolve questions about Warren's relation to being Ojibwe or to Indigeneity broadly, this chapter is interested in what it means to write against removal. How Indigenous writers situated in the midst of, and who in multiple ways participate in, emergent policies of removal critically and generatively oppose those policies. For Warren, writing against removal meant developing methods of interpretation agile enough to be sensitive to a world in catastrophic transition. At his best, Warren offered salient accounts of how removal recurs and of methods of opposition that could be leveraged from within and between its recurrences. Living and writing between recycling structures of colonial power is not a heroic position or one liberated from ideology, as Warren knew. While he was deeply connected with Ojibwe communities, he was also proximate to colonial power, and this ambivalence was a source of unyielding misery, alienation, and poverty during his short life. In other words, Warren was, by trade, an interpreter: someone who traffics in-between. The lessons this chapter draws about his work have to do with how a life in-between is also a condition for organizing history against—which is to say, in proximity and confrontation with—the formal rearticulation of colonial power and violence. Warren's strange and heartfelt grappling with the contractions of writing against removal in *History of the Ojibway People* is both an achievement of political analysis and a response to fundamental questions about the politics of Indigenous history writing that continue to preoccupy Indigenous intellectuals and communities in and beyond the Twin Cities.

Sovereignty as a Condition of Aid

During Warren's lifetime the most notorious removal of Indigenous people was that of Cherokee communities from tribal homelands in the colonial southeast—a removal driven by Andrew Jackson, settler mining, and the plantation/slaver class in Georgia. That removal was famously adjudicated in the Marshall Trilogy (*Johnson vs. McIntosh, Cherokee Nation v. Georgia, Worcester v. Georgia*). In these cases, Chief Justice John Marshall established many of the key principles of Federal Indian Law as it operates today, including the understanding that tribes are "domestic dependent"/semisovereign nations whose primary diplomatic relation with the United States occurs at the federal level. The removal of Cherokee people to make way for settler miners, speculators, and the expansion of slavery was the occasion of these cases, but not their primary question. Rather, the cases were principally concerned with the balance of power between the US federal government and states and between the federal executive and judiciary. The trilogy arguably marks the most significant constitutional crisis in US history because the decisions sought to intervene in a moment in which states openly challenged federal power over control of Indigenous land, and the president attempted to assert independence from the Supreme Court. The court's decisions opposed Georgia's removal of Cherokee people, but it did so to express the superiority of federal power and to balance executive and judicial power. In other words, although Marshall ruled that the state of Georgia had no standing to violate Cherokee sovereignty, he never outlawed or opposed removal. What these cases reveal is that removal was significant not as a matter of right but as an occasion for the United States to renarrate its own political, historical, and spatial coherence as it pivoted between the equally genocidal policy mandates of war against Indigenous people and the extension of humanitarian aid to them.

At stake in the question of Cherokee removal for colonial officials was control over the politically consolidating, if plainly untrue, historical narrative of Indigenous disappearance. Despite the fact the Cherokee communities had sustained a robust political and economic system and a thriving cultural life through centuries of US colonial incursion, state and federal officials were engaged in a rivalry over what O'Brien calls "lasting": the production of narratives of colonial modernity based on "the myth . . . that Indians can never be modern because they cannot be the subjects of change, only its victims." Lasting "locates Indians in an ahistorical temporality" in order to articulate "a rupture that enabled [colonial] modernity and demonstrated [colonial] progress."[13] For both the Marshall court and its rivals (President Andrew Jackson and Georgia officials) that rupture is the end of the explicit political disposition of war against Cherokee communities, marked by the Treaty of Hopewell (1785). War provided ideological stability for settlers and state and federal forces, all of whom could be aligned via orientalist narratives of "civilizing" conquest. The language of the Treaty of Hopewell troubles this alignment by guaranteeing Cherokee people state protection against unsanctioned violence and land seizure. While that protection was neither seriously offered nor provided, the treaty raised the question of how to narrate colonial power in the aftermath of the ideological stability war made possible, a question that was intensified by the "discovery" of gold on Cherokee land in 1827.

For Jackson and Georgia officials, the end of war was a chance to narrate the United States in terms of racist, military domination. In 1830, Georgia governor George Gilmer wrote: "Treaties were the expedients by which ignorant, intractable, and savage people were induced without bloodshed to yield up what civilized peoples had a right to possess by virtue of that command of the Creator delivered to man upon his formation—be fruitful, multiply, and replenish the earth, and subdue it."[14] Here, Gilmer links the compatible discourses of white supremacy and white Christianity to depict US colonialisms as a historically coherent project entering its modern phase. This is a gesture echoed in Jackson's first speech to Congress where he describes Cherokee communities as having "*lately* attempted to establish an independent government within the limits of Georgia and Alabama"—an interruption, in his mind, in the historical continuity of US colonialisms that could effectively be resolved by removal.[15]

For Marshall, the end of war was a chance to narrate US power as a structure of aid. In a letter to Justice Story, he wrote: "It was not until the adoption of our present government that respect for our own safety permitted us to give full indulgence to those principles of humanity and justice which ought always to govern our conduct towards the aborigines when this course can be pursued without exposing ourselves to the most afflicting calamities. That time, however, is unquestionably arrived, and every oppression now exercised on a helpless people depending on our magnanimity and justice for the preservation of character."[16] Marshall links a construction of colonial modernity with a lasting narrative, one in which holding Indigenous people at the brink of disappearance through aid is both source and proof of the integrity of the state.

Although Marshall's stance seems like a turn away from extraction in comparison to Gilmer's vulgar appeals to mineral access and enslavement, he was in fact interested in intensifying the state's extractive capacity. Especially in *Johnson v. McIntosh* and *Worcester v. Georgia*, Marshall relies on a close reading of the Treaty of Hopewell to clarify what he calls the US-Cherokee relation as one that "resembles that of a ward to his guardian."[17] Here, Cherokee political life is defined as a special and sustaining relation with the United States characterized by the exchange of unequal political recognition and by a US monopoly on the acquisition of tribal land in exchange for "protection."[18] This is a position Marshall defends by rooting his theory of tribal sovereignty in the commerce clause and the Trade and Intercourse Acts, which, in his words, "consider the several Indian nations as distinct political communities, having territorial boundaries, within which their authority is exclusive, and having a right to all the lands within those boundaries, which is ... guaranteed by the United States," and that "provide that all intercourse ... be carried on exclusively by the government of the union."[19]

In the long term, the United States has benefited immeasurably from Marshall's construction of Indigenous sovereignty as a condition of aid, as it administrates individual settler access to Indigenous land while reserving the federal right to seize tribal land, water, or minerals. I am especially interested in two specific aspects of Marshall's pivot between the logics of war and aid. The first is that, by positioning tribal people as beneficiaries of aid, Marshall intensifies the US extractive relation to tribes via the biopolitics of colonial racialization. Wardship as a horizon of sovereignty marks tribal people as nonidentical with whiteness and is thus a way to justify the brutalities of colonial boarding schools and the disparities of social, agricultural, and health care services within the broader logic of colonial uplift. And like all US racial regimes, the racialization of Indigenous people under the terms of sovereignty is subtended by anti-Blackness in the sense that Marshall defines Indigeneity as a social position between the complete freedom of white, male settlers and the belief in fundamental absence of freedom for Black people that animated both Marshall's life and his judicial rulings.[20]

The discrepancy between Marshall's and Jackson's/Georgia's position on sovereignty has little to do with tribal political autonomy in any material sense. The cases in the Marshall Trilogy did not stop the removal of Cherokee people in the mid-nineteenth century; neither did they challenge the entrenchment of racism as a defining aspect of US law.[21] However, the cases did codify an aid relationship around which the United States could narrate and justify a new ideological infrastructure of extraction. After the Marshall Trilogy, the fiction of a coherent colonial state increasingly depended on disguising its own resource dependency with racializing narratives of the ideological dependency of the Indigenous people and land it dominated. As Edward Said observes, the construction of Indigenous ideological vacancy is a common supplement to and justification for projects of colonial expansion that depend on myths of territorial vacancy: "Neither imperialism or colonialism is a simple act of accumulation and acquisition. Both ... *require* and beseech domination, as well as forms of knowledge affiliated with domination: the vocabulary of classic nineteenth-century imperial culture is plentiful with words and concepts like 'inferior,' or 'subject races,' 'subordinate peoples,' 'dependency,' 'expansion,' and 'authority.'"[22] For Marshall, too, the racializing language of colonial aid recodes domination as a cultural requirement, a tactic that, unlike Jackson's simple territorial seizure, is a renewable form of extraction after the (supposed) completion of US territorial expansion.

The second aspect of Marshall's rulings I want to emphasize is how his shift between the logics of war and aid is enabled by granting the US narrative authority over tribes. In *Worcester v. Georgia*, the last of the three cases and the decision in which Marshall most assertively argues for Cherokee immunity from removal by the state of Georgia, he writes:

> Indian nations had always been considered as distinct, independent political communities, retaining their original natural rights, as the undisputed possessors of the soil, from time immemorial ... The constitution, by declaring treaties ... the supreme law of the land ... admits [Indian nations] ... among those powers capable of making treaties. The words "treaty" and "nation" are words of our own language ... We have applied them to Indians, as we have applied them to the other nations of the earth.[23]

This famous definition of sovereignty is as vague in its account of tribal power ("original natural rights," "possessors of the soil") as it is clear that sovereignty means incorporation into structures of US political and historical narrative. Through constructions of political precedence ("discoverer," "supreme law of the land"), history ("time immemorial," "first discoverer"), and narrative authority ("Indians nations had always been considered," "the constitution, by declaring ... admits," "words ... of our own language," "applied ... to Indians") Marshall indicates that federal power depends on retaining a position of unilateral narrative authority—"the power," as Said puts it, "to narrate, or to block other narratives from forming and emerging ... [that] constitutes the main connection between [culture and imperialism]."[24] Marshall's careful narrative control over tribal history and colonial violence and aid is a gesture of epistemic removal even as it is one ostensibly made in opposition to territorial removal. While the legal legacy of the Marshall Trilogy is mixed, these cases are defining examples of the multivalence and the complex utility of removal within colonial systems of power. Removal occurs in them as a political and moral logic and as a narrative practice coincidentally with the way it occurs as a matter of land and history. In this sense, the Marshall Trilogy demonstrates how removal creates the opportunity for colonial systems in crisis to recompose themselves as coherent, a task that always involves the cooperating projects of text- and territory-making.

The Genre of Survey

In addition to the Marshall Trilogy, a key point of origin for mid-nineteenth-century Ojibwe removals, as well as other Indigenous removals in the Great Lakes, was the Louisiana Purchase and the formation of the Missouri Territory. As a simple jurisdictional declaration—made in the aftermath of the War of 1812 and the Haitian Revolution—the creation of the territory is itself a gesture of removal, an overwriting of Indigenous claims to and concepts of land, that asserted US control of nearly a million square miles of land and led to 222 tribal land cessions over the next century and a half. Beyond this, the creation of the Missouri Territory was also the precondition for a proliferation of political and cultural removals under the terms of colonial aid established by the Marshall Trilogy and the inauguration of an era of intensive colonial textual and territorial production. One figure whose career exemplifies the multivalence of removal in the context of this territorial expansion—and who became a central figure in Warren's *History of the Ojibway People*—is Henry Rowe Schoolcraft. Schoolcraft came to national prominence in 1819, amid the United States' first financial crisis, as the author of a geological survey, *A View of the Lead Mines in Missouri*. The book launched the country's first mineral rush, and almost immediately Schoolcraft was asked to join the Michigan Territorial administration as an "Indian Agent" in 1820.[25] Schoolcraft's sudden promotion from mineralogist to administrator responsible for dispensing aid and conducting land seizures reveals a common generic structure, the colonial survey, that links colonial projects of removing Indigenous people and natural resources in this era. Schoolcraft married an Ojibwe woman named Bamewawagezhikawquay, or Jane Johnston, and, in his position as a territorial official, he began collecting information about Indigenous people in the Great Lakes, eventually publishing several ethnographic texts, including *Algic Researches* (1839) and the six-volume *Indian Tribes of the United States* (1857). After Johnston's death, Schoolcraft married a woman from South Carolina named Mary Howard, who, with his support, wrote the proslavery novel *The Black Gauntlet: Tales of Plantation Life in South Carolina* (1860). Part of Schoolcraft's process for collecting ethnographic data on Indigenous people was to send a 347-question survey to colonial officials and prominent settlers. In 1847, the trader Henry Rice received Schoolcraft's survey and passed it on to be completed by his clerk, a young man named William Warren. Warren did, and he also published his response in a St. Paul newspaper, the *Minnesota Pioneer*, in a four-part series. The newspaper's editor eventually asked Warren to expand that response into a book that would become *History of the Ojibway People*.[26]

Warren's book is a survey written in response to Schoolcraft's survey, itself a text invested in the link between ethnographic salvage and access to natural resources. As such, *History of the Ojibway People*'s relation to removal and the essential role removal plays in US resource extraction conducted under the terms of aid is intricate and unavoidable. Reading the book in this context explains some of Warren's peculiar formal choices, including the desperate language with which he frames the text's stakes: "The red man has no powerful friends (such as the enslaved negro can boast), to rightly represent his miserable, sorrowing condition, his many wrongs, his wants and wishes. In fact, so feebly is the voice of philanthropy raised in his favor, that his existence appears to be hardly known to a large portion of the American people, or his condition and character has been so misrepresented that it has failed to secure the sympathy and help which he really deserves."[27] Here, Warren commits to representation as an aspect of colonial aid. He argues that if settlers have greater epistemic access to tribes, they are more likely to extend to Indigenous people sympathy and protection, in addition to (not instead of) genocidal violence. It is an argument underpinned by the anti-Black implication that enslaved people were more protected by being deeply incorporated into US power, one that erases Black and Indigenous histories of solidarity and ignores the possibility of tribal autonomy outside of colonial power. But it is also an argument that is directly contradicted by the organizing Warren did concurrently with the drafting of *History of the Ojibway People*, including his efforts to expose the cruelty and hypocrisy of many of the most powerful settler officials responsible for genocide and enslavement, and his attempts to consolidate Ojibwe communities in order to oppose further removal.

The gap between what we might call Warren's activism and his text suggests that it was a conscious decision of his to commit, in the course of drafting *History of the Ojibway People*, to the genre of the colonial survey on its own, dubious terms. And it is fair to assume that both implicitly and explicitly Warren learned that genre from Schoolcraft. Warren studied *Algic Researches*, corresponded directly with Schoolcraft, and cites him frequently in *History of the Ojibway People*. For Schoolcraft, the cultural survey is a genre with a specific, if contradictory, relation to removal. Like Marshall, Schoolcraft understood the territorial and discursive administration of Indigenous people to be an essential practice of state production. Schoolcraft characterizes Indigenous difference specifically as an ahistoricity intrinsic to US modernity—a historical absence that US cultural history produces itself by erasing. In his *History of the Indian Tribes of the United States* (1857), a text funded by and addressed to the US government, Schoolcraft describes Indigeneity as the quality of being "a man without history" and "having produced no historian."[28] It is a relation to history that, for Schoolcraft, is explicitly racial. He writes, "[Indigenous people] appear to be branches of oriental stocks who relapsed into the nomadic state at primeval periods, and of whom no records . . . can be found."[29] Indigeneity is a "declension from [civilization]," the condition of "man in ruins."[30] Crucially, this is a quality of social difference internal to the US colonial project: "The Indian tribes constitute an anomalous feature in our history. . . . Their geographical position, and their prior occupation of the continent, constitute the basis of an appeal . . . they have a just claim on our nationality."[31] For Schoolcraft, the racializing ahistorical construction "our Indians" is the precondition for epistemic and ideological extraction and the production of a coherent colonial modernity.[32] In Schoolcraft's mind, US modernity is characterized by the benevolent and nonconsenting incorporation of Indigenous people and land into colonial modernity. "In depicting [Indigenous] history," Schoolcraft writes, "the task [is] . . . to furnish a true basis for the governmental policy to be pursued with them as tribes and nations, and for the pursuit of the momentous object of their reclamation and salvation as men."[33]

Warren's investment in cultural survey means he inherited a generic relation to removal in which Indigenous displacement is a threshold of cultural production. For Schoolcraft, as it was for Marshall, that production is textual and territorial. Indigenous displacement is how they made the United States thinkable as an expansive and coherent cultural project. In this sense, the survey, as a genre that subtends colonial territorial seizure and culture-making, is an order of knowledge characteristic of what Michel Foucault calls the "age of history."[34] Survey is a genre that resolves Indigenous difference via narratives of development and that depends on the contradiction that colonial coherence requires an unrelenting action of incorporation possible only at the horizon of difference. Schoolcraft's *History of the Indian Tribes of the United States* admits this in the way its declaration of Indigenous ahistoricity inaugurates a "History of Indian Tribes" both narratively structured as a history of colonialism and explicitly named as a colonial possession (a "History of the Indian Tribes *of* the United States"). History, here, is the condition of production for fictions of colonial belonging that resolve difference via "principles," as Foucault puts it, of "analogy and succession"—that is, principles that do not measure differences but administrate "the identity of the relation between" them.[35] The obvious contradictions of Schoolcraft's version of history were in some sense resolved for him by what he understood the genre to be good for: controlling the terms of cultural difference through comparison, and producing the United States as an idea and a space that had history. If Foucault had been thinking about the context of colonialism, his suggestion that "history *gives place* to analogical organic structures" would be an apt and literal assessment of Schoolcraft's method.[36]

For Warren, the stakes of the contradictions and productivity of colonial history in general, and of survey in particular, were reversed. History could not be textually or territorially productive in the same way because, unlike Schoolcraft, Warren was committed to the sustenance of Indigenous knowledge and land, neither of which is a political fiction produced through extraction. Indigenous knowledge and land are what fictions of colonial culture erase in order to obtain, and so the political yields of participation in colonial survey never accrue to Warren or to the Indigenous social and material worlds of which he was a part. While other scholars justifiably read Warren's text as one that produces a written archive of tribal knowledge, I am interested in the analytically generative disturbances he creates by participating in cultural logics of removal without the desire or the position of authority to make them productive to colonial power. In particular, I am interested in his approach to cultural logics that, at the time Warren was writing, were essential to the transformation of colonial power into a structure of aid and to the colonial construction of Indigenous sovereignty as a condition of aid. In the more than a century and a half since Warren's death, colonial power has increasingly narrated itself as provider of peace, political stability, and basic provisions of human life. At the same time, colonial power constantly renews and administrates the conflict, scarcity, and destruction that are its preconditions. In the context of political and ecological emergency, however, it can be hard to argue against the relief colonial power offers from its own violence. Warren's experience of these dynamics may have been local and literary but, as such, are no less significant to laying bare the contradictions that structure colonial power and challenging its benevolence.

Against Originality

History of the Ojibway People is organized into thirty-five chapters that adhere to the generic norms of the cultural survey in three major ways. First, they describe Ojibwe communities in static geographic terms (e.g., "Ojibways of the Upper Mississippi"). Second, the chapters move chronologically from the third chapter, "Origin of the Ojibways," to the last chapter, "Events from 1818 to 1826." Third, the chapters scale between the incidental and abstract in a way that positions details about Indigenous life as evidence and colonial methods as explanatory. In this section, I turn to two places where Warren invokes and then disturbs these generic norms, specifically around the cultural and methodological frameworks of originality and analogy.

After one chapter that describes the "Present Position and Numbers of the Ojibways" and another that offers a structural analysis of Ojibwe kinship, Warren begins *History of the Ojibway People* with a chapter on the "Origin of the Ojibways." Here, the concept of Indigenous "origin" indexes a powerful alignment with colonial survey. As opposed to a supposedly claim-bearing concept of political beginning like "discovery," origin is a mythologizing and racializing formulation. Origin suggests a specific and delimited spatiality (as in a site of origin) and a progressive or evolutionary temporality (as in Darwin's *On the Origin of Species*, published six years after Warren's death). As a description of Indigenous beginning, *origin* submits to the dynamic scalarity of cultural survey: it is a word that simultaneously suggests an abstract structure of comparison and (as it does when, for instance, Indigenous origin stories appear at the beginning of American literary anthologies) a singular cultural artifact. As an organizing concept, originality situates Warren's text within the survey genre and, more broadly, at the site of contradiction between colonial war and aid. Originality is a discourse that vacates Indigenous claims to land, to intellectual sovereignty, and to modernity, and as such is a "lasting" narrative. At the same time, it is a discourse that implies aid via incorporation. Narratives of Indigenous beginning are saved as cultural property by colonial texts that absorb their supposed ancientness, as in Schoolcraft's line "The Indian tribes constitute an anomalous feature in our history."

However, Warren's engagement with originality almost immediately departs from the generic standard. He argues that Ojibwe originality—while essential to include in his text—is untransmissible in the context of the ethnographic survey because Warren himself is too proximate to Ojibwe communities: "Ever having lived in the wilderness, even beyond what is known as the western frontiers of white immigration, I have never had the coveted opportunity and advantage of reading . . . [western accounts of Indigenous history to] compare with . . . [those that] obtained possession in my own mind, during my whole life, which I have passed in close connection of residence and blood with different sections of the Ojibway tribe."[37] Warren is being disingenuous here, as he in fact did have access to education in Ojibwe and US contexts. Growing up at his father's trading post in La Pointe, Wisconsin,

Warren was primarily taught by his Ojibwe grandmother and great-uncle, but he also spent much of his adolescence in boarding schools in Wisconsin and New York.[38] This life between educational experiences is arguably an ethnographic advantage, so the fact that he denies it suggests his awareness of a contradiction intrinsic to the genre—namely, that to position himself and his text as an authentic and worthy object of colonial preservation, he has to disavow his authority as an agent of cultural comparison. Having studied the genre, Warren is aware that the structures of comparison on which survey depends require the distribution of subjects and objects of cultural analysis. The genre does not allow for Warren to be both, so he has to remove himself, in his own text, from the position of agent of cultural comparison. It is a bizarre and alarming moment in *History of the Ojibway People* that marks one of the limits of its genre. Because survey is a product of extraction, it is a genre that cannot sustain Indigenous textual or territorial production.

In response, Warren makes the brilliant and necessarily strained gesture of trying to reassert himself as cultural authority by rephrasing the terms of Ojibwe originality. He invokes and challenges Schoolcraft, who, Warren writes, "has made the unaccountable mistake" of translating a word that Ojibwe people use to describe themselves, Anishinaabe, as "common people." In contrast, Warren insists that "spontaneous man is . . . the literal translation." The belief," he writes about Ojibwe people, "that they are a spontaneous people [accords with the fact that] . . . they do not pretend, as a people, to give any reliable account of their first creation."[39] Although Ojibwemowin linguists have rejected Warren's etymology, it is possible to read this moment as one that points to the contradiction intrinsic to Indigenous originality—that it is an extractive framework for narrating colonial modernity. Further, Warren's etymology opens a space of creative analysis that, impossible to disprove by colonial officials or scholars, steals back the posture of authority under almost surrealist terms: spontaneity as an unreconcilable rephrasing of originality. This is a moment of colonial critique but not of outright generic antagonism, and, as such, it is an occasion to consider the generative sleights that open the space between colonial orders of knowledge and experiences of Indigenous writing against removal.

Later in the chapter, Warren opens that space further through another generic detour, this time via analogy. Having distanced his approach from colonial scholars and texts (which Warren names but claims not to know) and from the particulars of sacred tribal stories (which Warren also knew), he spends the majority of his "Origin" chapter considering what he calls an "analogy" between Ojibwe cosmology and "the ancient and primitive customs of the Hebrews—their faith in dream, their knowledge and veneration of the unseen God, and the customs of fasting and sacrifice."[40] Warren's long and abstract comparison between the histories and cultural structures of Ojibwe and Jewish people is anomalous in *History of the Ojibway People*, but it is formally characteristic of the genre of the colonial survey and of the logic of colonial inclusion. Analogy organizes surveys like Schoolcraft's *History of the Indian Tribes of the United States* and is how colonial ethnographers justify the confusion of all Indigenous people into singular, racializing social categories, as in: "The Indian tribes . . . [are] recognised as a strongly-marked variety of mankind, they appear to be branches of oriental stocks relapsed into the nomadic state."[41] Analogy also structures removal policy including Marshall's theorization of Indigenous sovereignty: "Their relation to the United States resembles that of a ward to his guardian."[42] Analogy is a "principal figure" to colonial orders of knowledge, as Foucault makes clear—a tool for reducing difference to what he calls a logic of "resemblance" or "similitude."[43] For Foucault, the power of analogy is its abstraction, the way it changes material conditions of human experience into "the marvelous confrontation of resemblances across space."[44] Within colonial orders of knowledge, analogy produces space and history by reducing difference to abstraction.

But like his reinterpretation of originality, Warren works analogy against the grain of colonial power. If survey reconciles contradictory colonial demands for Indigenous erasure and preservation, Warren analogizes contemporary Ojibwe and biblical Jewish people to displace and disturb objectification. By comparing these cultural systems, Warren uses the abstraction intrinsic to analogy to protect sensitive aspects of tribal religious and intellectual practice from being reduced to artifact. In his chapter, such details become evidence of "identity of relation between elements" rather than of the particularity or accessibility of Anishinaabe culture.[45] Further, by analogizing Ojibwe and Jewish cultural systems, Warren challenges confusions of Indigenous people in general and of Ojibwe and Dakota people in particular. He argues: "The writer is disposed to entertain the belief that, while the original ancestors of the Dakota race might have formed . . . a tribe of the roving sons of Tartary . . . [Ojibwe people] may be descended from a portion of the ten lost tribes of Israel, whom they also resemble in many important particulars."[46] Finally, Warren uses analogy, if not to directly challenge the presumption that only colonial scholars could be agents of comparative cultural analysis, to worry that presumption. He reports that he "sometimes interpreted to [Ojibwe elders] . . . portions of Bible history, and their expression is invariably: 'The book must be true, for our ancestors have told us similar stories, generation after generation, since the earth was new.'"[47] Here, the reduction of specific histories to abstract relation opens interpretive authority beyond the conventions of survey, muddying the taxonomies of ancientness and modernity, center and periphery that the genre conveys. Like Warren's reinterpretation of originality, this is not a moment of heroic decolonization, but one in which the generic conventions that naturalize removal are subtly and significantly destabilized.

Interpretation as Interruption

Originality and analogy are not narrative structures of direct opposition to removal for Warren. Rather, they are aspects of a text, written during what is now understood as the "removal era," that demonstrate that Indigenous removal is ongoing and unfinished, a recurrent site of colonial textual and territorial production. Writing even as Minnesota began to announce its occupation of Ojibwe and Dakota lands complete, Warren reveals how, for colonial cultural and political structures that depend on extraction, removal is never over. Further, one way that Indigenous writing against removal succeeds is by thinking beyond and between the terms of erasure and preservation. Warren's short life coincided with the first mineral rushes in the Great Lakes and Southeast, a series of colonial removal orders, the judicial codification of tribal sovereignty, and the rise of the geographic and ethnographic survey. Each of these directly shaped his thinking and writing, but not strictly in terms of loss or displacement as we might expect.

From a very young age, Warren was unusually positioned between the United States and Indigenous communities in a way that is often theorized as aligning with ideological fluidity, instability, and alienation. As a one-year-old, Warren was specifically named in the Fond du Lac Treaty of 1826 in an article setting aside land for "half-breeds," the same treaty that established Ojibwe "acknowledge[ment]" of US "authority and jurisdiction," and "grant[s] the government of the United States the right to search for, and carry away, any metals or minerals from any part of their country."[48] This treaty and the 1837 White Pine Treaty, which provided Ojibwe land to Warren's white father, racially marked Warren's relation to Ojibwe land, which might otherwise have been organically included in Ojibwe kinship systems, as an element of US political and resource extraction. By 1842, Warren was hired by the United States as a primary interpreter for the Copper Treaty, which traded settler mineral access for Indigenous "right of hunting on the ceded territory, with the other usual privileges of occupancy, until required to remove by the President of the United States."[49] In 1847, Warren interpreted during negotiations for a treaty that ceded Ojibwe land on which removed Ho-Chunk tribal communities would be temporarily situated. In 1850, he was employed by Ojibwe communities to negotiate against Zachary Taylor's executive order to remove Ojibwe people from their tribal homelands, a negotiation that ended catastrophically with hundreds of Ojibwe people starving or freezing to death while waiting for government annuities.[50] Finally, in 1851, Warren agreed to help administrate another Ojibwe removal effort, a decision that cost him his credibility with Ojibwe communities in Minnesota.[51]

As Theresa Schenck's biography of Warren makes clear, what it meant for Warren to live and work between the United States and tribes during this intensive period of removal was not an experience of ideological inconsistency or ambivalence. Warren was unremittingly committed to the Ojibwe communities he recognized as his relatives, and who recognized him in kind. Rather than understand Warren's position as one of alienation, I argue that his life and work spent between colonial and Indigenous worlds was an intense, specific, and analytically generative immersion in the contradictions intrinsic to removal that displaced (and continue to displace) Ojibwe people and ecosystems in the Great Lakes. This specific quality of experience was particularly acute for Warren in the course of treaty negotiations, when he was tasked with reconciling two irreconcilable political and cultural systems: one based in racial capitalism and colonial nationalism, and the other based in nonenlightenment practices of reciprocity and relation. Here it is essential to think about that experience using the term Warren himself used: *interpretation*. I understand interpretation here as a something other than the translation of meaning from one language to another under the rubric of transparency. And while no translation achieves or tries to achieve pure transparency, the gap between English and Ojibwemowin in treaty negotiations is particular because what Ojibwe leaders were not given to understand always became a site of the extraction, while what colonial officials did not understand was ignored or racialized and diminished. What it meant for Warren to interpret was to confront irreconcilable gaps and contradictions in meaning, to understand that such gaps were constitutive not anomalous to living against removal, and to help sustain Ojibwe life and thought nonetheless.

In a personal letter to a government agent, Warren reported that after many years of being denied access to elders' stories, he was able to use treaty negotiations in 1847 to "mention to the chiefs my anxiety to collect all events of importance that had happened to their tribe ... to write these events on paper, that they might last forever." In response, an elder named Old Buffalo gave Warren a "talk," which Warren recounts:

> My Grandson . . . you have now become as one of us, you have now arrived to the age of thinking and discretion . . . Since the White faces have come and resided among us our young men have become unsteady and foolish. . . . The traditions and customs of their fathers shall be buried with them. . . . My Grandson . . . you had often asked me what I knew of former times but I did not open my heart to you for you was then a child. You are now a man you know how to write like the whites you understand what we tell you. Your ears are open to our words and we will tell you what we know of former times. You shall write it on paper that our words may last forever.[52]

Old Buffalo affirms Warren's status between tribes and settlers as a position of relation. Further, he indicates that he waited to be sure that Warren's disposition toward these stories was not fetishizing or transactional, and that Warren was asking from the position of an epistemic collaborator. That Warren prompted this exchange in the midst of treaty negotiations suggests that he understood interpretation to be something other than a matter of achieving political consensus through translation. More than the production of a new text, Warren produced what Christopher Pexa calls a "pause" within translational practice of textual production: a gesture of "listening and remembering" that is "born of the embodied encounter" with people and "with a specific place."[53] Interpretation, for Warren, was a way of grounding and holding open the production of Ojibwe texts; it was social, and it was a way to interrupt the broader extractive political conditions that occasioned it.

By framing Warren's relation to interpretation as a literary and political practice of interruption, I want to underscore the ways his work destabilizes the territorial and textual processes through which the United States creates fictions of its coherence and of Indigenous erasure. Mohawk scholar Audra Simpson theorizes Indigenous interruption as a way "to stop a story that is always being told," specifically the story that "settler colonial states tend to tell about themselves . . . that they are new; they are beneficent; they have successfully 'settled' all issues prior to their beginnings."[54] Similarly, Pexa frames practices of generative refusal Indigenous translators use to intervene in colonial ethnography as a "subversive withholding."[55] As an interpreter, Warren was hired to help produce Indigenous consent to removal, a story of colonial territorial and political realization. In such a role he was never in a position to challenge that expansion directly. If officials thought he was thwarting negotiations, Warren would be fired (as he sometimes was) and replaced. As powerful if not more so than direct opposition, his interpretation became a scene for interruption, as an occasion to open up pauses, gaps, and breaks that necessarily structure colonial negotiation and to fill them with Indigenous epistemic production and sociality. In a political sense, Warren's interpretation interrupted the story of jurisdictional consolidation and Indigenous erasure of which treaties are an archive. In a literary sense, I also understand his interruptive interpretive practice as a critical modality that echoes in deconstructive approaches to literary comparison.

Although comparative literature would not be established in US universities for a half century after Warren, its early conceptual and methodological development was (as it was for the literary survey in 1840) a direct extension of colonial removal. Comparative literature was conceived as a way to expand literary studies beyond national boundaries without jeopardizing white literary traditions' separateness from Black or Indigenous thought. A disciplinary new-world-making, early comparative literature measured its transnational traversals via racializing surveys and a temporality of social evolution toward "a synoptical view" of white literary studies.[56] As a discipline, US comparative literature's epistemic erasures and abstractions were also materially sustained by Indigenous displacement, at first through the rise of both private and public (and, in many cases, land grant) universities and, later, in an effort to support wars overseas, via Department of Defense funding.[57] Critiques of early comparative literature from Said forward have drawn attention to the colonial logics at work in comparative scale enlargement schemes from transnationalism to world literature to the Anthropocene. But these critiques have also invited focus on comparative modalities that do not reconcile to existing or enlarged jurisdictional forms or recapitulated progressive temporalizations. Following Natalie Melas, I am interested in comparison that centers textual, territorial, and temporal "incommensurability," and in particular what she calls a "minimal form of incommensurability, which produces a generative dislocation without silencing discourse or marking the limits of knowledge . . . [but] instead opens up the possibility of an intelligible relation at the limits of comparison."[58] Melas roots her theory of incommensurability in concepts like Édouard Glissant's formulation "equivalences that do not unify" and Gayatri Spivak's elaboration of Jacques Derrida's term "teleopoiesis" as "affect[ing] the distant in a poiesis—an imaginative making—without guarantees," which Derrida himself puts in terms directly relevant to Warren: "Teleiopoiós qualifies . . . that which *renders* absolute, perfect, completed, accomplished, finished, that which *brings* to the end. But permit us to play too with the other *tele*, the one that speaks to distance and the far-removed, for what is indeed in question here is a poetics of distance at one remove."[59] Comparison that "does not gather," that makes "without guarantee," and that holds open the space of the "remove" speaks to Indigenous intellectual production against removal in that it invites a refusal to reconcile difference and remembers that the sites of contradiction intrinsic to colonial power are opportunities to elaborate Indigenous life and thought.

Warren's work as an interpreter should be considered a part of the genealogy of incommensurability as comparative analytic, an analytic that recognizes the cooperation of the production of "completed" or "settled" cultural formations and the extractive production of colonial territory itself. As an interpreter, Warren held open space in the midst of processes of colonial production for remembering and inventing tribal knowledge. His interpretation was a mode of Indigenous meaning-making that unsettles totalizing colonial jurisdictional and epistemic systems; it is a practice that marks the gap, distance, or remove between those systems and Indigenous knowledge traditions. I also argue that Warren's interpretation became a principal literary methodology for *History of the Ojibway People*. In biographical terms, this argument is supported by the fact that interpretation was Warren's primary literary training as a young person. But it is also an argument that clarifies some of the unusual narrative and formal aspects of *History of the Ojibway People* and, more importantly, establishes an ethic of Indigenous literary intervention against colonial extraction that lives on and through the other texts I consider in this book—an ethic, therefore, that is essential to understanding the cultural politics of the modern Twin Cities and US colonialism broadly. In formal terms, to say that Warren's interpretation shapes his composition of *History of the Ojibway People* means that his text is distinguished by the interruption of generic conventions of colonial history. Warren understood colonial history to be a genre of removal dedicated to temporal and spatial similitude. For writers that Warren studied, colonial history is the backdrop against which Indigenous difference is staged and reconciled by linking Indigenous disappearance with modernity. This is a pattern that, throughout *History of the Ojibway People*, Warren poses and interrupts. In the remainder of this chapter, I focus on two generic structures of colonial history that Warren interrupts: discovery and incorporation. Both are narrative forms that produce singular constructions of colonial history and territory via removal and which Warren interrupts with scenes of Indigenous social and epistemic invention.

In the title of his seventh chapter, "Era of the Discovery," Warren invokes the colonial concept of discovery as an "era"-making concept that inaugurates the written history of Indigenous people. But as soon as Warren positions discovery as a historically and territorially stabilizing gesture, he begins a series of interruptions and refusals of conventional discovery narratives. First, he points out that the singularity of discovery narratives is always specious: "Those who have carefully examined the writings of the old Jesuit missionaries and early adventurers, who claim to have been the first discoverers of new regions, and new people, in the then dark wilderness of the west, or central America, have found many gross mistakes and exaggerations, and their works as a whole, are only tolerated and their accounts made matters of history, because no other source of information has ever been opened to the public."[60] Warren argues that colonial history is unreliable and intrinsically linked to the removal of competing histories, of Indigenous people as subjects of history altogether (sardonically suggested in Warren's terms, "new people"), and of Indigenous people from the community that narratives of history are designed to produce (a suggestion Warren's encodes, mirroring the language of frontier extraction, in the phrase "opened to the public").

Next, Warren considers the specific mythology of Jesuit "discovery" of Anishinaabe people, a mythology he questions ("imagination in some instances, outstripped their actual progress, and missionary stations are located on Hennepin's old map, in spots where a white man had never set foot") and then strangely affirms by way of a kind of archeological reversal. Warren tells the story of "an old Indian woman" who

> dug up an antique silver crucifix on her garden at Bad River near La Pointe, after it had been deeply ploughed. This discovery was made under my own observation, and I recollect at the time it created quite a little excitement amongst the good Catholics at La Pointe, who insisted that the Great Spirit had given this as a token for the old woman to join the church. The crucifix . . . has since been buried at Gull Lake, in the grave of a favorite grandchild of the old Indian woman, to whom she had given it as a plaything.[61]

Here, Warren reinterprets a remnant of colonial incursion as an artifact kept and curated by Ojibwe people and thus upends discovery as a colonially productive narrative structure. Colonial discovery becomes an object of Indigenous discovery and, far from an instrument of totalizing redescription, a vehicle for Indigenous generosity, joy, and memory.

Via narrative interruption, Warren remakes colonial discovery as an interruption in Indigenous life and thought, a gesture that becomes a theme for the rest of the chapter, in which he offers a survey of the Ojibwe tradition of prophesizing colonial discovery:

> The Ojibways affirm that long before they became aware of the white man's presence on this continent, their coming was prophesied by one of their old men . . . He prophesied that the white spirits would come in numbers like sand on the lake shore, and would sweep the red race from the hunting grounds which the Great Spirit had given them as an inheritance. It was prophesied that the . . . the white man's appearance would be [the] . . . "ending of the world."[62]

In this account, and those that follow in Warren's chapter, even the threat of discovery, the end of the world, no longer belongs to or produces colonial modernity. In his text, discovery—the concept that organizes the genre of survey and justifies, according to Marshall, colonial sovereignty—is reduplicated and destabilized as a basis for an ongoing tradition of Indigenous interpretation. Warren holds out against the generic expectation that discovery produces singular narrative coherence and instead takes it as an occasion for interruption. Discovery is no longer a historical event at all but a formal disjunction that Warren opens and fills up with lively and unreconcilable trajectories of Indigenous intellectual life. Against the expectation that discovery marks a singular threshold of colonial modernity and Indigenous vacancy, the term is multiplied beyond stable meaning: a form whose interruption incites questions about narrative and political singularity and proliferates incommensurable spatial and social histories.

For figures like Marshall and Schoolcraft, discovery is a stabilizing precondition of political, cultural, and territorial coherence, one invoked any time colonial power needs to rearticulate itself: as a federal power, as a resource frontier, as a nation with cultural history. Without figures like Warren, who show that discovery is never singular and that it always takes place amid and from Indigenous life and thought, the principles it anchors (sovereignty, culture, territory) are easy to normalize and accept. Discovery is a method of removal and a way that all colonial stories start. How they end is in structures of Indigenous incorporation. For Marshall and Schoolcraft, the transition and sustenance of colonial power depends on shifting its disposition toward Indigenous people from antagonism to absorption. In Marshall's case, it occurs in the movement from removal via eviction to removal via inclusion; in Schoolcraft's case, it occurs from Indigenous antihistoricity and antiterritoriality to Indigeneity as U.S. antehistory and anteterritoriality.

Like discovery, incorporation is a key narrative structure that Warren invokes and interrupts. As a political logic, incorporation was a powerful and emergent force in Warren's world, symbolized in part by the shifting physical infrastructure of settlement in his lifetime. When he started interpreting, the Twin Cities did not exist. The principal settler political structure was not the city but the fort, and, like all colonial forts, Fort Snelling (where Warren interpreted between the United States and Ojibwe and Dakota people) is a structure of pure anti-Indigenous and anti-Black antagonism which figures the noncolonial world as alien and threatening. But by 1853, when Warren was no longer an interpreter but a territorial legislator, pure anti-Indigeneity was no longer sufficient to sustain colonial power. One of the votes Warren participated in as a legislator established the locations for a future state capitol, university, and prison. In Minnesota, as everywhere in the United States, the capitol, university, and prison are the fundamental structures of colonial power via incorporation, structures that extend and renarrate the terms of Indigenous removal; they are places where removal is described in legal, ideological, and therapeutic terms as ending, but where in fact removal is reinvented, intensified, and normalized. It is, of course, necessary to criticize Warren for his participation in this transition in colonial power and, worse, for hoping that it would represent a relief for Indigenous communities. But it is equally necessary—and, arguably, more important—to see how *History of the Ojibway People* creates a method that refuses to allow colonial incorporation to operate on its own terms. Like discovery, incorporation is a form that Warren interrupts in order to insist on the instability of colonial fictions of political and cultural coherence and on the steadfastness of Indigenous intellectual and social life against removal.

Warren interrupts the generic conventions of incorporation throughout *History of the Ojibway People*, often in unannounced structural or categorical gestures. For instance, where colonial histories and political discourses collapse Indigenous people into singular, homogeneous, and racializing categories, Warren distinguishes histories of separate Ojibwe bands such that the figure "Ojibway People" he names in his title becomes unnarratable outside the rubrics of ethnography. Where cultural and territorial surveys depend on immutable Indigenous ideological or economic difference that inevitably deteriorates, Warren traces histories of colonial dependence on Indigenous adaptation and improvisation that suggest how the fiction of Indigenous deterioration is itself an epistemic and economic horizon without which colonial cultural and industrial systems fail. To conclude my reading of Warren, however, I want to focus on a single chapter in which Warren stages the explosion of colonial incorporation in a way that metaphorizes the broader political commitments of his project.

Almost halfway through *History of the Ojibway People*, Warren interrupts a sequence of thirteen chapter-long microhistories of different Ojibwe bands and their diplomatic relations with Dakota communities. Here, he adds a pair of chapters—"Ending of the French Supremacy" and "Commencement of British Supremacy"—that narrate a shift in structure of colonial occupation in the Great Lakes. The first of these is presented as a lamentation over the deepening political domination that came with rising British power. But the chapter immediately interrupts itself with an account of the Indigenous insurgency, Pontiac's War, focusing on the Ojibwe overthrow of the British-occupied Fort Michilimackinac. Now a well-known story in the history of that war, Warren describes how the Indigenous community living around the fort in 1763 organized and disguised their assault on that fort as an intertribal lacrosse game, ostensibly held to celebrate the British king's birthday. After a planned, errant throw over the fort's walls, the Ojibwe warriors/players, ostensibly in the midst of a game, rushed into the fort and overthrew the British soldiers guarding it. Warren's recounting of the episode is perhaps most interesting in how he frames the story with relation to questions of history and removal. Warren begins the narrative by introducing a figure utterly ancillary to the Indigenous insurgency and to the intra-European struggle for power in the Americas: Alexander Henry, a British ethnographer and historian who was working in the area, unprotected by British forces. Warren details the uncertain and intense interrogation Henry faced from tribal elders before he was allowed to continue his research, prior to the uprising. Then, after Warren's retelling of the attack on the fort, he quotes Henry's own account of that event, ending with Henry being spared by the Ojibwe warriors and identified as an Ojibwe "friend and relation." The chapter ends without further contextualization of the political stakes of the insurgency or of the odd and interwoven narrative of Henry's temporary integration into the Ojibwe community.

Like many of Warren's chapters, this is one that seems to prompt more questions than answers. Why tell the story of the insurgency and Henry together? What were the lasting effects of the uprising on Ojibwe communities? How was that uprising understood in the context of the longer tradition of Ojibwe militarism and political self-defense? However, questions like this, that situate the story of the uprising in abstract argumentative, historical, or political frameworks are aspects of the structures of colonial history and culture writing that Warren is committed to interrupting. Conventions of colonial history are not ignored in this chapter but displaced onto the figure of Alexander Henry to whom Warren attributes "the most authoritative record of [the uprising] that has been published," and whose presence marks the advent of British military and cultural occupation.[63] Much like the fort in a political geographic sense, Henry figures as the site of the resolution of Indigenous difference via incorporation into colonial literary and cultural convention. And much as Warren does in his work on discovery, he invokes Henry here as an avatar of incorporation not to oppose or contextualize him but to interrupt him.

The uprising and the overthrow of the fort (as a temporary lapse in colonial operation) is one trajectory of interruption in Warren's chapter, but even more relevant to Warren's historiographic intervention is the reversal insurgent Indigenous organizers enacted in their disguising of the attack. On the occasion of incorporation into British domination, these organizers deployed a performance of capitulation (a celebratory lacrosse game) in order to reassert narrative and military control over the space. For Warren, the success or failure of that insurgency are less interesting than the way the story becomes a site—amid the staging of colonial incorporation—to perform the liveliness and resoluteness of Ojibwe social life. Similarly, Henry, as a representative figure of colonial history-making, becomes important because of the almost comedic reversal that occurs as he is incorporated into the tribal community and history, a gesture that becomes a chance for Warren to fill one-fourth of a chapter framed by the politics of colonial occupation with the words of tribal leaders, quoted either by himself or Henry. In both cases, Warren focuses on interrupting colonial military and cultural forms to create space for Indigenous interpretation. The fact of that interpretation is the most pressing stakes of history and culture writing for Warren, particularly insofar as it demonstrates that as often as removal is reconceived and recapitulated by colonial regimes it is thwarted by the presence of Indigenous life and thought.

My reading of Warren has situated his life and his only book in a theory of removal as a polyvalent and recurrent structure that never signals the singular elimination of Indigenous people but, rather, the reorganization of colonial power as it adapts develops new extractive demands. In Warren's life, and in the decades that followed, removal specifically signaled a shift from a colonial political and cultural logic of war to one of aid/incorporation, a shift in which Warren's career as an interpreter and administrator deeply entangled him. In this context, the brilliantly interruptive and unreconcilable formal qualities of History of the Ojibway People throws into relief the way that generic conventions of colonial history and culture are necessary to creating the fictions that make extraction thinkable as a coherent modality of living.

Domestic
Affects   2

I n the previous chapter, I argued that removal is a multi-valent and recurrent threshold that consolidates colonial governance and culture. In his classic analysis of settler colonialism, Patrick Wolfe quotes James Mooney's account of Cherokee removal to describe removal's multivalence in terms of the coincident incursions of "the lawless rabble" and the army:

> [Cherokee] families at dinner were startled by the sudden gleam of bayonets in the doorway and rose up to be driven [out] with blows. . . . Men were seized in their fields or going along the road, women were taken from their wheels and children from play. In many cases, on turning for one last look as they crossed the ridge, they saw their homes in flames, fired by the lawless rabble that followed on the heels of the soldiers to loot and pillage. So keen were these outlaws on the scent that in some instances they would drive off the cattle and other stock of the Indians almost before the soldiers had fairly started their owners in the other direction. Systematic hunts were made by the same men for Indian graves, to rob them of the silver pendants and other valuables deposited with the dead.[1]

Here, Mooney recounts the soldiers' eviction of Cherokee families from pastoral homes as well as the vigilantes' uncannily simultaneous ("almost before") obliteration and plundering of those homes, their food, and their burial sites. For Wolfe, this account reveals the cooperation of colonial law and lawlessness and establishes that cooperation as the defining military logic of settler colonialism as well as its "principal means of expansion."[2]

Wolfe's rigorous analysis of Mooney is useful for understanding the inextricability of classes of violence that colonial states try to distinguish in order to make claims to political innocence or justice. Two aspects of that analysis, however, I want to draw together and slightly reconsider. First, Wolfe understands removal as part of settler colonialism's "replacement" of Indigenous people that is always preceded by their "elimination." He considers removal as fundamentally precedent to the installation of colonial economic and social structures which depends on, among other things, enslavement: "[The] removals whereby Indians from the South East were displaced west of the Mississippi . . . [made] way for the development of the slave-plantation economy in the Deep South."[3] This approach misunderstands the geographic and historical relationship between US colonialisms and enslavement, in which enslavement was always an ideological and economic premise rather than a localizing and secondary phase of US power. Moreover, as I suggested in the first chapter, it is a mistake to overstate the finality and stability of what removal makes room for. Colonial societies are nothing other than engines for the repetition of their own violence. However their pronouncements of supremacy and autonomy seek to disguise this fact, nothing succeeds removal or any other vector of extraction. Second, I want to recenter the affective dimension of settler violence, something registered in one sense by Wolfe and Mooney both in terms of the startling proximity of the army and rabble, which ominously and correctly implies that settler vigilantes always lurk "behind the screen" of official colonial war-making systems. In another sense, they both also dwell on the avidity and brutality of settler violence, a feeling admitted, for instance, by a soldier who participated both in removal and in the Confederacy, who later reported: "I fought through the civil war and have seen men shot to pieces and slaughtered, but the Cherokee removal was the cruelest work I ever knew."[4] The anticipation Mooney describes in addition to the soldier's admission of extreme (and eventually regretted) violence exemplifies that extraction is something constantly and variously felt by colonial subjects and that organizes national structures of feeling including pride, contrition, and nostalgia.

A principal question of this chapter is how to understand these two aspects of US colonialisms together—that is, how can we describe the emotionally rewarding and libidinally charged drive of colonial violence that does not establish a replacement structure other than its repetition. In territorial terms, the recurrent and violent colonial production of nothing (other than the repetition of violence) has been figured in terms of the discourse of the cartographic fantasy terra nullius that precedes and justifies Indigenous removal and state expansion. In terms of political economy, a similar sense is captured by Glen Coulthard in his critique of Marx's theory of "primitive accumulation" and "proletarianization" and his recentering of unceasing "dispossession" as the guiding logic of settler colonialism.[5] Even in aesthetic terms, we can describe the (re)production of the colonial sublime by photographers like Ansel Adams and Carleton Watkins in terms of the preservation and identification with landscapes emptied of human life. In this chapter, I describe this colonial drive toward nothing other than the repetition of violence in affective terms, which is to say as a quality of attachment that organizes everyday life within US colonialisms. Affect, here, is not separable from the territorial, political, or aesthetic investments in nothingness, and, as such, I bookmark its iteration in relational and cultural contexts with the phrase *social vacancy*.

Social vacancy is an attachment to and by absence that both conditions social life within colonialism and normalizes and justifies the recurrence of extractive policies like removal. Just as the cartographic fantasy of terra nullius is a way for states to imagine and justify expansion, feeling alignment and identity with vacancy (in spatial, aesthetic, and relational senses) links ordinary life in colonialism with the repetition of "elimination" and justifies its own reproduction at any cost. As a social condition, vacancy feels safe, private, and indicative of unobstructed reproduction at the same time it oppositionally defines what is outside that secured vacancy, what Fred Moten and Stefano Harney evocatively call "the surround," as dangerous, public, and pathological.[6] Social vacancy is an affect that originates in and recurs through extraction, and it would be possible to trace its genealogy through racialization and fantasies of whiteness. However, in this chapter, I offer a legal and cultural genealogy of social vacancy—inextricable from the regulation of race and gender—by following its shifting relation to the forms and policies of the domestic.

Within US literary and cultural studies, the domestic is conventionally interpreted and historicized as either a generic or a jurisdictional concept.

As a genre, or category of cultural production, the domestic describes the gendering and racializing organization of social reproduction under colonial capitalism.[7] As a jurisdictional idea, the domestic is a spatial and biopolitical demarcation—a national or personal threshold that qualifies matters of power, access, and justice around binaries of externality and internality, publicity or privacy, reproduction and pathology. In this chapter, I depart from these conventional approaches to theorizing the domestic in two ways. First, I approach the domestic as a category of cultural activity that specifically reproduces social vacancy, or the array of cultural and political forms and performances that redescribe the alienating work of reproducing colonialism in terms of kinship, safety, and identity. As such, I define it as a genre of political and cultural activity that is intrinsically extractive and colonial and thus not as a generally descriptive sociological "site" or social structure that has comparable, proximal, or "coterminous" iterations in "tribal-national" or "settler colonial" contexts.[8] Second, following colonialism studies scholars including Anne McClintock and Amy Kaplan, I attend to invocations of the supposed distinction between cultural and jurisdictional expressions of the domestic as an illusion employed in order to stabilize, justify, and expand extractive colonial worlds.[9] This approach is equally guided by analyses of the domestic in Native American and Indigenous studies—for instance, K. Tsianina Lomawaima's study of domestic education in boarding schools. As Lomawaima shows, the disciplinary reproduction of Indigenous women as colonial laborers and subjects via cultural performances of domesticity was a way for settlers and settler governments to expand territorial holdings through allotment.[10] In the readings that follow, I approach the cultural and jurisdictional operations of the domestic as coextensive. The power of the concept to reproduce restricted or vacant colonial social worlds is inextricable from its use as a threshold of colonial regulation with which Indigenous social world-making is restricted, criminalized, and alienated. However the domestic is invoked in colonial contexts, what is stabilized is gendering and racializing social reproduction that guides the management of political and social meaning toward vacancy.

This chapter focuses on the specific invocation of the domestic in the 1887 Allotment Act, a piece of legislation that made collective Indigenous landholding illegal and subdivided tribal homelands into individually held, taxed, inherited, or sold plots. Allotment coordinated the social and jurisdictional sense of the domestic in three ways. First, it imposed on Indigenous people the framework of the nuclear family household and its attendant cultural investments in domesticity. By aligning the domestic household with the only means of maintaining control of land, allotment remade Indigenous kinship systems into mechanisms for the reproduction of social vacancy including the racialization of belonging via blood quantum and the financialization of reproduction via inheritance.[11] Second, it created a context in which tribal communities would (as a result of their interpolation into capitalism) likely be measured as failing to meet the economic standards of proper landholders. By demanding that Indigenous people suddenly invent revenue streams to pay for property taxes, allotment set cycles of economic and social crisis in motion, cycles that often resulted in disrupted support systems, land forfeiture, and children lost to social services and boarding schools.[12] Finally, allotment limited the numbers of acres an individual or family could possess and declared the remainder of what a tribe had previously, collectively held as "surplus" and sold that remainder to settlers. Here, landholding is the domestic horizon of the alienation of the expansive human and more-than-human relations Indigenous people sustained through land (beyond their allotted plots).

Allotment's weaponization of the domestic means that it, like the other key concepts in this book, is a shifting threshold of extraction rather than a stable structure or concept. The domestic was not something simply applied to US jurisdiction, to settler families, or to Indigenous people but is, rather, a volatile condition for social reproduction to become an engine of extraction. This chapter tracks how extraction proceeds and is exceeded and undone in four minor histories of the domestic. The first two concern the jurisdictionalization of the domestic—the histories of its codification and policing. The first of these shows how the idea of the United States as a domestic polity is a function of extraction. Here, *displacement* indexes the recurrent disavowal of Indigenous self-determination across boundary lines of nation and household, a gesture that produces the sense of interiority to and through which colonial attachment proceeds. The second demonstrates how the forms of the allotment and the reserve normalize the political and economic distributions of colonial publicity and privacy as vehicles of affectively generative exchange. Although the allotment and the reserve are advertised as forms that hold and distinguish public versus private property, I argue that they are both vectors of exchange through which Indigenous claims are traded and repressed and through which the cooperating fictions of colonial public and private life obtain.

The second two sections take up the domestic as a genre of cultural belonging that is always an effect of the attempted restriction and moral correction of Indigenous human and ecological kin relations. Here I argue that the genre of the domestic, including the domestic novel, is characterized by the repression of but also the failure to foreclose Indigenous projects of social and territorial recovery. These sections center a reading of Louise Erdrich's connected novels *Tracks* (1988) and *Four Souls* (2004) within the extraction histories of the domestic described above and critical accounts of the domestic as a genre and a site of ideological consolidation. *Tracks* and *Four Souls* are both part of Erdrich's eight-novel sequence that begins with her first book, *Love Medicine* (1984). Erdrich is a member of the Turtle Mountain Band of Chippewa and resident of Minneapolis, and many of her novels are set in or between Minnesota/North Dakota reservation spaces and the Twin Cities.[13] Her fiction is characterized by an attentiveness to the co-constitution of language, place, and social relation, a quality that has led critics to situate her work within comparative studies of American modernism, diaspora, and gendered analyses of colonial violence.[14] It is also a quality that becomes jarring when (as in *Four Souls*) the setting shifts between reservation and the city, or when (as in both *Tracks* and *Four Souls*) the social and ecological world of her characters' land is threatened by extraction. These two novels in particular dramatize the colonial political and affective productivity of extraction as they are set in the immediate aftermath of the Allotment Act.

Erdrich's *Tracks* begins in 1912 as the novel's central Anishinaabe community confronts a tuberculosis epidemic, on the heels of a smallpox epidemic, at the same time that the twenty-five-year allotment trust period ended, marking the moment when colonial taxes became due for the first time, and land became forfeitable to the state. The novel ends as the land belonging to the main character in *Tracks* and *Four Souls*, Fleur Pillager, is seized and timbered. Fleur leaves her land and walks to Minneapolis, in the first pages of *Four Souls*, to confront the lumber magnate, John Mauser, who took possession of her land and trees. Unlike *Tracks*, *Four Souls* explicitly alludes to the generic conventions of the domestic novel. It is set in a paradigmatically colonial domestic space—a pastoral, urban mansion built with stolen timber and stone, on seized Dakota land, in which the social and economic choreography of white supremacy is established and spatialized via the household administration of Mauser's wife and by his sister-in-law, Polly Elizabeth. It is also a novel whose plot initially invokes a crisis of social reproduction, as Mauser (a World War I veteran) is, at the outset of the novel, apparently too physically and mentally ill to father a male heir to his fortune. Fleur enters the domestic world of the Mauser house and the critical history of the domestic novel as a character positioned to be incorporated through racialized wage labor, and, indeed, she is hired by the family as a cleaner. It is a position Fleur seems to accept at first, but then, almost as immediately, her actions in the house make clear that her incorporation into the Mausers' domestic world is impossible, because she refuses to relinquish her relation to the stolen wood and stone out of which the mansion is built and aims to force Mauser to return her stolen land. Fleur cannot be incorporated into the house or the generic structure of the domestic novel as long as she insists on the primacy and reality of the relational system out of which the house and the genre have been extracted.

In this chapter, I refer to Erdrich's *Tracks* and *Four Souls* as *allotment novels* to signal how the Indigenous social and ecological relation they narrate emerges against (both in opposition and proximity to) their repression by colonial formations of social vacancy, like the allotment. In the chapter's third section, I track that repression as a generically defining operation through a reconsideration of the discourse of haunting or the ghostly that produces formations of the domestic in canonical psychoanalytic and Marxist theories of modern power as an obfuscation and a trace of extracted Indigenous kinship systems. This is an approach driven by Erdrich's unnerving depiction of Fleur herself, who first appears to Polly Elizabeth at the threshold of the Mauser mansion as a "negative . . . the image of a question mark set on a page . . . a keyhole . . . [a] deep black figure layered in shawls . . . more of an absence, a slot for a coin, an invitation for the curious, than a woman come to plead for menial work."[15] As the novel progresses, however, Fleur's insistence on the materiality and presence of her relation with the stolen timber, stone, and land out of which the mansion and the city are transformed into a space avid for colonial attachment helps clarify how critical and theoretical dependence on haunting as a constitutive aspect of the modern domestic extends systems of colonial resource and economic extraction.

In the chapter's final section, I turn back to the ways Fleur orchestrates social and ecological relation beyond the descriptive or regulatory power of the colonial domestic. Here, I bookmark Fleur's recovery of relations that the domestic classifies as fundamentally foreign, dangerous, or lost within the interpretive framework "land back" commonly deployed in decolonial organizing spaces today. I argue that central to Fleur's commitment to relational generativity is a quality that distinguishes that work from the social vacancy of the colonial domestic: the ability to experience and interpret loss and repair together. What Fleur imagines and what land back performs is rejection of the jurisdictional and generic distinctions—presence and absence, privacy and publicity, reproduction and pathology—through which the disavowal of Indigenous life and land is naturalized and repeated.

Domestic Displacement

We should not mistake judicial invocations of the domestic as being coextensive with the colonial interior—the fortified, emptied, and unobstructed space of colonial reproduction. The domestic is not the same as the interior, but it is a condition of its production. The domestic is invoked not at the center but at the edges of colonial control, and it works under the rubric of incorporation to the exact opposite effect. In the cases and cultural histories that I consider in this section, the domestic is marked at sites or in times when the reproduction of colonial power is in question, and in every instance it is invoked in order to disavow, jettison, or dispossess people or land to demonstrate the autonomy and coherence of what remains. As a gesture, the domestic is anxious and panicked. It indicates what belongs by fixating on what it can expel. It lays the groundwork for colonial belonging, and for colonial attachment in general, by emptying existing relations out from the sites it marks for or as itself.

I begin here with legal rather than literary articulations of the domestic to challenge the expectation that the domestic is a cultural abstraction and to show how it is an essential, material theater of colonial reproduction. At the same time, I want to emphasize how tenuous and uncertain is that colonial reproduction. Colonial power is especially vulnerable where and when the domestic is invoked because colonialism depends on and only produces extraction. Fleur understands this when she refuses to be separated from her trees and enters the Mausers' house. Conventional legal historiography may be another matter, but it remains the case that we can follow Fleur's analytical lead and refuse to read colonial legal constructions of the domestic as either absurdist demonstrations of racist authoritarianism or as the unideal precedent for the more nuanced laws of today. The legal history of the domestic is a history of colonial expansion in crisis, and unpacking that history holds open the interval of its nonreproduction and begins to practice seeing how tenuously the United States holds its claims of belonging.

In its narrowest political and jurisdictional construction, the domestic references the politically fortified spatial and social vacancy that conveys a normative and reproductive sense of belonging—a sense, in other words, of home in a colonial world. Although the United States has never been nor will ever be a spatially or politically coherent project (insofar as it has only ever relied on the seizure, absorption, and administration of people and resources conducted via a global network), it became essential to develop, in the first decades of its existence as a Western power, a theory of itself as a domestic polity. With that said, the domestic is not possible to historicize in terms of an originary event but is, rather, like removal, a recurrent threshold of political reproduction. Thus, although I begin here with Justice John Marshall's decision in *Cherokee Nation v. Georgia* (1831), it would work just as well to start with Frederick Jackson Turner's frontier thesis (1890) or Justice Henry Billings Brown's famous construction of Puerto Rican sovereignty as "domestic in a foreign sense" in *Downes v. Bidwell* (1901).

One central question in *Cherokee Nation v. Georgia* was whether Cherokee people—and by extension, any tribe the United States colonized—had sovereignty separate from US federal and/or state power. Marshall's now famous answer to that question strikes a middle ground between the positions taken by many of the court's judges (that either Cherokee nation was a completely foreign nation or that its claim to sovereignty was superseded by US "discovery"):

> Those tribes that reside within the acknowledged boundaries of the United States can, with strict accuracy, be denominated foreign nations. They may, more correctly, perhaps, be denominated domestic dependent nations. They occupy a territory to which we assert a title independent of their will. . . . They look to our government for protection; rely upon its kindness and its power; appeal to it for relief to their wants; and address the president as their great father. They . . . are considered by foreign nations . . . as being so completely under the sovereignty and dominion of the United States, that any attempt to acquire their lands, or to form a political connexion [*sic*] with them, would be considered by all as an invasion of our territory, and an act of hostility.[16]

As a legal definition, "domestic dependent nations" is unprecedented, meaningless, and intentionally unenforceable. While the case has endured as the defining precedent for constructions of Indigenous sovereignty in colonial law, its backdrop was a struggle between US federal and state power, as I observed in chapter 1. Marshall's terms are primarily about establishing the coherence of the United States as a federal authority, a definition he makes by contrasting the United States with Indigenous "domestic dependent nations," and that he protects by embedding in a decision that could not be challenged because it was not attached to a political order.[17] US power is not only articulated in terms provided by the politically nonsalient conceptualization of Cherokee sovereignty and the political nonperformance of juridical decision, but it is also, here, utterly theatrical. No citation of the acknowledgment of US borders or of an exclusive relation between the United States and tribes is provided or possible, especially given that the other parties, the Cherokee Nation and the state of Georgia, are present because they refused to make those acknowledgments in the first place. In one sense, Marshall's decision is completely unilateral; it depends on dismissing non-US power and constructing Indigenous power in the negative. In another sense, his language is all about agreement and interrelation. Even as that agreement is obviously a fantasy, its theatrical deployment exposes the nonunilateral, nonautonomous quality of US power. His articulation of that power depends on the displacement of domesticity onto Indigenous people, a gesture that is both a negation and an intimate engagement with Indigenous politics as a constituent aspect of the United States. The fact that tribes are not allowed to be nondomestic by the United States is what constitutes US domestic power.

Throughout his decision, Marshall marks every such gesture of invention and inversion with theatrical declarations of consensus—what he calls "acknowledge[ment]" and mutual "consider[ation]" in the passage above. This habit—the declaration of consensus via the performance of unilaterality—is, according to Jacques Rancière, paradigmatic of modern power. Rancière writes: "Consensus consists in the attempt to dismiss politics by expelling surplus subjects . . . [it] means closing spaces of dissensus by plugging intervals and patching up any possible gaps between appearance and reality."[18] Consensus is not about actual political agreement between parties but about securing the apparently seamless relationship "between sense and sense . . . between a mode of sensory presentation and a regime of meaning."[19] Marshall's construction "domestic dependent" does not describe tribal politics, but it does name the occasion of its disavowal as a performance of consensual US power. *Cherokee Nation v. Georgia* posits the US domestic as a threshold for producing political consensus, the alignment of an obviously fictive description of US and tribal relations and the interpretive apparatus of the law, that is itself dependent on the presence and negation of Indigenous structures of political autonomy. Further, it positions the domestic as a space where the performance of spatial and sovereign coherence is produced via the disavowal of what Rancière calls politics and what we might call the multitude of relations irreducible to power.

Marshall is uninterested in establishing the domestic as a space or a spatial scale but, rather, understands it as a theater for spatial and jurisdictional motion, specifically the consolidation of US federal power under the terms of consensus and the transformation of the management of Indigenous politics from the colonial public to the private. In this sense, the domestic is not a legal structure at all but the invocation of a repertoire of cultural norms on behalf of US law at a moment of constitutional crisis. In the decades that followed *Cherokee Nation v. Georgia*, the Supreme Court relentlessly invoked the domestic in precisely this way, as a cultural regulation of political change, as it continued to define federal power over and against tribes. Many of these cases occurred contemporaneously with allotment and, following the central logic of that legislation, asserted jurisdiction over tribes by classifying intratribal activities as a matter of US domestic concern. At the same time, the court maintained the ostensibly paradoxical position that because tribes were not fully included in the US legal domestic, nontribal citizens could not be subject to tribal law when they committed crimes on tribal land. The court laid the groundwork for this position in a sequence of cases—*Ex Parte Crow Dog* (1883), the Major Crimes Act (1885), and *U.S. v. Kagama* (1886)—that immediately preceded the passage of the Allotment Act in 1887 and that share with allotment a specific justification for expanded US domestic jurisdiction. As Grand Traverse scholar Matthew Fletcher puts it, the "lack of [tribal] consent" in cases like *Cherokee Nation v. Georgia* "actually generated the legal and political justification for congressional (and federal) plenary power over Indian affairs."[20] Because there is no statutory justification for controlling tribal boundaries or self-governance, officials cited the performance of colonial political and cultural consensus (which Fletcher phrases tribes' "lack of consent") in cases like *Cherokee Nation v. Georgia* that established that colonial domination was necessary and benevolent.[21]

The culmination of these cases' expansion of US control over intratribal affairs was *Oliphant v. Suquamish*, a case decided by the Rehnquist court in 1978. The court affirmed US control over tribal self-governance and added that nontribal US citizens that commit crimes on tribal land are not subject to tribal jurisdiction—a ruling that meant that the United States is responsible for prosecuting those crimes, something it almost never does.[22] In *Oliphant v. Suquamish*, the court faced and evaded a contradiction produced by the use of the domestic as a logic of colonial seizure: if tribes were internal to the United States, so, too, ought to be their right to protect themselves from non-tribal members under the constitution. In his decision, however, Rehnquist argued that tribes are not statutorily included in the United States but are so only as a matter of US spatial coherence or as a matter of white impunity, a decision designed to privilege the protection of white perpetrators over tribal jurisdiction.[23] It perhaps seems like it is tribal law itself here that is disavowed, but the immediate stakes of that case are the continued trajectories of racialized and gendered violence committed on tribal land by nontribal citizens. *Oliphant v. Suquamish* granted ironclad impunity to individual perpetrators of crimes that always have but still increasingly target Indigenous women and gender nonconforming people (people who experience violence at among the highest rates of any demographic group and who experience that violence, unlike other groups, almost entirely at the hands of nontribal perpetrators).[24]

Oliphant v. Suquamish was a culmination of a century-long intensification of colonial domination under the rubric of the domestic, a structure that reproduces at the threshold of colonial interiority and that secures itself by alienating Indigenous people at increasingly intimate political scales. Thus, in the sense that it made the right to commit colonial violence privately a matter of the colonial public interest, it is also a case that aligns with the development of domestic violence law, broadly speaking. As scholars of nineteenth-century US law have observed, legal approaches to domestic violence have interpreted the domestic as a site for the rearticulation of power against the expansion of national rights structures. For instance, Reva Siegel marks a shift from the sanctioned abuse of women in heterosexual marriages under "the right to chastisement" to the development of anti-abuse laws, developed during Reconstruction, that almost exclusively targeted Black and immigrant men.[25] Domestic violence law was a tool of social control in such cases, adopted to challenge the postbellum expansion of citizenship. In states like Alabama, this approach was particularly explicit, as laws against domestic violence penalized perpetrators with disenfranchisement.[26] At the same time, regulation of white domestic violence was increasingly made noncarceral. Courts in the late nineteenth and early twentieth centuries found that criminal intervention in cases of domestic violence violated patriarchal families' right to privacy, culminating in the decriminalization of domestic violence via the creation of family courts.[27] Elsewhere, the regulation of white domestic violence was carried out by vigilantes including the Ku Klux Klan, the Regulators of South Carolina, and the White Caps.[28]

From the late nineteenth century to the second half of the twentieth century, US policing of domestic violence shared with the expansion of colonial domestic power an investment in the public protection of the domestic as a space of sanctioned, private violence. By 1978, the autonomous white male settler was the horizon of domestic power in both cases. But in the following decades, federal regulation of the domestic shifted toward a civil rights approach with the passage of the Violence Against Women Act (VAWA) in 1994, reauthorized in 2000, 2005, 2013, 2019, and 2021. While VAWA made the protection of women from violence a federal responsibility, it did so with a multitude of loopholes and contradictions inherited from the previous century's legal theorization of the domestic. For instance, included in VAWA's original language is a provision (Title III) that classifies violence against women as a violation of federal protections against sex discrimination. However, conservative opponents of VAWA (ostensibly to keep federal courts from being overwhelmed by domestic violence cases) ultimately limited that classification to crimes committed because of "an animus based on the victim's gender."[29] Here, US officials sought to differentiate domestic violence from hate crimes, or, in the venomous idiom of Senator Orrin Hatch: "If a man rapes a woman while telling her he loves her, that's a far cry from saying he hates her. A lust factor does not spring from animus."[30] In contrast, when a "Tribal Title" provision was finally added to VAWA in 2013, it extended tribal jurisdiction over nontribal perpetrators (previously limited by *Oliphant v. Suquamish*) only to nontribal men who had "sufficient ties to the tribe"— that is, to those perpetrators who commit domestic violence as opposed to violence in the context of anti-Indigenous racism or violence in which the nontribal perpetrator simply does not know his tribal victim.[31] Although VAWA represents increased public awareness of violence committed against non-Indigenous and Indigenous women, it ultimately deepens the conditions for colonial state and state sanctioned violence to occur. The vast majority of the funds distributed through VAWA support police and carceral systems that enact violence against Indigenous people (women and gender nonconforming people in particular) at a greater rate than any other structure in the United States. In general, the law organizes safety, belonging, vulnerability, and protection around the domestic as a theater for conceptualizing and justifying colonial distributions of violence—one specifically that protects white domestic violence from prosecution, and that withdraws protection from Indigenous women under the rubric of legal inclusion.

Across the convergent histories of colonial sovereignty and domestic violence law, the domestic is variously articulated as a space, a classification of belonging, and a jurisdictional horizon. In these contexts, it has no conceptual identity or stability, even as it is often linked to the denial of the political autonomy of Indigenous, Black, and other racialized women and the communities they organize. That patterned recurrence is not because those people or communities have any inherent relation to colonial domesticity, but because the domestic is invoked in colonial legal situations in order to control and evacuate the meaning of social and political reproduction.[32] Where Indigenous people advance or sustain trajectories of social and political invention, colonial law intervenes, using a repertoire of cultural affects (e.g., belonging, safety, fear, vulnerability) to manage or directly dismantle Indigenous communities. This pattern of colonial intervention is one, as Marshall and the courts that followed his made explicit, on which the ostensible autonomy of the United States itself depends. Colonial sovereignty, citizenship, and the social and spatial choreographies of settlement depend on absorbing and disavowing Indigenous people and land, a quality overwritten or disguised by fictions of colonial coherence and the concepts of consensus, consolidation, fortification, and interiority that US officials invoke when they mobilize the state around the domestic.

Like all settler cultural formations, the domestic does not index a stable set of social or political relations. As the histories of sovereignty and of domestic violence law indicate, the domestic shapes political meaning, at the threshold of colonial consolidation, around the culturally regulated conditions of attachment and alienation. These histories also show that it is a way of producing and protecting fictions of colonial autonomy even as those fictions are constantly undercut by the nonautonomy of their material conditions of production. Finally, these histories suggest that the domestic is a site of productive exchange. Colonial concepts of the public and private are coproduced and refined as legal structures shift power, access, and capital between them. In the following section, I elaborate on this third quality of the domestic both to disaffiliate the domestic from the private sphere alone and to suggest how the conceptual and material exchange between the public and private subtends multiple extractive systems simultaneously. I am not arguing here that the domestic bears an essential relation to neoliberalism or any particular framework of colonial political economy, but that the spatial and cultural terms of colonial private and public control are coproduced when and where the domestic is invoked. The domestic is a site of what Jodi Byrd calls "transit," where "U.S. empire orients and replicates itself by transforming those to be colonized into 'Indians' through the continued reiterations of pioneer logics."[33] In the histories of colonial sovereignty, gendered and racialized violence, and, as I will consider now, resource development, the "Indian" marks the antecedent and effect of the domestic: the ground for extraction whose classification shifts along with the demands of the state.

Allotment and Reserve

It is tempting to trace a trajectory of the steady privatization of power under the rubric of the domestic, from *Cherokee Nation v. Georgia* to *Oliphant v. Suquamish*, that is then slightly inflected back toward the public in the aftermath of the civil rights movement, by VAWA. But histories of the colonial domestic actually reveal that the private and public always coproduce each other and always depend on the extraction of Indigenous land and life. These histories belie the opposition of the private and public emphasized by both liberal exponents of a benevolent colonial public and conservatives crusading for the free market. One way to sense the cooperation and shared extraction dependence of private and public articulations of the domestic is to track the convergences between the histories of the domestic I have already traced in this chapter and the shifts in natural resource policy conducted by the same colonial administrations. To do this I draw attention to two forms—the allotment and the reserve—that link the social and political histories of the domestic that I have already considered in this chapter with extraction in a more explicit and familiar sense: the legal framing of the lumber and mineral industries beginning in the late nineteenth century. At first glance, these forms might seem to indicate opposite trajectories of private-public exchange. The allotment is a form for moving public land into private, individual or corporate title, while the reserve is a form that keeps land for the colonial public, from or against private claims. However, these forms not only emerge in explicit political relation to each other; they also, together, structure the domestic as a modern colonial affect.

Prior to the 1862 Homestead Act, settlers petitioned the federal government for land, which they often received via states. After 1862, settlers could buy land individually, for as little as $1.50 per acre, often with federal financing, and in tracts as large as 640 acres.[34] This way of distributing seized Indigenous land was not a part of an existing colonial property system but the start of one. The plots are most accurately understood, at least in the moment of their initial dispensation to settlers, as grants or allotments provided by the colonial administration, rather than as purchases made within an existing land economy. Settler allotments were not only a way to convey Indigenous land to individual settlers but were also a scheme for extraction management. Settlers with new allotments deforested millions of acres of land in order to initiate the US farming economy, and, when federal officials realized that the land had almost instantly been overtimbered, they were tasked with reforesting the same land they had cleared.[35] Further—and in direct contravention to the mythology of permanent, individual agrarian settlement—the dispensation of allotments to settlers via the Homestead Act fueled the corporate consolidation of land owning. Lumber companies, for instance, immediately capitalized on the severe undervaluation of timber lands by buying vast tracts from individual settlers, only to refuse to pay taxes on that land and ultimately forfeit it back to the federal government once it was deforested.[36] By 1911, the federal government, newly concerned with conservation, began to incentivize the process of corporate divestment by creating a process to formally purchase extracted land under the Weeks Act. By 1920, actual land ownership ceased to be the most lucrative territorial relation for resource extraction industries that simply leased public land for the duration of temporary and ecologically exhaustive operations.

This pattern of temporary, ecologically devastating landholding follows the logic of allotment, rather than that of a stable, individually based property system. Allotment, as an extractive form, is not a withdrawal from but a reimagination of the colonial public as a way to displace the risk of sustaining nonalienating and nontemporary relations with land. This same logic subtends the production of the land grant university system, also devised in 1862, which apportioned allotments of land seized from Indigenous communities to universities to sell to settler individuals and corporations in order to create the endowments for those public universities.[37] And finally, the allotment form was the primary instrument for dismantling Indigenous governmental, social, and cultural relations with land by reorganizing tribal landholding around individually owned, taxable, sellable, and forfeitable plots and appropriating the rest, which it classified as "surplus."

In none of these cases does the allotment form move land or resources simply from public to private property holding. Instead, it orchestrates an exchange in which surplus value accrues to individual or corporate settler interests, and risk is absorbed by the public. The allotment is a form that correlates belonging with value and that produces domestic economic, social, and institutional structures that depend on the public as a permanent financial backer and trading partner. As such, it is neither a form available to racialized, disenfranchised, incarcerated, or poor people, nor one that organizes equitable protection through structures like the private household, the corporation, or the colonial public, whose political coherence depends on social exclusion. The allotment separates Indigenous women and gender nonconforming people from social and political relations that offer relief from violence enacted by settlers, and it often intensifies their exposure to environmental harm.[38] Further, the protections against violence committed in the context of allotted spaces often open Indigenous people to incorporation into colonial public systems equally committed to their victimization, a pattern evinced in the history of Indigenous experiences in boarding schools and universities, nonrepresentation in US politics, and the failures of federal policing to protect Indigenous people.

In the same years that allotment became a principal form for positioning the settler individual and corporation as beneficiaries of private-public land exchange, US officials developed a complementary form, the reserve, to administrate and financialize the affective and ideological consolidation of post–Civil War colonial nationalism. As a way of managing the environment, the reserve form emerged only two years after the Homestead Act, in 1864, with the establishment of Yosemite Park. As a way of managing Indigenous people, the form emerged in the decade before allotment with the passage of the Indian Appropriations Act in 1871.[39] In both cases, the reserve form was used to manage and monetize the colonial fascination with wildness.[40] In the case of the National Parks and forest reserve system, the "preservation" of landscapes manufactured to appear pristine and undeveloped animated the growth of a new tourist economy.[41] As a way of managing Indigenous people, the reservation system was justified by colonial officials as a protection from settlers and a tool for installing "civilization."[42] But much like the park and forest reserve system, it, too, inspired a new colonial economy, one predicated on delivering social improvement via extractive educational institutions, health services, and selling treaty-protected resources to settlers. Administrated by the Bureau of Indian Affairs (BIA), reservation land after 1871 was understood as being held separate from both private settler incursion and, by way of a "trust" relationship, from total tribal control. More accurately, however, we ought to understand that position between settler and tribal control as a mode of management through which the BIA administrates tribal landholding via the permitting of settler access and of extratribal sales of Indigenous land and labor.

As the allotment rewards settler citizens and corporations for temporarily holding land for extraction, the reserve is also a form that coordinates political production along an axis of resource exchange. Specifically, the reserve organizes permanent public landholding and temporary private access, which is often coded as "leasing." Leasing is a familiar way of describing land use—for instance, when mining companies lease public lands to extract ore. But we can also think about tourist access to parks as leasing, and even tribal land use in general, given that the BIA asserts that it holds Indigenous land "in trust" for tribes. The lease is a mode of conditional access that produces private users as a class dependent on land or property holders, and on property holding as a primary political function, a source of political meaning, in general. It is also, therefore, an ideological scheme in which land or property holding is recast as necessary and benevolent: an expression of pastoral power in which dependent subjects are moved toward social improvement.[43] In the context of US forest reserves, public landholding is an ideological infrastructure of private social and economic improvement.[44] In the context of the reservation system, the colonial public is explicitly described as providing for the "civilization" of Indigenous people. In both cases, the manufacture and maintenance of the spatial form of the reserve is also implicitly the condition for the production of the public as an ideological site. The reserve is how the public becomes the source and achievement of political good, even when it can only do so via unceasing Indigenous dispossession. Moreover, the lease structures the juridical function of the reserve form. From *Cherokee Nation v. Georgia* to *Oliphant v. Suquamish* to VAWA, the United States has rejected assertions of separate tribal jurisdiction over nontribal citizens because it interprets Indigenous people as lessees or "occupants" of US public land. In addition to questions of protection against racialized and gendered violence, the environmental consequences of this logic are severe. From the denial of tribal water rights to biodiversity protection, to the remediation of corporate and US military ecosystemic toxification, tribes are prevented from making claims as separate, private entities and are instead positioned as beneficiaries of much broader, and more conditionally enforced, public legal protections.

The allotment and the reserve are forms that organize the private-public exchange that makes the United States seem domestic. That is, they organize the exchange that produces fictions of colonial cultural, spatial, economic, and legal interiority. The material histories of the US domestic confirm that it is not a space or concept that marks a coherent internality, but is rather a threshold effect and a boundary marker that seizes and stabilizes at moments when the reproduction of colonial power is uncertain. The histories of the domestic I have given in this section concentrate on the ways the domestic creates conditions of attachment or alienation around colonial forms in crisis (the jurisdiction, the home or homestead, the park)—forms that in turn give shape to everyday life in empire. Because the domestic is extractive, it produces absences, gaps, and disjunctions at the same time that it produces colonial forms, particularly around Indigenous people and texts that do not resolve to colonial orders. For instance, the inaugurating problem of this book—how to theorize Indigenous cultural production from colonial cities—is an effect of the gap between the allotment and the reserve established by the legal and cultural consolidation of the domestic. The allotment and the reserve not only became central forms for understanding the colonial domestic during the nineteenth century; they also became the forms associated with Indigeneity. Although Indigenous people always lived in the places colonial cities developed, and although those cities were populated by Indigenous people from the beginning, cities have been culturally coded as non-Indigenous as an effect of the persistence of the allotment-reserve binary. Thus, when Fleur appears at the threshold of the Mauser mansion in Minneapolis as a "negative . . . an absence," Erdrich is giving voice to a colonial discursive limit. The evident attachment, which Fleur carries with her, to the material relations out of which the mansion and city are made is irreconcilable to the terms of the domestic. In the section that follows, I turn to the negative spaces and negated relations the domestic produces to think about how multispecies Indigenous relations sustain and transform in the context of the colonial city. To do so, I read Fleur's return to the Mauser mansion via analytical discourses of haunting central to theories of the modern, colonial domestic, paying particular attention to the way Fleur's relentless kinship with stolen trees and stone eludes, exceeds, and ultimately undoes the fantasies of extractable Indigenous relationality that found and secure the colonial domestic.

Ishkonigan, the Leftovers

Even writing about histories of the domestic is, in a sense, to indulge colonial fictions of interiority, heteroreproductivity, and the naturalization of racialized and gendered labor and vulnerability to violence. The material conditions of production of those fictions are the absences, disjunctions, and elsewheres that are rendered within the conventional terms of colonial culture as parafictional, metaphoric, artifactual, or altogether unnarratable. Thus, as the administrator of the house, Polly Elizabeth, trying to observe and make sense of Fleur, standing on the threshold of the urban mansion, becomes caught in a litany of metaphors of absence. Fleur is a "negative," "a question mark," "a keyhole," "a cipher." As Nancy Armstrong argues, the domestic novel is a generic alignment with and a theater for the changing political meaning of gender, and of white English cis-womanhood in particular. What Armstrong does not attend to is how historical shifts in the meaning of gender and desire include and depend on broader cultural, political, and generic dispositions toward Indigenous and Black women. If the first modern subject was a (white cis-)woman, the trajectories of desire that produced her also produce the unnarratability of racialized modern subjects, Indigenous and Black women especially. Fleur's unnarratability is a matter of colonial desire and reproduction, a generic effect of the broader conditions of epistemic

constraint that Laura Wexler, for instance, describes as the generically manufactured "unhearab[ility]" of colonial violence.[45]

Erdrich's *Tracks* and *Four Souls* are novels about the conditions of production of the colonial domestic. In one sense, that means that they are novels
sensitive to the shifts in the meaning of colonial gender articulated both
through the changing economies of extraction and, as Armstrong famously
argues, the domestic novel itself. In another sense, it means simply that they
are novels about land. Specifically, they are novels about struggles over the
classification of land on which the production of colonial gender, race, and
the domestic broadly depend. *Tracks* begins with the catastrophic classification
of land under allotment that made it sellable ("in the past, some had sold
their allotments for one hundred poundweight of flour"), taxable ("others,
who were desperate to hold on, now urged that we . . . pay a tax and refuse
the lumbering money that would sweep the marks off our boundaries like a
pattern of straws"), and generally extractable.[46] But the novel also begins with
the land that land classification is made out of and against: "The other place,
boundless, where the dead sit talking, see too much, and regard the living as
fools."[47] The avatar of that land, the negative and the antecedent to classification, is Fleur's, the lake called Matchimanito, and ground around it—a place
the principal narrator of both novels, Nanapush, describes as thick with living (human and other-than-human) and no-longer-living beings in relation.
The animating drama of *Tracks* is the question of whether Fleur's land will be
lost via allotment to lumbering, an event initially stymied by the tremendous
force of relation hosted there, which Nanapush narrates: "I heard in those
months she was asked for fee money on all four allotments. . . . The Agent
went out there, then got lost, spent a whole night following the moving lights
and lamps of people who would not answer him, but talked and laughed
amongst themselves. They only let him go at dawn because he was so stupid.
Yet he asked Fleur again for money, and the next thing we heard he was living
in the woods and eating roots, gambling with the ghosts."[48]

By the end of the novel, Fleur's land is lost to a lumber company. But
in a gesture of brilliant and terrible sabotage, she secretly cuts through the
bottoms of her trees so that they blow down, in a sudden and conjured gust
of wind, crushing the lumber crew sent to steal them. Like the beginning of
the novel, the moment just before the trees fall is one in which the stillness
and suspension of the forest, at the threshold of being violently subjected to
colonial classification, is heightened by the fierce and kinetic sociality that
the standing trees host. Nanapush describes Fleur's forest as a space saturated
with relation: "I heard the hum of a thousand conversations. Not only the

birds and small animals, but the spirits in the western stands had been forced together. The shadows of the trees were crowded with their forms. The twigs sun independently of the wind, vibrating like small voices. I stopped, stood among these trees whose flesh was so much older than ours, and it was then that my relatives and friends took final leave, abandoned me to the living."[49] One by one, each in a moment of collapsing past and present, Nanapush encounters people he used to know, whose more-than-corporeal presence it was that had electrified the atmosphere of the forest—last of all his father and his first love:

> Kanatowakechin, Mirage, as thick snow came down ... confusing the soldiers and covering the body of my mother and sister ... I felt the snow of that winter and then the warmth of my first woman, Sanawashonekek, the Lying Down Grass. I smelled the crushed fragrance of her hair and full skirt. She took my arm, showed me how simple it was to follow, how comforting to take the step. Which I would have done happily, had only the living called from that shade.[50]

The trees fall, Nanapush mournfully chooses the living, and Fleur begins her long walk to Minneapolis. The end of *Tracks* threatens to mark the end of land, which is to say, the end of the materialization of multispecies and multitemporal relation and the beginning of the reservation in the sense of a space constituted by classification and loss. *Ishkonigan* is the Ojibwemowin word that Nanapush uses to describe what's left: "This scrap of earth. This ishkonigan. This leftover," in a way that may seem to suggest such a trans- formation.[51] *Ishkonigan* means what is left over but, more precisely, what is held back, what is saved. It shares a root (*iskw-*) with verbs like *ishkonazh* (to spare someone from killing), *ishkozh* (to leave a living thing uncut), and *ishkwii* (someone remains). The end of *Tracks*, a depiction of allotment at its most venal, is a moment of transformation from the dense, boundless land of Matchimanito to *ishkonigan*. But that transformation does not only occur in terms of loss, as colonial cultural narratives that link the rise of the domestic with the dissolution and replacement of Indigenous relations would have it. It is also a moment of the intensification of Indigenous relation under duress. Here, Erdrich attends to gestures—made by Nanapush, Fleur, their relatives, and the land itself—of restraint, of holding back, and of remaining as elaborations of relation along with loss.

When Fleur reaches the Mauser mansion, she appears to the members of the Mauser family as a ghost, a negative and illegible presence and as someone out of place and time. But Fleur is not there to haunt the family or even, as a very first priority, to retake the land Mauser stole from her. First, she simply returns to be with the material out of which the house is built:

> Copper. Miskwaabik. Soapstone. Slate for the roof shingles. A strange, tremendous crystal of pyrite traded from a destitute family in the autumn of no rice. The walls were raised and fast against them a tawny insulation of woven lake reeds was pressed tight ... Iron ... mined on the Mesabi Range. ... Water from the generous river ... mantels and carved paneling ... wooden benches ... and heavy doors ... all this made of wood, fine-grained, very old-grown, quartersawn oak that still in its season and for many years after would exude beads of thin sap—as though recalling growth and life on the land belonging to Fleur Pillager and the shores of Matchimanito and beyond.[52]

Because Erdrich is writing in the context of an American and English domestic novel tradition in which plots are shaped by relations that are property-based and heteroreproductive, Fleur's return just to be with these materials cannot register, itself, as a structuring event. But what happens when she rejoins those materials is a practice of decolonial relation, the terms of which exceed the descriptive frameworks provided by theories of the domestic novel, the city, or colonial constructions of the environment. By simply and strenuously insisting on rejoining or rather remaining with these materials, Fleur makes land back out of and against colonial terms of spatial and specific order. Much as the trees' sap connotes memory *and* continuity of living, Fleur re-anchors and reorganizes those materials as land. She does so not in any way that pretends that it is the same as before, but that insists that Indigenous practices of grounded and somatic relation have the capacity to regrow with loss.

I begin this section with this reading of the transition between *Tracks* and *Four Souls* to underscore two arguments about the domestic that emerge from the novels themselves. First, even beyond the extraction dependence evident in legal histories of colonial sovereignty and safety, the domestic also indexes a specific cultural and affective relation to loss, temporality, and ontology that depends on Indigenous extraction. Fleur's appearance to the Mausers as a specter is an aspect of both the inability of the colonial domestic to conceptualize Indigenous presence and complex temporal and ontological relation around loss, broadly speaking. Here I understand Erdrich as invoking metaphors of haunting in order to point out a limit of the imaginary of political domination at moments of political crisis. This is an argument particularly relevant to the question of how US disciplines and political institutions face the prospect of world-ending environmental change. Although those questions are usually structured by universalizing discourses like the human, the planet, and the epoch, they are, even at their grandest, extensions of the political logics of the domestic that conceptualize belonging as an aspect of sovereignty and safety and always depend on extraction. Second, I use Erdrich's allotment novels to think about the formulation and invocation popular within Indigenous activist spaces: *land back*. In the context of the jurisdictional problem of the city in general and the Twin Cities in particular, I argue that Fleur insists that the city is a site of taking and making land back. And in the context of the question of how to face world-ending political and environmental change, I argue that Fleur's nonlimitation to the terms of the domestic coincides exactly with her practice of remaking lost land—her practice, that is to say, of remaining with land with loss.

In 1924, when Fleur arrives in Minneapolis, the US timber extraction industry was collapsing. Old growth forests were almost completely eliminated, the Great Depression drove most lumber companies out of business, construction was increasingly accomplished with cement and steel, and conservation was gathering momentum. As an aspect of that extractive history, the mansion Fleur enters at the start of *Four Souls* is a memorial. Its owner, John Mauser, would not make more money from stealing trees. Correspondingly, his position of authority within the household was, by the time Fleur arrives, almost purely honorary. The house and its staff are not organized by deference to him any longer, but by the administration of his sister-in-law, one of the novel's two principal narrators, Polly Elizabeth. Polly Elizabeth is a character and a narrator who emerges at a moment of uncertain colonial reproduction both in the historical sense of the transition between extractive regimes and global wars, and in the sense of a reproductive crisis within the house as Mauser and his wife, Placide (Polly Elizabeth's sister), are actively repressing their sexual desire through a practice Placide called "Karezza."[53] As a narrator and a conductor of discourses around the family's economic and social nonreproductivity, Polly Elizabeth is the apotheosis of the modern woman, in Armstrong's terms, a figure whose cultural and historical ascendance the domestic novel, as a genre, stages. Fleur, on the other hand, arrives in the midst of this productive crisis of colonial reproductivity as the counterpoint to the modern woman. Her decisions to join the house, to kill or heal, marry and coparent with Mauser are not structured by repression in the same way. Fleur's otherwise "successful" entrance into the colonial domestic world is never affirmed by lasting social power in Minneapolis. Most importantly, she remains silent. The novel's chapters, narrated alternately by Nanapush and

Polly Elizabeth, pivot around Fleur's narrative absence, even as her experience remains the primary animating force of the book.

From the vantage of Polly Elizabeth and the genre of the domestic novel, Fleur's presence is disturbing not because she is so alien, but because she is too familiar. She is and she activates what the domestic marks as raw, excessive, charged, what comes before and what must be repressed. Fleur haunts the Mauser mansion, in that she can only be reconciled to the temporal and spatial terms of the domestic as a revenant, as a return of what was supposed to remain or to be rendered as remains. As such, Fleur fulfills a necessary position in the cultural economy of the domestic, what Sigmund Freud calls the *unheimlich* the unhomely, the uncanny. Freud points out that *unheimlich* is a constituent aspect of domestic belonging, that historical use of the term "*heimlich* . . . becomes increasingly ambivalent, until it fully merges with its antonym *unheimlich*."[54] That merger, for Freud, is figured specifically as an unwelcome, anachronizing return: "The uncanny [the unhomely] is something familiar [homely, homey] that is repressed and then reappears."[55] In *Four Souls*, what it means for Fleur to (re)appear as the uncanny specter of and in the colonial domestic has to do with the political, social, and resource negations—the dialectics of sovereignty and safety—through which the domestic is articulated. The interlocking and systematic assaults on tribal land, knowledge, and women register to Polly Elizabeth as historical curiosities ("as I've since learned, [Mauser] plundered their land and took advantage of young women") and to Nanapush as the unfolding catastrophe of the present: "In his earliest days, handsome and clever, [Mauser] had married young Ojibwe girls straight out of boarding school, applied for their permits to log off the allotment lands they had inherited. Once their trees were gone he had abandoned his young wives. . . . Stumps and big bellies was all he left behind."[56]

However, as Freud predicts and Nanapush implies, although the political architecture of the domestic expresses nothing other than a separation of its present and proper terms from what it leaves behind and leaves as behind, it cannot sustain that separation, because it has no way of proceeding as a political form other than consuming and repressing Indigenous relation. Erdrich exposes the specific and unavoidable extraction that constitutes the domestic, what it requires to progress, eerily suspended between its own dissolution and rearticulation. As scholars of the American domestic novel have observed, the racialization and gendering of domestic space is dedicated to stabilizing precisely this volatile threshold of interiority—political work that Lora Romero figures as "expung[ing] imperialist conflict from the Jacksonian cultural memory," and that Kaplan describes as a "bulwark against and embodiment of the anarchy of empire."[57]

Freud observes that the uncanny "often arises when the boundary between fantasy and reality is blurred, when we are faced with the reality of something that we have until now considered imaginary."[58] For the Mausers, and for the array of colonial systems and histories they stand for, there is nothing unsettling about the boundary between reality and fantasy per se; colonial worlds depend on administrating that boundary, particularly with regard to value, beauty, and power. But what makes that boundary "blur," as Freud puts it, is land: the complex of multispecies and multitemporal relations that colonial political and cultural attachments depend on consuming and repressing. Land haunts colonial affect, particularly that which cathects at the critical thresholds of social and political reproduction that I index with the term *domestic*. To conclude this chapter, I concentrate on that impossible contradiction, that blur, inspired by the proposition shared by Fleur and by modern Indigenous communities and activist movements: that land can and must return, that it can be returned, that it can be remade and that people must remain with it, even with the catastrophes that colonialism rebrands as structures for living. The proposition that land can and must return is, as I have suggested, anathema to the domestic because colonial sovereignty and safety depend on the fantasy of political and economic progress sustained no other way than the unceasing extraction of Indigenous land. When Indigenous people and the ecosystems they live with reassert the materiality and complexity of land, beyond what colonial structures can manage, those structures turn to metaphors of ghosts and haunting as a last gesture of culturally scripted repression. However, the insistence land back names an altogether more nuanced and robust framework for living with and through the social and ecological catastrophe of colonialism.

Land Back

In its contemporary use, *land back* began as a meme made by Niitsitapi artist Arnell Tailfeathers in 2018.[59] Land back is a retort and a critique of liberal constructions of justice, specifically the discourse of reconciliation that so felicitously coexists with the intensification of pipeline and fracking development, economic exploitation, and militarization all on Indigenous land. Land back is also an anagrammatical invocation and a performative. It is a way of calling for and calling together in which land blurs between subject and object and in which the meaning of the word *back* resonates beyond possession. It is a demand and an articulation of yearning that attends less to originality than to what it means to return from and with loss. As a kind of cultural expression, land back is a meme, a genre uninterested in defensible boundaries, repression, or inheritance, and one that flourishes with repetition and elaboration that is always social beyond measure. Unlike the domestic novel, the genre of the meme does not make heroes or romances or try to hold a total world; neither does it suggest a politics of innocence. Memes are shared across corporate media networks whose ecologically exhaustive infrastructures intensify environmental inequities for poor, racialized, and Indigenous communities globally. As such, memes—and, in particular, land back memes that have been instrumental in organizing support for land and water protection movements from Standing Rock to Wet'suwet'en—share with Erdrich's novels an ability to indicate the limits and contradictions that constitute supposedly autonomous colonial political and representational systems.

Premised on a decolonial theory of return, land back deconstructs progressive temporalities that subtend liberal legal reform. Laws like VAWA, which expand US carceral power and incentivize its reproduction by tribes in the name of safety and sovereignty, establish a progressive timeline from discovery to the present (the period of legal establishment) and from the present into the future (the period of legal improvement). Land back, on the other hand, names a mode of repair and reparative temporality impossible within US cultural and legal frameworks. Land back is irreconcilable to US colonialisms that depend on unceasing land extraction, and it suggests a temporality predicated on a multidimensionality of repair that does not repress but proceeds with loss. Within deconstruction there is a separate and convergent tradition for thinking about the kind of temporal aporia posited by land back. Jacques Derrida's proposition in *Specters of Marx*, for instance, of what he calls "hauntology," suggests an apposite theory of temporality. The sense of "spirit" or "specter" Derrida draws out—starting with *The Communist Manifesto*'s famous opening—finds revolutionary potential in the temporal potentialities of haunting and mourning. As a mode of being and thinking with loss, Derrida observes that mourning "consists always in attempting to ontologize remains, to make them present . . . to know *who* and *where*" the dead are, so that, "in what remains of [them], [they] *remain there*."[60] In mourning, we face the critical ontological convergence of being and nonbeing through a radically unstable temporal frame, a frame that disorients past and future from the present and does so inexorably via the equally unstable relation, the blur of presence, between self and other. The present and presence are both always constituted by the anticipation of loss (of ourselves and/as other, of the temporary illusion of discrete past and future) and by the remembering of return (of presence through the blur of time and subjectivity).

For Derrida, this temporal and ontological aporia is also the premise for "the possibility of justice," the "absolute *pre*cedence" as he puts it, of other modes of being and other temporalities: "The heterogeneity of a *pre-*, which . . . means what comes before me, before any present . . . but also what . . . comes from the future or as future. . . . The necessary disjointure . . . of justice, is indeed here that of the present—and by the same token the very condition of the present and of the presence of the present."[61] Derrida's concept of a present/ness constituted by the possibilities and difference of being and time is itself a powerful analogue to many contemporary abolition and decolonization discourses. As Gayatri Spivak puts it in her elaboration of hauntology, this "ethical relation with history" depends on "the uncontrollable, sporadic, and unanticipatable periodicity of haunting."[62] Thinking about haunting as a framework with abolitionist or decolonial potential, what Derrida calls the "disjointure of justice," Spivak insists that it posits a "future anterior, not a future present, as is the case with the 'end' of most narratives of social justice"—not a "guarantee of a future present," but the necessary gesture of "surrender[ing] to undecidability . . . as the condition of possibility of responsible decision."[63] From cultural and political perspectives produced by way of the colonial domestic, land back can only be (mis) understood as a messianic project, a reverse domestication of property and capital into tribal power, a (mis)understanding that demonstrates the powerful conceptual delimitations the domestic enacts.[64] But the actual political invocation land back performs is even more threatening to the United States than such a reversal of property-holding and sovereign exclusion. As Spivak puts it, revolutionary return of this kind, "because it coordinates the future in the past . . . is not only a revenant . . . but also an arrivant."[65]

What land back calls together are precedent and anticipated temporal and ontological relations in the context of which colonialism is not merely displaced but is impossible. What it requires to imagine and enact is at once the spectacular and unstable revolutionary horizon that Spivak describes and something altogether simpler: a theory of relation in which regeneration with loss is possible. Turning back to Erdrich, now as a theorist of the politics of return, we find that one of the reasons the Mausers' understanding of Fleur's appearance as a haunting fails is because of the political, temporal, and ontological limitations of the domestic itself, the lens through which they interpret not only Fleur but also their own uncertain position at the threshold of colonial reproduction. Mauser confides to his sister-in-law Polly Elizabeth (who, by the middle of the novel, has begun to think of Fleur, not Mauser, as her family): "[Fleur] expects that I will return her land and give her all my money . . . but she doesn't understand . . . I could hardly make restitution to a people who've become so depraved. . . . The reservations are ruined spots and may as well be sold off and all trace of their former owners obliterated, That's my theory. Let the Indians drift into the towns and cities. . . . There's nothing left!"[66] Mauser mistakes Fleur's presence as a call to reverse the terms of progressive temporality, property, and subjectivity. He pathologizes Indigenous people and land as the wasted, barely lively remains of the social and ontological orders of the present/ness because the domestic depends on that discursive exclusion to produce fictions (e.g., "towns and cities") of its coherence and totality. Finally, his understanding of Fleur and her purpose is fundamentally constrained by his inability to conceive of repair that could occur with loss.

Mauser, as a denizen and producer of the colonial domestic, never could understand what Fleur meant when she arrived at the mansion and made it clear that she was there to get her land back. Perhaps most importantly, he did not understand that she was not alone. Fleur arrives in Minneapolis, after her long walk from Matchimanito, having taken the name Four Souls. As Nanapush explains, that name comes from her mother, who had also been named Anaquot, "the fourth daughter of a fourth daughter in a line of dawn women healers going back across the miigis water and farther back yet, before the oldest remembers."[67] Anaquot herself received the name Four Souls from her mother, who, in an act of unutterable grief, buried herself alive after smallpox killed members of her family and community, including her mother. Anaquot's mother became Anamaiiakikwe—Under the Ground Woman—after emerging from the earth with healing power and having taken on herself some aspect of the death that had taken her mother: "She was wearing a red dress and smelled of the beginnings of a powerful decay, a smell of bear, a smell of the dead lashed high in trees, an odor that came and went the rest of her life."[68] Anaquot inherited this understanding of healing from Anamaiiakikwe, the idea that "you heal by taking on the pain of others, by going down to argue with death itself, by swallowing the sharp bone and vomiting the sickness out in your own blood"—a theory of repair that depends on sharing and staying with harm and loss, rather than excluding it or erasing it via classification.

The name Four Souls names the process of healing by sharing loss as a generational practice. When, as a child, Anaquot nearly freezes to death, Anamaiiakikwe saves her by throwing out one of her souls, and thus invoking the ancient name that signifies "exactly what [it] . . . tells us, four souls that she could use. Four times she knew in her life that within the year she was meant to die, and so, those four times she threw out a soul. That soul . . . roamed here and there, gaining knowledge of things, then came back and reported to its owner. So Four Souls grew wiser."[69] Therefore it was with generations of women, working together outside of progressive temporality, ontological or subjective rigidity, or a theory of healing that depends on purification, that Fleur arrived at the Mauser mansion to take or, rather, make her land back. The extrasubjective sociality, the multitemporality, and the sense that healing occurs by taking on, not escaping loss, are inseparable from what Fleur is taking back when she takes her land back. She is not simply reseizing land, but she brings to the Mauser mansion a social, temporal, and ontological system capable of holding the loss, the social vacancy, that the colonial domestic enacts. That is, rather than the performance of a claim or a grievance, Fleur's return is an elaboration of a critical and social continuity—a "haunting," in Avery Gordon's terms, that is "a way of life" and a "method of analysis."[70]

In the end, what the moment of the return of land looks like for Fleur is indeed nothing Mauser could have imagined. Fleur uses the son she shares with Mauser to trick the trader, who bought the land from Mauser, in a card game to win back the title to Matchimanito. Fleur returns to her land, carrying the bones of her ancestors that she took with her to and from Minneapolis, not triumphant but exhausted and in need of the generosity and company of Anishinaabe women. Nanapush's partner, Margaret, provides this company by supporting Fleur in a brutal process of reckoning, one that ends with the taking of a new name. Margaret insists:

> [Fleur] needed help from her neglected spirits, and would find it only by fasting on the dark rock eight nights with all her memories and her ghosts. "You must suffer with your relatives," I told her. "The living and the dead . . . you will remember every dear one you lost, those you have forced yourself to forget in order to survive. You threw your souls out. You lived. Now you must weep over those who died in your place. Mourn your dead properly so you can live properly. . . . If you make it through the next eight days, I will give you my medicine dress. Not only that, I will give you the name that goes with it. . . . Your name will help you heal . . . [and] when the time comes for you to die, you will be called by that name and

you will answer.... It will comfort you to finally be recognized here upon this earth."[71]

In *Four Souls*, land back is a movement toward regeneration that attends to and with what colonialism leaves as remains. Margaret keeps company with Fleur, for whom the return of land is not coextensive with the receipt of a land title, the quality of sovereignty that title implies, or with the fantasy that land can be whole or safe while colonialism continues. The return of Fleur to her land, and her land to her, continues a process that has the capacity to hold relation and lost relation together—a process that, as Margaret explains, is rigorous, taxing, and communal.

This moment in *Four Souls* is in some sense a fiction, an aspect of a narrative invention that bears an adjacent relation to the domestic novel. However, one of the implications of the argument I am making in this chapter about the domestic is that the boundary between what we interpret as fiction or not is a site of material extraction and social regulation. Although Erdrich is a fiction writer, the space she opens beyond the conceptual parameters of safety and sovereignty that the domestic marks as the threshold of real colonial life is more than imaginative. Against the interpretive constrictions of the domestic, I read Erdrich's allotment novels as theory—that is, as elaboration and invitation for material practices of Indigenous remaining and return that are always multitemporal, always social beyond subjectivity, and always sustained by Indigenous women and gender nonconforming people. These books intervene in the disciplinarily managed tradition of the domestic novel, but as expressions and practices of extradomestic relation they also extend the theoretical and embodied tradition of Indigenous people opposing extraction. Even within the last few years, Indigenous women and gender nonconforming people in particular have assembled at the front lines at the Unist'ot'en camp, the Sacred Stone camp, and the installation sites in Minnesota for the Line 3 Enbridge pipeline. Often these are the first people arrested by police at these thresholds of colonial reproduction, and texts like Erdrich's allotment novels help clarify why. As the genealogy of the domestic I offered in the first part of this chapter shows, US officials and settlers who commit and legalize violence against Indigenous people understand that fictions of coherent colonial life depend on displacing the robust and expansive practices of repair that Indigenous women and gender nonconforming people elaborate when they assert their ability to take their land back.

The Ruins
of
Settlement 3

In his 2017 book, *Extreme Cities: The Peril and Promise of Urban Life in the Age of Climate Change*, Ashley Dawson theorizes a specific relation between the modern city and climate change. "Cities," he writes, "are at the forefront of the coming climate chaos. . . . They house the majority of humanity, they contribute the lion's share of carbon to the atmosphere, and they are peculiarly vulnerable to climate chaos."[1] Because they are situated at geographic borderlands (e.g., shorelines, foothills), and because they are powerful engines of capitalism's expansion, waste, and inequalities, Dawson argues that cities are where the most grievous crises of climate change will increasingly occur: devastating flooding, water and food scarcity, inexorable exposure to weather, state violence, and disease. For Dawson, cities are the exemplary subjects and objects with which to interpret the devastations of climate change, at once "peculiarly vulnerable" forms and powerful agents of possible remediation.

Cities are useful for describing histories of climate change because the temporal and spatial formalisms their analyses reproduce almost automatically imply a relation both to the environment and to colonialism as the condition of their alignment with power and capital. How they symbolize modernity, industrialization, and global power is inseparable from the way they symbolize environmental alienation, displacement, and vulnerability. In approaching cities this way, Dawson synthesizes environmental justice, post-colonial, and Marxist frameworks in which cities are understood as dynamic political and material forms and as theaters for analyzing systems that create social and economic inequality.[2] But in doing so, his book also reproduces a disciplinarily conventional stabilization of the city as a spatial and historical form in which conditions like inequality, vulnerability, or relief can be under-stood to be internal. When he proposes that "it is in extreme cities that the most important struggles for human survival will take place," or speculates how might "extreme cities become ecocities," he intensifies rather than inter-rupts an underlying liberal formalism, a spatial and historical distribution of interiority, that inspires climate change in the first place.[3] To conceive of cities like New York or the Twin Cities in formally positivist terms that might aptly describe social and ecological vulnerability or that might be figured as a source of relief is to forget the ongoing histories of world-ending environmental harm through which colonial cities are made and sustained. It is also to obscure the fact that anything colonial cities can be said to do, including remediation, occurs on and with seized Indigenous land. Colonial cities cannot be subjects or objects of action, analysis, or anything outside of extraction, the structuring logic of climate change.

This chapter argues that the city form is itself an aspect of extraction and thus that histories of cities are always already histories of colonialism and climate change. Instead of framing the city as a form through which to measure social and ecological harm or relief, I treat it as an unstable formal threshold that obtains where the unrelenting colonial drive for extraction is contradicted by the fantasy of spatial and historical immunity from extrac-tion's devastations. In this chapter, I use the term *climate ruin* to index this methodological intervention, where social and environmental destruction is both precedent and product of the processes through which the colonial city is made to seem real and stable. One aim of this approach is to develop new ways to narrate the historical and spatial relationship between cities and the social and ecological displacement they inherently reproduce—a relationship I bookmark with the pair of terms *location* and *relocation*. Within conventional histories of the Twin Cities, relocation might refer to various discrete eras or events including the convergent movements of people (e.g., settlers and migrants) coming to live in the cities at different times from the mid-nineteenth century onward, the specific and largely coerced relocation of

Indigenous people to the Twin Cities beginning in the middle of the twentieth century, or the present and future phenomenon of people moving to, away from, or within the cities to protect themselves from environmental vulnerability (sometimes called *climate migration*). However, in this chapter I read histories of relocation—always animated by colonial fantasies of immunity from climate ruin and sustained by the racializing displacement of harm—as constitutive of the form of the city itself and the sense that form gives of an experience of location or locatedness that is never actually stable.

Within this broader approach to the city as an effect and engine of climate ruin, I attend closely to two convergent shifts in the relation between location and relocation in the Twin Cities: Indigenous relocation, and urban renewal. For colonial proponents of Indigenous relocation, increasingly unregulated urban wage labor was advertised as a kind of redemption from what they depicted as endemic moral and economic ruin of post-allotment reservations.[4] Instead of sudden economic advancement within capitalism, however, relocated Indigenous people were actually routed into the most precarious housing structures and neighborhoods and into the most dangerous jobs, thus reproducing them as a class associated with the discourses of "blight." As urban renewal intensified along with deindustrialization and white flight in the Twin Cities, those urban Indigenous neighborhoods were among those first and most regularly to be "cleared" or redeveloped for white homebuyers and businesses. They were, in other words, also the site of the systematic recycling of the kind of ruination and displacement from which the city, initially, was offered as a form of relief. In the context of these histories, neither the city nor the social and environmental harms it produces or remediates are geographically or temporally stable; however, they are made to appear so, depending on how we read or narrate histories of the coerced or rewarded relocation of Indigenous people and settlers, and their differential exposure to social and environmental harm.

This chapter approaches relocation not as an era or as stable description of geographic movement, but as the infrastructural management of distributions of ruin and immunity through which places like the Twin Cities project their jurisdictional and historical coherence. Here, building on Susan Leigh Star's observation that "the normally invisible quality of working infrastructure becomes visible when it breaks," this chapter tracks how infrastructures manage the politics of the appearance and interpretation of ruin in addition to the material resource distributions associated with it.[5] Here, I understand climate ruin as a process and a point of convergence between form and deformation, where it is not only an effect but a founding and sustaining condition of US colonialisms.[6] Climate ruin begins in the discursive attributions of emptiness, ancientness, and social pathology with which colonialism clears the way for its reproduction. It continues, as a practice of sanctioned forgetting, through projects of improvement and protection that render Indigenous lifeways anachronistic or dangerous, including historiographic projects that cast colonial history as the only history. In these ways, climate ruin is also always made to seem slightly outside the colonial present and center such that colonial expansion can be narrated—mournfully or eagerly—as progressive. This understanding of climate ruin extends this book's larger reframing of US colonialisms as extraction—that is, as producing nothing other than the conditions of its own violent reproduction.

As with this book's chapters on Warren and Erdrich, this one is interested not only in the establishment and operation of colonial infrastructures but also in the way they are reinhabited, reinterpreted, and exceeded by the Indigenous people and land that those infrastructures intend to manage. To consider the limits of the relocation here, I turn to *The Hiawatha*, a novel by Leech Lake Ojibwe writer David Treuer. Treuer was born in 1970 and in 1992 earned a degree in anthropology and creative writing from Princeton University, where he studied under Toni Morrison and Paul Muldoon. Treuer is an academic, the author of four novels, and three books of nonfiction. *The Hiawatha*, his second novel, is set in the midst of the transformation of the Twin Cities from a dense, industrial urban center to a suburbanized metropolitan area—a transformation characterized by the installation of a massive interstate highway system and downtown district from which poor, working, and racialized people were largely expelled. Published in 1999, the novel considers urban renewal in the Twin Cities from the experience of the Indigenous people who were relocated to so-called blighted neighborhoods beginning in the 1950s and who served as a wage labor class involved in the construction of the cities' new transportation infrastructures and financial districts. For Treuer's characters, ruin is not strictly a precursor or outcome of urban renewal but a continuity of the experience of Indigenous incorporation into US colonialism: from the economic and ecological impacts of logging and mining on reservations post-allotment, to the precarity of living in urban spaces targeted for renewal, to the manufacturing of a new suburban city form whose infrastructures of security were never intended to insulate Indigenous people from neoliberalism's intensification of environmental and social destruction.

In formal terms, one of the critical contributions of this novel is the way its depiction and understanding of ruin departs from the political and aesthetic conventions of the colonial literary canon. Within US and European literary history, ruin is a site for the reproduction and renewal of cultural representation, whether a site of romantic contemplation, politically mobilizing realism, or materialist critique. In Ann Laura Stoler's terms, it is a "privileged site of reflection"—an assessment particularly suggestive if we underscore the dialectical action signaled by "reflection," a gesture of semantic exchange as well as of personal meditation. In *The Hiawatha*, however, the vectors of political and formal reproduction indexed by ruin trace an intensification and repetition of extraction that is both aestheticized and repressed in the new shape of (and the shape of newness in) the Twin Cities. In one sense, therefore, the novel works as a gesture of critique; it reveals the fallacy of ruin's externality to US power that is the condition for the reproduction of colonial form. In another sense, the novel is also a creative archive of the possibility of living amid ruin. Such a proposition is at once unthinkable within the framework of immunity from ruin on which urban renewal depends and also the precondition to develop new theories of history beyond the formal operation of extraction.

This chapter, like the novel itself, is organized around sites where Indigenous dwelling vexes and exceeds the conventional cultural and political meaning of ruin: a modest house in South Minneapolis, a tourist hotel destroyed by highway expansion, and a skyscraper. Readings of these three sites are paired with three historical and conceptual frameworks: concentration and clearance, immunity, and infrapolitics. The readings of the first two sites, the house and the hotel, draw attention to the critical force of *The Hiawatha* by showing how Treuer clarifies the relation between ruin and extraction, a relation formalized via colonial investments in concentration and clearance and that ultimately naturalizes a politics of white immunity from climate crisis. My reading of the last site, the skyscraper, develops an approach to the novel as a speculative archive of survival with and through extraction that invites a retheorization of the history of the Indigenous Twin Cities that exceeds the critical framework of ruin.

Like previous chapters of this book, this one refuses easy methodological distinctions between the way it reads jurisdictional and narrative forms. Both the city and the novel are forms whose conditions of production and whose imagined worlds are critical for understanding how US colonialisms work and how they might be dismantled. Thinking about *The Hiawatha* as the convergence of these forms is a generative problem in literary historical terms, particularly in the way we might interpret the novel's interest in ruin in relation to modernist critiques of state power and to traditions of Indigenous literary and intellectual world-making. On one hand, the way *The Hiawatha* operates as a critical intervention against (that is, in opposition to) the Twin Cities bears a resemblance to a stance characteristic of postcolonial modernism. Here, the way modernist texts leverage their entanglements with colonial infrastructures is a chance to expose and press the limits of state power. Simon Gikandi describes this as modernism's "staging" of colonial failure: "We have become so accustomed to reading the modernist text as an attempt to keep out the contaminants of the world outside the aesthetic sphere that we have forgotten how often modernist art forms derive their energy from their diagnosis of the failure of the imperial enterprise.... Modernist narratives are about failure—the failure of traditional authority, inherited modes of representation, and the European subject—but they also derive their authority from the staging of failure in the colonial space."[7] Within the context of the twentieth-century Twin Cities, it is true that *The Hiawatha* clarifies how Indigenous relocation, and the discourses of ruin it authorizes, points back at a city on the brink of economic and environmental failure, revealing it to be a structure unable to reconcile competing demands for economic growth and white immunity. In this sense, *The Hiawatha*'s critical engagement with ruin throws into relief—in the way breakages do infrastructures—the city as a condition of extraction rather than an autonomous civic or cultural form.

On the other hand, the novel cannot only be understood in terms of an antagonistic intervention into what Jacques Rancière calls the distribution of sensibility, of which decolonial and postcolonial literary modes of critique are a part.[8] The novel also attends to Indigenous art- and community-making that sustains continuities of urbanity having very little to do with the colonial concept or form of the city. Through practices of transgeographic constellation, narrative production, memory, and kinship, relocated Indigenous people brought cities with them, and made new cities against (i.e., proximate to) places like the Twin Cities. This understanding of Indigenous urbanity builds on work in Indigenous studies, including Shari Huhndorf's "Native transnationalism" and Sean Teuton's "Indigenous cosmopolitanism" that itself extends an argument about Indigenous cultural geography made in Renya Ramirez's anthropological study of relocation, *Native Hubs*.[9] Ramirez's work rethinks the "usual opposition between 'Native' and 'diaspora' by emphasizing that Native Americans bring their own sense of culture, community, identity, belonging, and rootedness with them as they travel."[10] From this perspective, homemaking, political organizing, and the production of imaginative forms like *The Hiawatha* extend practices of world-building into a political and jurisdictional sphere in which Indigeneity might otherwise be given as a sign of displacement.

But because the urban Indigenous worlds described and produced in texts like *The Hiawatha* are also reduced, by way of colonial cultural and material infrastructures, by discourses of ruin, the work of reading the novel for its participation in that world building also means interpreting the erasures and absences the form of the city enacts. In this, I follow Indigenous literary critics like Seneca scholar Mishuana Goeman, whose work in *Mark My Words* does not attempt to fill or rename the archival gaps produced by colonialism but, rather, acknowledges and holds open those spaces to "demonstrate how the silenced are living and maintaining their culture while acting as important agents of global restructuring."[11] For Goeman, this requires "remapping" forms like the city as fundamentally unstable and nonsingular: as "connected to multiple stories that move across time and space."[12] To attend to spaces and forms that colonialism simplifies through extraction also requires imaginative criticism of the kind Osage writer Robert Warrior models in his work on Pequot writer William Apess. At the end of Apess's life, he moved to New York City, where he lived without leaving behind a record that we can access now. In the face of this archival gap, Warrior develops a critical practice of "speculation . . . a way of trying to grasp from the shreds and shards of evidence . . . [an] act of imagination [that] reveals its own kind of truth, however little we might be able to ascertain of the facts from the sparse historical record."[13] I approach *The Hiawatha* as an articulation of the critical imagination Warrior describes: a novel that participates in the Indigenous world-making that occurs amid and against the Twin Cities without bearing a specific or affirmative relation to genres like realism or the historical novel that imply the stability of colonial civic, cultural, and temporal forms.

The No-Numbered House

A house, a hotel, and a skyscraper are all identifiable and historical features of the appearance of US colonialisms. They are products and producers of colonial power and they are also symbols of the promise, the sense of stability and scalability, it conveys. US colonialisms have a look, and, despite the relentless brutality of their constituent structures, they look ordinary most of the time: like places and structures where people live, work, and move, even as those are only possible through systematic killing, exploitation, and confinement. The aggregation of forms through which power in this context appears—and appears as banal and durable—is what I call *settlement*, a term that underscores both the sense of US colonialisms as uncontested (i.e., settled) and as a stable entity: something obviously there, with obvious boundaries. Settlement is inextricable from the material structures that settlers install, but it is not reducible to them. It also includes the way those structures appear, and the way they police what can or cannot appear. In the context of US colonialisms, a house is a structure with apparent shape, but it is as much a reduction of the possibilities of the meaning of shelter to an administrable and repeatable form, possibilities we learn to forget as we learn to recognize the form.[14] This phenomenological aspect of settlement is essential to its reproduction and is thus a principal challenge for decolonization. It means that describing power against the grain of the apparent as a part of political organizing, is crucial to decolonization—work *The Hiawatha* does from the outset.

The plot of Treuer's novel centers an Anishinaabe family—a mother, Betty, and her four children, Simon, Lester, Caroline, and Irma—who move to South Minneapolis in 1960 after Betty's husband, Jacob, is killed in a logging accident, on their allotment, to which Simon is a witness. Jacob's death is not so much an accident as it is a predictable effect of colonially manufactured climate change. "In 1958," Treuer writes, "there were no more furs left, and no one was buying the few stray beaver that remained tucked into boggy ponds away from trappers on snowmobiles. . . . The fisher and marten were long gone and since muskrat and weasel only gave twenty-five cents each, they were ignored and left to rut in the broken slashings and rice beds. Simon and his father took the minimal logging roads along the river and cut pulp off their family allotment ignored by the white land-grabbers."[15]

Logging, for Jacob and Simon, is a desperate act of survival amid a catastrophically damaged ecosystem, and it is also an occasion for an intimate exchange of environmental and social knowledge between generations, a quality that makes Jacob's sudden death a cataclysmic and life-altering trauma for Simon. The scene of Jacob and Simon's logging and the tragedy of Jacob's death establishes a pattern of precarious survival and unbearable loss that continues to shape the family's life in Minneapolis. There, Betty rents a house in an Indigenous neighborhood, a house that "had a number, on paper anyway. The stamped metal numbers above the door had lost their black paint, corroded, and dropped off long before she carried her boxes inside during a light rain and set up window curtains. The numbers were ground right off the boards by the weather before the porch began to sag, long before Betty unboxed the kids' clothes and ordered them to make their new beds."[16] In one sense, Betty's "no-numbered house" is precisely the kind of structured distribution of Indigenous people into invisibility that settlement needs and normalizes. Even as Betty and Simon start jobs (as a nurse and an ironworker) essential to the growth of the cities, they are positioned outside the coordinates of civic location—the sense, for instance, of the house as part of a sequence, as mappable, reachable by civic services, as geographically named. The no-numberedness of the house is an explicit announcement that although Indigenous people were necessary to the reproduction of the cities, that reproduction would actively discount or disremember them. More than this, the very "illegibility" of their domestic lives, to use James C. Scott's terms, is an essential "tool of legibility"—that is, of the regimented reproduction of the cities themselves.[17] To that point, even as Betty's family begins to make a life in the no-numbered house, the neighborhood is being torn down around them. This destruction eventually includes the house itself, which is demolished and replaced by a gas station.[18]

In another sense, however, because the no-numbered house is situated at the horizon of the il/legibility of settlement, there is nowhere better from which to witness the production of settlement as a phenomenon. Almost immediately after Betty's family moved in, they are taken by a neighbor (a Ho-Chunk man named One-Two who, like many relocated Indigenous people, worked demolition and construction crews) to witness the destruction of the Twin Cities' first—very modest—skyscraper, the Metropolitan Building. From the thin, caution-taped threshold of safety the family notices the quiet and relentless violence of the crew's work:

> There was no sudden transformation. . . . So the children remember the sounds of wrecking. The bone deep crunch of stone, again and again. The cranes swept their arms back as if preparing for a ponderous stiff-armed hug. . . . Until now the building had always been treated with care, with tenderness. Simon watched with a sense of license, that in the city there were times when you . . . were encouraged to rip something apart. After it was clear that this would continue, that architectural death, at least, was a monotonous process, they and the others drifted away . . . [back] toward South Minneapolis.[19]

What the family learns (unlike the white suburban families whose inability to read the city Treuer examines elsewhere in the novel) is that the distinction between form and deformation is an illusion of settlement. Colonial form depends on the unceasing manufacture and remediation of ruin, which is both the antecedent and the aftermath of what they sensed as the city's "care" or "tenderness." It is a lesson that the family also understands includes and predicts their own experience. They have been included and even made demographically constituent of the condition of ruin against which the city establishes the devastating and incremental pace of its reproduction. Beginning with this encounter, Treuer's novel establishes a counteranalytic to the way settlement in general conditions people to misread it. Treuer roots this approach in the negative space of settlement, the no-numbered house, a site suspended between what I will elaborate in the next section as the forms of concentration and clearance that is the crucial and obfuscated link between Indigenous relocation and urban renewal.

Concentration and Clearance

Beyond but intimately connected to Treuer's novel, the mid-twentieth century in the United States was distinguished by two apparently opposite but both politically salient ways of visualizing ruin. In one sense, ruin was a spectacle through which the United States consolidated Cold War–era nationalism. The "national contemplation of ruins," specifically the "ritual" attention to curated fantasies of nuclear annihilation, as Joseph Masco observes, characterized both the abstract discourse of politicians justifying the globalization of US military power and the everyday life of school children, forced to rehearse duck-and-cover drills.[20] In the same years, the spectacularization of ruin was an animating practice of city planning. As cities suburbanized and transformed downtowns into spaces emptied of all but the structures of finance, urban renewal was mobilized by racist discourses of ruined or "blighted" housing and slum clearance. Like fantasies of nuclear destruction, urban renewal primarily benefited corporate interests but was offered as a matter of broad public welfare. In cases like *Berman v. Parker* (1954), the Supreme Court declared "slum clearance" a question of "public safety, health, morality, peace and quiet, law and order" even as hyperbolic and moralizing descriptions of poor, Black, Brown, immigrant, and Indigenous neighborhoods were actually used to spur new sectors of real estate speculation, investment, and development and justify an unprecedented expansion of policing and prisons.[21]

At the same time, and toward the same goals of political, economic, and ideological consolidation, ruin—real ruin, which is to say, politically manufactured social and ecological devastation—was systematically obfuscated. While the United States invested in fantasies of its own nuclear annihilation, the actual, world-ending consequences of nuclearization were realized by Indigenous people and land: from the permanent devastation visited on the Marshall Islands and Southern Paiute land in the United States (the most nuclear-bombed place on earth), to the catastrophic biological, economic, and agricultural legacies of uranium mining and remediation. Irradiated ecosystems and precipitously rising cancer rates among people whom the United States understands as disposable did not, during the middle years of the twentieth century, rise to the level of public or corporate visibility. These histories of ruin are examples of what Rob Nixon calls "slow violence"—"violence that occurs gradually and out of sight, a violence of delayed destruction that is dispersed across time and space, an attritional violence that is typically not viewed as violence at all."[22] These slow and silenced histories of nuclear ruin also parallel those of urban renewal. Where assurances of housing relocation for those displaced by slum clearance failed and combined with de jure and de facto racist lending practices and white community covenants, urban renewal marked the advent of multigenerational housing and economic precarity, increasingly inaccessible education and health care, and exposure to violent policing and incarceration. These aspects of the social ruin of urban renewal were, to the extent that they were acknowledged at all, racialized and moralized—which is to say that they were delinked from their actual colonial purposes—while other aspects, like the uneven distribution of ecological toxification directly correlated to urban renewal, were erased from public concern altogether. While Rachel Carson's *Silent Spring* did establish a vocabulary for describing the obfuscation of the social effects of ecological ruin, neither her work nor the legislation it inspired addressed the catastrophic extractive exposures to unremediated industrial pollution that poor, Black, Brown, immigrant, and Indigenous communities faced in the aftermath of urban renewal.

One goal of this chapter is to specify the relation between the phenomenology of ruin and colonial extraction. To do so requires reading against the grain of the narratives that US cities create about how ruin justifies and proves their development as coherent historical and political formations. Specifically, I bring together two interventions in the critical assessment of ruin by scholars in American and colonialism studies. First, the insistence that although ruin is often depicted as a spatially and historically discrete place or event, it is more accurately understood as an ongoing process on which colonial regimes depend. This is an intervention Stoler makes by way of a shift in the conceptualization of ruin from "a privileged site of reflection [and]... pensive rumination" (a description that accords with Masco's account of the ritual fantasy of nuclear annihilation) to a multivalent process she calls "ruination."[23] For Stoler, ruination captures the complex descriptive and temporal enactments of ruin: "Ruination is an *act* perpetrated, a *condition* to which one is subject, and a *cause* of loss. . . . To think with ruins of empire as ruination is to emphasize less the artifacts of empire as dead matter or remnants of a defunct regime than to attend to their reappropriations, strategic neglect, and active positioning with the politics of the present."[24] Here, Stoler's framing returns our understanding of what ruins do from the convolutions of defensive anticipation or self-justifying nostalgia to the spatial and social fictions through which empire works in the present. This approach corrects the displacements intrinsic to conventional approach to ruin—that it already happened, has not yet happened, or happened elsewhere—thus drawing attention to the more pressing question: "how," throughout the history of colonialism, "people live *with* and *in* ruins."[25]

A second and related intervention is the rethinking of the relation between ruin and the politics of form. Rather than treat ruin as a form itself, or even a formal process, this chapter considers ruin as the condition for the production of colonial form. This approach departs from assessments of modern political and economic systems that frame ruin as a formal counterpoint to creativity. For instance, in rehearsals of imperial nostalgia, ruin is the form of past political creation (whether that production is imperial or is, as in what Jean O'Brien calls "lasting," Indigenous). In other cases, for scholars and commentators concerned with the neoliberalization of cities, ruin is a form of economic creation, or Marxist critics identify as the systemic stabilization of capital after overproduction, otherwise called "creative destruction."[26] In still other cases, interrogations of ruin treat it as a form of deformation, the form in which colonial devastation occurs. For instance, Eyal Weizman's work on "forensic architecture" examines buildings and other sites destroyed by colonial violence by treating the destroyed structures, "the bruised materiality of buildings," as sensors and archives.[27] How buildings explode or crumble tells practitioners of forensic architecture about the fleeting and terrible presents that are too spectacular or too obscured to be assessed within conventional justice systems. In each of these cases, a formal approach to ruin yields generative insights into structures of culture, economy, and militarism. However, these are still too specific to address the role extraction plays in colonialism broadly, a role that precedes because it produces formal taxonomies of empire. I argue that ruin is not a spatial or social category that exists outside of colonialism, or the binary construction of waste and value that colonial systems use to normalize domination through race, capital, and property. Even as, and because, colonial systems define re/production against ruin, ruin is internal to the formal operation of colonialism. This approach invites questions that further denaturalize colonial spatial and social orders, questions I use Dan Nemser's and Francesca Ammon's work to frame in terms of concentration and clearance.

For Nemser, "concentration" indexes the material and structural production of race in the modern Americas, a process that depends on "the construction of more or less durable structures like roads, walls, ditches, buildings, boundaries, and towns, into which both human and non-human objects were concentrated."[28] Nemser argues that concentration not only signals "confinement," as in the calamitous restrictions of spatial and social divisions through which the availability of housing, work, and well-being is managed, but also "certain forms of mobility"; as in histories of people and ecologies "displaced from one another."[29] The concentration of people and ecosystems with relation to new trajectories of harm and capital accumulation is how racialization operates under colonialism. Moreover, the structures through which concentration is achieved always bear a relation to ruin, even before they are specifically deployed on behalf of colonial racialization. That relation is detectable in, for instance, the vastly different durabilities of highways and prisons that displace Black, Brown, immigrant, and Indigenous communities and the housing structures (if any are provided) to which they are made to relocate; or in the different scales of response to potential, spectacular threats to cities (i.e., those indexed by "terrorism") and the actual, already-existing toxifications and resource deprivations that determine what Ruth Wilson Gilmore famously calls "group-differentiated vulnerabilities to premature death."[30] Concentration is a racializing form that organizes people and environments for extraction by linking them more proximately and more permanently to ruin.

As a complementary formation, what Ammon calls "clearance" represents the manufactured immunity to ruin associated with whiteness under colonialism. In her cultural history of the bulldozer, Ammon traces the US national ideological investment in clearance from World War II through urban renewal into the explicitly cultural theaters of children's literature and land art. At every stage, clearance is an enactment of (actual) ruin against (declared) ruin, in which state-sponsored demolition is depicted as racial purification—"ordering and cleaning," as Ammon puts it.[31] From the origins of the term *bulldozer* as an extrajudicial practice of anti-Black violence to the machine's ability to symbolize anti-Asian sentiment during World War II, Ammon demonstrates how images of destruction were reframed as the precondition for the alignment of whiteness with national power.[32] In the decades the followed the war, federal sponsorship of housing and land demolition extended a fantasy of racial purification into urban spaces across the United States.[33] And while the destruction of hundreds of thousands of houses and millions of acres of land was justified by discourses of national security and revitalization, much of what was ruined was never rebuilt: a process that left massive greenfields and parking lots in the midst of downtown districts in place of vibrant human and ecological communities.[34] Thus, clearance indexes a complex process in which the racializing description of social and economic ruin is met with physical ruination and leaves behind uninhabitable space officially coded as safe and clean. In this way, clearance is a material process and an ideal metaphor for the social vacancy of whiteness in a colonial context.

In the Twin Cities, and in South Minneapolis in particular, concentration and clearance were the forms that structured its physical and political transformation into a neoliberal city. As Treuer shows, but as most canonical accounts of the neoliberal city elide, Indigenous people were central to this transformation in multiple ways. First (and as I will elaborate in the next section), post-relocation Indigenous neighborhoods were made ruinous through racializing policies and sociological narratives of concentration. University- and state-sponsored studies, including a report by the Governor's Human Rights Commission in 1965, depict communal, seasonally mobile, and economically precarious Indigenous households as pathological and avid for state aid.[35] The ruination of Indigenous people and neighborhoods became the precondition for the enactment of demolition projects, the justification for the reorganization of the cities' economy and social hierarchy under the sign of white suburbia, and the solidification of what Joanne Barker calls the racialization of Indigenous people as a way of separating their political status from sovereignty.[36] In other words, the remaking of Indigenous people and neighborhoods as examples of ruin was how the cities justified, realized, and mapped its renewal.

Second, Indigenous people were an essential labor class who built the most spectacular architectural symbols of renewal—skyscrapers, highways, suburban commercial structures—at the same time that they bore the most intense economic and environmental costs of that development. Not only were such buildings and roads constructed by Indigenous people over Indigenous homes, but the severe pollution of the demolition and construction processes were displaced onto Indigenous neighborhoods. For instance, starting in 1928 and throughout the decades that saw the highest numbers of Indigenous people moving to the Twin Cities, a South Minneapolis manufacturing plant distributed massive levels of arsenic into local soil and water. In 2007, the historically Indigenous Philips, Longfellow, and Powderhorn neighborhoods were all declared a Superfund site, based on residual arsenic exposure.[37] In this second sense, then, Indigenous people and spaces were remade as structures of economic and environmental absorption and as invisible countersites against which a new architecture of white civic reproduction was deployed.

Relocation and White Immunity

Concentration and clearance are typically given as opposing formal articulations of ruin. The way cities and other structures of settlement curate ruin always implies one or the other formal intentionality. As I suggested in the previous section, each of those forms organizes a specific relation to sensibility. In historical terms, I am interested in the emergence of this binary formalization of ruin in the decades characterized by urban renewal in the United States—a period, and political operation, that depended on a specific, extractive relation between colonial reproduction and Indigenous people. In this section, I explore that relationship further, using Treuer's novel to resituate the Indigenous history of this period, typically bookmarked as Termination and Relocation, within my broader consideration of ruin. Specifically, I observe that the coerced movement of Indigenous people to urban spaces like the Twin Cities was not only materially essential to urban renewal and reproduction but also essential to disguise the fundamental connection and simultaneity of concentration and clearance. Novels like *The Hiawatha* are key to this analysis because they animate a space in which concentration and clearance and the phenomenal operations they organize coemerge and commingle.

The story *The Hiawatha* tells of Betty's family's move to South Minneapolis is in many ways exemplary of how Termination and Relocation in the 1950s and 1960s are conventionally understood. Within standard histories of Federal Indian Law, Termination (the attempted dissolution of tribal governments) is narrated as a backlash against BIA administration of the New Deal era, which supported tribes in establishing constitutional democracies in the style of the United States. Beginning with Dillon Myer's appointment to lead the BIA in 1950, the United States sought to dissolve tribal governments and assimilate Indigenous people into the political economy—a move that for the protolibertarian Myer was described as a gesture of freeing Indigenous people from a relationship of dependency with the United States.[38] Relocation, a policy that closely followed Termination and was ultimately more impactful, extended Termination's assimilatory logic; it was a jobs bill that provided apprenticeship, job training, and direct employment to Indigenous people who moved to cities. And while these provisions did not meaningfully soften the brutal economic and social transition relocated people negotiated, they did extend a systematic and multifaceted interest in extracting Indigenous land and labor. Relocation was "successful" in this regard because allotment had so profoundly upended tribal economies and governance structures, and because cities needed nonunionized labor to execute demolition and renewal projects cheaply. The most commonly cited effects of Relocation are, first, the geodemographic shift such that by the end of the twentieth century more than two-thirds of all Indigenous people in the United States lived in cities. Second, the correlation of growing urban Indigenous populations and their increasing subjection to racialization and a related shift in organizing tactics of which the founding of AIM in South Minneapolis in 1967 is a hallmark.

However, it is also possible to situate relocation and its racializing effects in a much broader political, environmental, and cultural crisis of whiteness, and of white immunity specifically. That crisis can be understood as the intersection of two new, and newly scaled up, axes of vulnerability: the increasingly catastrophic recurrence of global war (and the spectacularization of nuclear ruin during and after World War II in particular) and the growing awareness of toxification caused by unregulated manufacturing and industrial farming.[39] In the last half of the twentieth century, these cooperating threats amounted to what we would now call a climate crisis, a phrase that I take to mean both the realization of potentially intractable social and ecological harm and the particular quality of harm that becomes politically significant and universalizable insofar as it affects white people.[40] In the context of this climate crisis, Indigenous relocation was a strategy of racial and geographic management that was not designed to address the causes of that crisis but, rather, to align whiteness with immunity from harm, and, as such, it is a revealing precursor to more contemporary responses to climate crisis that invest in fantasies of fortified white settlement or retreat as they accept the displacement of Black, Brown, and Indigenous people as inevitable.

As a response to a war in which the direct effects of nuclearization were most intensely felt by Japanese and Indigenous people, we can understand relocation as a system of racial management designed to produce whiteness as immune from nuclear vulnerability. This, first, axis of vulnerability coheres as a logic against which whiteness defines itself through the cooperating projects of Japanese American internment and Indigenous relocation. Administered by the same man, Dillon Myer, the WRA and Indigenous relocation both utilized colonial forms of concentration and clearance to justify the dispossession of thousands of US citizens and to advertise that effort as threat mitigation and the reinforcement of white immunity. One of Myer's most successful political strategies was to recode Japanese American and Indigenous communities as representative of the otherwise abstract and diffuse threats of nuclearization and environmental degradation. In testimony to the US Senate Military Affairs Subcommittee in 1943, on the subject of the relocation and internment of Japanese Americans, Myer argued:

> I sincerely believe, gentlemen, that if we don't handle this problem in a way to get these people absorbed as best we can while the war is going on, we may have something akin to Indian reservations after the war.... I am frankly hoping that quite a number of those people will get established in positions in different parts of the country other than on the Pacific coast ... where they can be absorbed ... and thus dispose of a racial problem that has been a pretty tough one for the coast people and for the United States.[41]

Myer's testimony frames Japanese American and Indigenous concentration as a tangible symbol of the kind of pervasive, internal, and existentially threatening risk to US settlement that nuclear war and the toxification of water, air, and topsoil actually were in 1943. But unlike those real dangers, racialized populations could be redistributed away from, or "absorbed" into, white settlement, in the name of the racist and capitalistic principles that precipitated global social and ecological crisis in the first place.

Myer intensified the entanglement of Japanese American and Indigenous racialization suggested in this testimony in the course of his administration of the internment camps. This was most acutely performed in the Gila River and Poston camps, which were situated within the Gila River and Colorado River reservations, and in which incarcerated Japanese Americans were forced to build irrigation systems and otherwise "develop" Indigenous land that Myer understood to be ruined by undercultivation or overgrazing. That agricultural work was said to prepare people held in the camps for economic integration into US capitalism, notably in rural places far from the western cities from which most were forcibly removed. Concentration—both exemplified by Myer's proleptic fantasy of Japanese American communities becoming "akin to Indian reservations" and by the camps themselves—was advertised as a style of racialized protection of people against themselves and a mode of transit toward a new relation more proximate to whiteness. It also created a discursive counterpoint to the formal process of release from the camps, literally a matter of "clearing" people for absorption into settlement. One of the many things people being vetted for clearance from the camps were made to promise was that they would "stay away from large groups of yourselves."[42]

Notably, while the policies of Japanese American internment and Indigenous relocation were established in sequence, Myer's racializing administration of both populations depended on defining them against each other throughout both policy eras. Before the WRA, Myer used Indigenous people and land to represent the potentially ruinous racial fate of Japanese Americans if they were left unmanaged—a threat clearly intensified in the context of the US nuclear assaults on Japan. During and after the WRA, the clearance of Japanese Americans into white settlements represented the possibility of racial renewal that justified and organized Indigenous relocation. This system of racial definition clarifies two things relevant to reframing relocation in the context of midcentury climate crisis. First, Myer's desperate attempts to assign stable racial meaning to Japanese Americans and Indigenous people through this system of ornate transits and comparisons indicates that what was actually produced by his policies was a construction of whiteness as immune and renewing. Whiteness is what the choreography of concentration and clearance produced both as its justification and as its outcome. Second, although relocation-era propaganda advertised to Indigenous people the idea that cities were places of economic relief from the devastation of allotment, the analogy between internment and relocation suggests that, for Myer, cities were viable sites to relocate Indigenous people because he understood them to be sites of social ruin. Myer intensified and recontextualized concentration via internment by removing Japanese Americans to spaces he understood to be ruinous. Likewise, cities, in Myer's mind, were laboratories for Indigenous economic extraction under the terms of retraining. This explains, among other things, why relocation only provided for job training instead of actually essential structures of support like housing, access to food, education, or health care.

The second axis of vulnerability against which whiteness defined itself as immune in the context of the midcentury climate crisis was a spatial sense of toxification. In the Twin Cities, like other suburbanizing places, the concentration and management of Indigenous and Black people in and as urban ruin was a powerful justification for new constructions of white social and economic life as "deconcentrated," pastoral, and private.[43] In order to sense how clearance is a response to this climate crisis, we have to take seriously the way its aesthetics intend a politics of white immunity at the same time we reject its justifying of racializing concentration with ruin. Suburbanization was a project in which the aesthetics of privacy and the pastoral were enactments of a fantasy of immunity as well as of racism and xenophobia, and as such were extensions of Cold War–era formulations of national immunity from nuclearization (like "Defense through Decentralization").[44] Clearance as immunity is a logic that subtends many of the key infrastructural developments of the US suburbs, including, in the Twin Cities, the separation of suburbs from urban waste and water management systems, the construction of the nation's first "climate-controlled" shopping mall, and the development of the interstate highway system, all of which took place within a year of the relocation bill Public Law 959 in 1956.

Among these material and spatial changes, the construction of the interstate system is perhaps the most dramatic symbol of the alignment of clearance with immunity from toxification insofar as it was conceived and continues to operate as an infrastructure of escape. Originally designed as a way to accelerate the movement of citizens away from, and troops toward, sites of military conflict that could occur anywhere in the United States, the interstate systems also famously facilitated the "escape" of white people from blighted urban neighborhoods (which we might also narrate as the escape of the white tax base from the civic responsibilities of urban infrastructure and social services support). Beyond this, the highways were, and still are, structures of escape from environmental toxification that was well underway in the Twin Cities in the decades before that toxification became a focus of Carson's *Silent Spring* in 1962 and thereafter of legislative concern. Like other cities whose economies had relied on manufacturing, the Twin Cities' most powerful companies' transition to globally decentralized production and an increasingly white and white-collar local workforce left behind devastated urban ecosystems. As suburbs grew, and the Twin Cities' economy was increasingly connected to the globalization of war, food distribution, and agricultural production, scores of toxic sites were left behind by major corporations like Honeywell (three petroleum brownfields, twelve active leak sites, two Superfund sites), 3M (thirty-one leak sites, one Superfund site), General Mills (nine leak sites, three petroleum brownfields), and Pillsbury (eleven leak sites, two petroleum brownfields).[45] Here, it does not matter if white people did or did not consciously invoke the proliferation of ecological harm to describe their "escape" from the cities. The discourses most familiar to them—of pastoral suburban safety and privacy, and those of urban "blight"—were chosen for them by the increasingly neoliberal governance and economic structures whose flourishing depended on local toxification prior to World War II and the export of toxification thereafter.

In the aftermath of Japanese American concentration camps, the coincidence of the infrastructural production of white immunity with Indigenous relocation reveals one way that colonial power reproduces through ruin. In the face of new scales of nuclear and ecological ruin, relocation is a re-racialization of space, one that was never designed to intervene in global catastrophe but to create administrable racial and spatial fantasies of identity with or immunity from ruin. In this sense it may be inadequate to think of relocation as a policy particular to the forced displacement of Indigenous people or any other racialized population; instead, we might understand it as an aspect of the "territorial project" of US colonialisms that is obscured by the premise that settlement is always a durable spatial project.[46] Relocation is a central principle of US colonialisms that is an effect of its unceasing production of and inability to live with ruin. It is a paradigm of racial and spatial management that reveals the fragility of settlement: its inability to create spatial meaning without domination and the unwillingness of those that belong to it to learn live with the disasters it produces.

The Curtis

Writing against the grain of settlement's constituent formations and the fantasy of separation between concentration and clearance they enact, Treuer's novel attends to the ephemeral spaces where ruin means both. The novel opens in the middle of the history of Betty's family: after Jacob dies while harvesting wood with Simon, after their move to Minneapolis, after Simon joins an Indigenous ironworking crew that builds the city's tallest skyscraper, and after Simon—in a paroxysm of grief—kills his beloved younger brother, Lester. Simon is incarcerated for ten years in the state prison and is released to a work-parole arrangement as a maintenance worker at a once prestigious and now decrepit hotel in downtown Minneapolis, the Curtis. Outside the novel, the Curtis was a tourist hotel built on the edge of the city's "Gateway District"—a park situated in the midst of skid row in an attempt to renew the downtown in the style of the "City Beautiful" movement. By the time Simon arrives at the Curtis, however, its role in the cities' transformation has shifted. Now a sign of spectacular degradation, its lingering on the brink of obliteration has become unseemly—a feeling Treuer captures in vivid, bodily terms:

> The brown brick is slicked with grime and stained with rust.... [Its] tan carpet is... spotted and worn, with what looks like dried vomit or blood ranging from the desk to the front door. A rubber mat has been laid over

the carpet at the entrance to protect it from the snow and salt, but the slush slips over the edges to pool on the carpet like dried semen. The walls [were]... finally, in desperation, covered... with paisley wallpaper, like throwing a blanket over a corpse.[47]

Treuer's description is not simply graphic; it captures one aspect of how the aesthetics of ruin are a mode of biopolitical and economic management in the context of relocation. Urban ruin is curated by building owners and investors, city administrators, and insurance contracts as grotesque, as the overconcentration of bodiliness, even in spaces that are largely empty. This alignment of economic and bodily ruin is, even for the proprietors of ruined places, a technique of "biosecurity," in Stoler's terms. It is a naturalization of the approximation of poverty and vulnerability that justifies the replacement of social support systems with carceral ones and incentivizes the maximally defensive separations between racialized poor people and white, wealthy urban spaces. Ruin is never isolated to a single built or embodied container but "multiplies," as Stoler puts it, "in content and form."[48]

For Simon (for whom the Curtis is unmistakably an extension of the logic of concentration that also organizes the toxification and incarceration), to live there, in its ruin, also affords an analytical perspective from which to sense the way the hotel's degradation means more than social pathology. Ruin is a temporally heterogeneous and spatially interconnected form in which the history and future of bodies, systems, and structures—as well as the larger infrastructural matrix in which they each are embedded—intermingle. Working in a ruined hotel in a downtown clearing itself of everything except finance means that Simon lives amid clearance and concentration, at the slight stall in the recycling system of infrastructural transformation. Walking there every day, he is relieved and devastated by a "renewed" downtown which empties itself of sensory density: "The streets of Minneapolis are too wide to box the sounds of urban life, and instead let them escape skyward like released balloons. The palette of smells from restaurants doesn't hang in the air.... The buildings are either too new or too far apart, the inspectors too intent on proper venting and the commissioner of transportation overattentive to garbage which... never collects more than a handful of blue bottles and yellow jackets."[49]

At the same time, underneath the hotel, where Simon and his coworker Dougan operate its heating and water systems, physical and sensory density not only characterizes the space but also delightfully exceeds the inspection processes established to hasten the hotel's condemnation: "Dougan makes him polish the pressure gauges though the dials no longer work. They are stuck and Dougan has long ago pried off the glass plates and wound the hands to the proper pressure. He says he doesn't need to look at them.... But the building inspectors feel better when they see the shiny dials pointing like compasses to true north, to safety. *They*, said Dougan smugly, *know nothing of the hotel's temperament.*"[50] In the waning months of the hotel's existence, Simon and Dougan participate in the dense, physical, and unadministrable labor of sustaining it. Rather than with any sense of obligation or profit, they do so with a sense of remembering and anticipatory mourning, a sense that attends to the history of the building, to the histories of racialized labor in it, as well as to the fragility and temporariness of their ability to protect it and to be protected by it from colonial clearance.

Just as it was outside the world of the novel, the Curtis is eventually destroyed in *The Hiawatha* because, as a ruined building and business, it could not conform to the fantasy of immunity that guided the Twin Cities' response to the midcentury climate crises of nuclearization and toxification. After 1956, the boundary lines and corridors of transit between spaces cleared of ruin in the Twin Cities' downtown and suburbs were the east-west Interstate 94 and the north-south Interstate 35. The Curtis was situated only a few blocks north of I-94, the dividing line between the downtown and South Minneapolis. Simon, of course, cannot experience the demolition of the Curtis in anything like the terms of escape or immunity designed to reassure city administrators and white suburbanites. For them, the hotel became an economic and symbolic threat—a sign of their own inability to manage the boundaries of social and economic crisis. For Simon, on the other hand, the hotel—as an extension of the city's racializing approximation of Indigenous people with ruin and as such as the conditions for his exposure to ecological and carceral harm—was actually threatening, yet his response to its demolition is not relief but utter dislocation:

> The hotel is gone. Where the Curtis used to be there is nothing but a pile of rubble on an empty lot.... Simon turns around and checks the street signs, but he had never been lost in the Cities. He is sure he is in the right place.... It is as if a bomb fell on this one building and blew out all the marble countertops, the ornamental iron, sinks, toilets, bathtubs, doorknobs and railings, leaving only a great mass of brick, tamped down into a rough road that must have been used by the bulldozers. He can't quit staring at what is left of the hotel. He can't believe it.[51]

The connection Simon articulates to the Curtis has nothing to do with co-lonial nostalgia, least of all for an array of decorations designed to signal, in the hotel's heyday, the exclusion of Black and Indigenous people. Rather, its intermediating aformality—that is, the condition the hotel takes between formations of concentration and clearance—provided a locating matrix of material and temporal relation. The objects Simon sees piled into wreckage bear traces of human life that are intimate and referential to structures of resource extraction, capital accumulation, and white supremacy on which the rise of the cities depended. What Simon achieves by living with the hotel during ruination is the ability to sense the mutation of colonial structures that can only conceive of themselves as settled. He understands how the most horrifying violence of systemic crises comes by way of their repression via fantasies of racializing vulnerability and immunity. For Simon, ruin is the clarifying blur between colonial forms and the historical, geographic, and political entanglement that is lost when they are cleared.

After Simon confronts the destroyed hotel, he is houseless, and after being harassed by police, he is rescued by a community member, Irene, who cares for him in her apartment. Simon is sick, unmoored, and still trying to hold onto the intimate knowledge of the city-in-ecological-crisis that his residence in the Curtis afforded him. Temporarily safe in Irene's apartment, Simon asks her what building they are in. "We're in the Balmoral, aren't we," Simon ob-serves. "This was the edge of the milling district. You know that after World War One Minneapolis was the artificial limb capital of the world? They needed the best white pine, no knots or weird grain.... Imagine that, these huge ware-houses full of feet and hand, legs." Finally, drifting into sleep, he turns his attention to the sounds of the city: "I can hear it.... I can hear I-94.... I can hear all those cars, those people. I know where we are."[52] What Simon accesses is something we might call location—not in a stable, nominal sense, but as in a process of historically informed being in place. Simon's sense of location is one, I have argued, that relocation's unceasing recycling between concentra-tion and clearance was designed to make impossible.

What Simon has learned living in the physical and historical space be-tween concentration and clearance is distilled in the strange image of the artificial limb warehouses. The Twin Cities' relation to global networks of power is symbolized by its supply of prosthetic limbs to participants/victims of an unthinkable rescaling of militarized violence using land and lumber seized from Anishinaabe and Dakota people in Minnesota. The image of warehouses piled with wooden limbs at the center of a growing settler city references devastating trajectories of loss and accumulation that are too many to account for in any socially or environmentally specific sense. However, it is also an image that dramatizes the convergent forms of concentration and clearance that displace and disguise the real effects of what colonialism calls relocation. That dramatization is available, almost paradoxically, only in and as actual locations—the Balmoral building or the Curtis Hotel—where concentration and clearance can be read against grain, as nondiscrete and contingent. Simon's reading of relocation is not an emancipatory position, but one that performs the critical work of novels, like *The Hiawatha*, that create ways of sensing and recording the formal production of settlement in the context of global crisis.

Infrapolitics of Settlement

One of the perceptual tricks of colonial power is that it always formally positions the ruin it incessantly produces as outside itself. Its ruin never belongs to it. And it is that displacement that is what relocation actually is. Indigenous relocation, therefore, cannot be understood as singular, as an elaboration of federal Indian policy alone but, rather, as interconnected with other relocations including but not limited to Japanese American internment and dispersion and white suburbanization in the same period. These interconnected relocations are organized by the formalism I call *concentration* and *clearance*, and they are reactions to a midcentury climate crisis. Relocation was not a solution to that crisis but a reorganization of its perception; it was a way of making climate crisis seem like a problem racial management could solve. These formal dynamics have not changed in the decades since relocation, as public anxieties about climate crisis have become more common. Even as climate crisis is increasingly inescapable, public and private responses among those proximate to colonial power continue to focus on displacement and immunity. Rather than accepting that climate ruin is something all people have to live and die with—an unavoidable epiphenomena of the existence of the United States—even supposedly leftist policy fixates on how to keep climate catastrophe at its current level, which is to say, contained by the boundaries of racialized exposure to vulnerability. This, all the while white people, from extremist preppers to the extremely rich, invest in more and more preposterous fantasies of immunity, from well-stocked bunkers to space colonization.

One intervention that novels like *The Hiawatha* make, even if they are not coded as works of environmental fiction or cli-fi, is that they show that because ruin is an effect and a precondition of colonial formalisms, learning to live with and in ruin depends on reading or perceiving it differently. Thus, I approach *The Hiawatha* less as a historical novel, in the sense of an imagined record of historically situated living, than as an elaboration of an ongoing history of Indigenous critical perception: an account and an example of what scholars of colonialism call *infrapolitics*. For James Scott, infrapolitics describes "the circumspect struggle waged daily by subordinate groups [that] is, like infrared rays, beyond the visible end of the spectrum . . . a tactical choice born of a prudent awareness of the balance of power."[53] Here Scott's immediate interest is about classifying an order of resistance not registered by studies of direct appeals to or antagonisms of domination—for instance, rights movements or revolutions. But more broadly, his framing through the metaphor of visibility underscores the political force of approaches to the phenomenology of power informed by living under domination. As Scott puts it, infrapolitics is not primarily about making an alternative, discrete archive of subaltern life subordinate to power but about making an archive of the production of domination and subalternity that is fundamentally indiscrete, that is enmeshed with and yet uncontrolled by the normative operation of power. Infrapolitics depends on proximity to regimes of domination but maintains the ability to change the meaning of that proximity because it never becomes coextensive with power. Scott describes it as "continually pressing against the limits of what is permitted on stage, much as a body of water would press against a dam"—a metaphor that aptly characterizes dynamics of repression and the immanence of insurgency, but that also dramatizes the critical force of proximity that infrapolitics denotes.[54] The "pressing" of the water is critical; it is a practice of gathering information about the coherence, integrity, and scale of the power that is otherwise, even to its designers, unknowable. As it pertains to *The Hiawatha*, I read the novel as an elaboration of the critical pressure that Indigenous living exerts on structures of ruin. Against the presupposition that the only response to ruin is relocation—in other words, that ruin is an anti-formalization and a pretext for the reproduction of power—*The Hiawatha*, and the histories of Indigenous attention it elaborates, insists on living in and knowing what ruin obscures.

In the context of the Twin Cities, an infrapolitical framework invites genealogies of Indigenous critical perception that extend back from a novel like *The Hiawatha* to include histories of labor, interpretation, and sociality associated with ruin and therefore understood to be definitively external to the central formalisms of the Twin Cities. Indigenous ironwork is one such historical practice, one that is responsible for the production of many of the most iconic buildings in cities like New York (including the Empire

State Building, the Chrysler Building, and the World Trade Center), and less famous but still significant structures in cities like the Twin Cities (including Minneapolis's tallest building, the IDS Tower). Despite having worked on structures central to the aesthetics and economy of colonial cities, the personal and labor histories of Indigenous ironwork are often externalized by settlement through racializing mythologies of ironworkers being unafraid of heights or otherwise naturally suited for the dangerous and often unregulated work. Although Indigenous ironworkers have strenuously denied them, these myths persist today as a way of associating cities' life-threatening and economically devastating conditions of production with a racial quality understood to be external to them. Reading against the grain of that externalization, *The Hiawatha*'s interest in Indigenous ironwork demonstrates and extends a history of Indigenous critical and spatial production that, although it is not understood to amount to a sovereign political claim, is more intimate than what settler users or designers of the buildings experience. Ultimately, the novel's depiction of ironwork extends a continuity of Indigenous life and thought that relocation is designed to avoid and obscure. Amid the ruin of the cities' Indigenous neighborhoods, the increasing exposure of Indigenous land to extraction, and the broader crises of global militarization and toxification, Treuer's novel holds open a zone of Indigenous social and spatial invention, where "One-Two, Simon, and the rest of the crews . . . were determined to glass the sky with the IDS Tower . . . in defiance of the dissolution affecting the rest of the country."[55] Like other modalities of infrapolitics, Indigenous ironwork never rises to the level of political organizing in the novel and even appears in quotations like this one as almost complicit with US civic reproduction. However, the world the ironworkers make on the unfinished girders of the IDS Tower is one that exceeds the logics that animate that reproduction. It is a world that literally disappears as the building is completed, but it is also the case that Treuer's attention to that threshold of disappearance reveals a spatial and social intimacy—a sense of location with and in excess of relocation—on which the phenomenological order of the city depends but cannot reconcile.

The IDS Tower

Simon joins the Indigenous high steel crew when he is seventeen to help his mother, Betty, provide for their family in the Twin Cities and to pay off their suburban landlord (who had been bartering a $50 per month rent reduction for sexual access to Betty).[56] To join the crew, Simon relies on

One-Two to vouch for him when the foreman goes through the motions of asking about Simon's age and work experience. Although this is a mundane moment, Simon's entry into the high steel crew dramatizes the formal operation of colonial ruin that I have described in this chapter. Relocated Indigenous people are racialized via their concentration around exposure to harm that is renewing for settlement, a framing that One-Two makes explicit: "I came back from Korea. I came back here and this place was jumping. They wanted to demo half the city. Wasn't much being built but they threw new crews together all the time. Now the buildings are going up. It's the only place we can get a good wage. The only way we can get union."[57] One-Two elaborates aggregating trajectories of concentration—global militarization, civic destruction, and labor exploitation—in addition to the histories of ecosystemic exhaustion, land expropriation, and gendered violence that shape Simon and Betty's family story in particular.

At the same time, Simon's job as an ironworker extends long and layered histories of colonial clearance that the novel distills in the construction of the IDS Tower. Finished in 1972, the IDS Tower was built to be the headquarters of two major companies: one, called Investors Diversified Services was started in 1894 by a lawyer named John Tappan, who made a fortune as a surveyor, lumberman, and homesteader near Duluth, as well as an Indian agent to Dakota people. The other company headquartered there, the Dayton-Hudson Corporation (now called Target), reshaped suburbanization in the United States when it built the first climate-controlled indoor shopping mall, the Southdale Mall, outside the Twin Cities in 1956.[58] It is not coincidental that these companies, both of which leveraged white immunity from ecological and social crises of settlement, established headquarters in a newly vacated downtown, in a massive glass building designed to seem powerful, impenetrable, and empty all at once.[59] Neither is it coincidental that these convergent expressions of clearance required the temporary reconcentration of Indigenous laborers in and above the same civic space from which the traces of Indigenous social and political claiming were being erased through renewal. It is a formalism that is the condition for the production of ruin, and one Simon incisively elucidates to his brother Lester, one night when they sneak up to the highest, unfinished floor of the IDS Tower, still under construction:

> There was the skeleton of the building swaying above them. [Simon] pulled his legs under and stood. His arms hung to his sides as if he were waiting in a slow checkout line at the supermarket. A thirty-one story fall on one side, a fourteen foot drop . . . on the other. . . . "You know what this'll look

like when we're done? All sided in glass, a huge lobby four stories high. The floor laid out in marble. Sixty-thousand fuckin square feet of marble. And it'll be theirs. It'll be all theirs. They'll have some black man in a uniform at the desk. And they'll tell him not to let me in. They'll tell him to ask me my business."[60]

However, in the same moment he describes the coloniality of the building, Simon, who does not to clip into the scaffolding (declaring, "Shit, I can fly. I can float.... I'm too light"), turns and "roar[s]" at his brother as he balances along the suspended I-beam, hundreds of feet above the city: "This is all mine. This is all mine."[61] Treuer draws our attention here to a contradiction of space, phenomenon, and sociality that the colonial city cannot reconcile. The city's claim to possession, security, and immunity depends on the concentration and disavowal of racialized people and labor. Nevertheless, the people who live and work amid the ruins of settlement continue trajectories of social and epistemic relation even if they remain officially illegible. Simon's intimate and brazen infrapolitical claim "This is all mine" hinges on the untranslatable demonstrative "this"—a reference to something he cannot point to or hold and so indicates with his body: "He thrust his hands out ... turning in a slow circle on the six-inch wide girder. He took a step forward."[62] What or wherever "this" is, it includes the space, the air (i.e., the land), and the history of Indigenous labor that he moves within.

"This" is also something that Simon needs to share with his brother Lester, a gesture that speaks to the sociality of Indigenous infrapolitics in the context of settlement's ruins. Elsewhere in the novel, Treuer is even more specific about that sociality—for instance, in his description of the secret languages the crew develops for communicating during and after work:

On the building the usual method of communicating by hand was of no use at night. So they developed their own version of Morse which they beat out on the beams with their spud wrenches. The crew spoke in a metallic staccato that cut through the diesel roar and hydraulic whine, above the rip of torches and grinders. After work, in the bars, the men still didn't talk; ordinary speech was too difficult. Instead they carried the principle of code with them. They shouted out names, buildings and dates that carried within them their own stores. *Quebec Bridge, 1907!* someone would shout and the rest nodded and drank. *Chosa! Empire State, 1931!* The bar was solemn. Then some joker yelled *Lenny White-bird, Sakura Massage Parlor, 1969!* They all laughed until it hurt. The list of fallen expanded to include those who got the clap.[63]

The crew's languages are created and sustained by a sociality that depends on a material and epistemic adjacency to and nonidentity with settlement. The conditions of their labor do not include formalized systems for sharing the knowledge they make about each other, about the building, or about colonialism. The crew is working too late and with too much urgency for any official language with which they could describe themselves or their space to be "of use." Their language, therefore, creates new trajectories of phenomenal transit—"out on the beams," "through the diesel roar," "above the rip of torches." Treuer uses these prepositions to signal the intimate proximity of and nonidentity between the crew's language and the conditions in which they share it. In James Scott's terms, this kind of "hidden transcript" is not invented to be either a discourse separate from or ascendent within the political economy of domination the building represents. Rather, their language "minimize[s] appropriation" of their labor, organizing, and knowledge production by the systems of property and profit that otherwise animate the tower.

In this sense also the crew's languages on and off the building are critical practices. In a built, economic, and political context in which Indigenous survival is sanctioned only insofar as it secures white immunity, the crew's strategies for knowing and remembering press against what Scott calls "the limits of the possible."[64] To create social and labor solidarity, to understand more intimately than colonizers how colonial infrastructures are made, to hold histories of production and loss for which there cannot be an official archive—these are strategies of "searching and probing" the tenuous and impermanent space that exists, at the threshold of colonial reproduction, for Indigenous flourishing. In the bars, the crew's interpretation of their experience on the IDS Tower is not narrative or archival; instead, it is repertory, which is to say that it depends on and sustains a repertoire of labor, geographic, and tribal histories that become descriptive in the way they are deployed. Which "names, buildings and dates" are invoked, when, where, or in what sequence, creates the conditions for interpretation shared and acknowledged ("the rest nodded and drank") if unuttered. In other words, while such hidden transcripts extend specific tribal social and intellectual traditions, they are also structures of contextual analysis. These repertories move in spaces that colonial political economies choose not to understand by naming them ruin. As such, their performances on or beyond the IDS are always analytical: ways of describing vulnerability or joy, camaraderie or loss, transgeographic intimacies, violence, and inventions, all held against domination.

The crew's languages are practices of Indigenous infrapolitical authorship that excavate the ruins of settlement, and that also, in Treuer's novel, resist becoming a new archive of Indigenous experience for readers to access.[65] To this point, I conclude by underscoring the way Treuer's account of the hidden Indigenous transcripts becomes a theoretical framework for understanding the novel's own fictionality. *The Hiawatha*'s interest in Indigenous inhabitations of and despite colonial ruin does not create a fuller or more authentic account of the history of the cities. In step with Warrior's theory of Indigenous critical speculation, which imagines around but always respects the formal specificity of the "shreds and shards of evidence" it engages, Treuer's novel participates in the production of special knowledge of the ruins of settlement without revealing or explaining it. What Warrior calls critical speculation's "own kind of truth" is what in *The Hiawatha* remains off-stage, even as the novel functions as a testament and extension of the persistence of Indigenous social and intellectual production in the spaces that colonialism marks as unlivable, uninterpretable, and unhistorical. Fiction, for Treuer, is not a new condition of access to Indigenous experience or relief from structures of domination like relocation. Rather, the novel's investment in and performance of infrapolitics—what I have called here a *practice of location*—marks a coincident and unreconcilable continuity of Indigenous organizing in which the novel itself participates. Location is a spatial and social practice that occurs amid the ruins of settlement, one whose political force is derived from its insistence, unthinkable within setter phenomenologies, that Indigenous space and sociality not only survives but is also the condition for the production of new analytical languages for understanding and ultimately dismantling relocation.

The
Right
to Gather   4

Gerald Vizenor's essay "Native Transmotion" opens
with a scene from a Minnesota district courtroom in
1968. It is an account of a case Vizenor covered and first wrote about during
his first weeks working as a journalist for the *Minneapolis Tribune*. For Vizenor,
the central drama of the case was an exchange between the presiding judge,
Miles Lord, and an Ojibwe witness named Charles Aubid. Aubid testified that
he had been told, by a man named John Squirrel, that a nineteenth-century
treaty negotiation included a guarantee that Ojibwe people could continue to
gather manoomin (wild rice) on ceded land in northern Minnesota. In court,
the judge rejected Aubid's testimony as hearsay, since Squirrel, now deceased,
was not present, and there was no other record of his testimony for the court
to consider. Vizenor writes that, in response, Aubid "pointed at the legal
books on the bench and then shouted that these contained the stories of dead
white men. 'Why should I believe what a white man says, when you don't
believe John Squirrel?' . . . Judge Lord was deferentially amused. . . . 'You've got
me there,' he said, and then considered the testimony of other *Anishinaabe*
witnesses.'"[1] Vizenor concludes that while Aubid's gesture is a keen rebuke

that exposes the hypocrisy of colonial constructions of legal authority, it is also more than that. The moment, he argues, was a kind of gathering. Aubid's testimony was a summoning, a socially generative and politically deconstructive performance of presence that revealed the basic epistemic and political limits of colonial law. "Aubid," Vizenor writes,

> created a presence of John Squirrel. That sense of present as sworn testimony in court, the fourth person pose of evidence ... The rules of evidence are selective, and sanction cozenage over native sovenance, boundaries over stories of sovereignty; however, evidence is never ultimatory. Squirrel was twice the tease of native evidence; the sense of his presence in stories, an actual presence in the memoires of others, and an obviative presence as semantic evidence. These stories and creases of native reason are evidence, a dialogic circle.[2]

What Vizenor describes here is the basic insufficiency of colonial justice, specifically the way it mandates maximally restricted definitions of representation, community, and land. Against this, Vizenor depicts an unruly gathering of memory, kinship, and a plant whose complex ecological and cultural significance exceeds the terms by which colonial governments endow or withdraw legal protection. This chapter traces a cultural history of the nearly two-centuries-old confrontation between colonial legal and environmental regulatory apparatuses in Minnesota and manoomin—a plant whose inextricable and expansive social and environmental connectivity is, as Aubid and Vizenor demonstrate, fundamentally unrestrictable to colonial distributions of subjectivity and objectivity.

The way Vizenor writes about Aubid in this scene is characteristically baroque, at once unwaveringly precise and a little windswept. As I will argue, this is not as much a style as it is a method—specifically, an enactment of the kind of disruption of colonial knowledge systems that he has elsewhere famously termed "survivance," "trickster hermeneutics," "varionative," and "transmotion." And while it is not within the scope of this chapter to offer a comprehensive genealogy of that method, I would suggest that it is one that emerges less from Vizenor's experience in the academy (despite having held faculty positions at nine institutions since the mid-1960s) and more from a life spent moving between structures of colonial power without allowing his work to become identical with them. Vizenor was born in 1934 and grew up between Minneapolis and the White Earth Reservation, after his father, an Anishinaabe man who had moved to the Twin Cities well before relocation, was murdered. Vizenor served in the US military and participated in the occupation of Japan following World War II. Afterward, and in addition to his academic work, he was a journalist, a minor literary celebrity, and a community organizer. Vizenor is a writer who has always worked in proximity to colonial structures, and who has also always insisted that their constructions of justice, expertise, and sociality are incomplete—moreover, that they derive their fictions of coherence and completeness from the erasure of Indigenous life and thought. This is, in fact, precisely the gesture he makes in his account of the exchange between Aubid and Lord in the 1968 manoomin case.

The Colonial Politics of Protection

When Vizenor describes Aubid's invocation of Squirrel as "the fourth person pose of evidence," he references a beautiful and complex linguistic structure in Ojibwemowin used to differentiate two third persons in a story. As Rand Valentine notes, "In Ojibwe storytelling... one and only one third person animate character... must serve as the story perspective," a position called the proximate.[3] "All other characters," Valentine writes, "are marked to show that their perspective is *not* being taken... characters [that] are said to be obviative," and who are grammatically identified as the fourth person(s) in a story.[4] Fourth personhood in Ojibwemowin is a structure of attention sensitive to the shifts and subtleties of relation out of which narrative, history, and knowledge always emerge but that, at least in English, are grammatically unaccounted for. As Valentine observes, a given character in an Ojibwemowin story does not necessarily stay in either the proximate third or obviative (fourth) position but, rather, moves between them as the central idea or question of the story articulates through the narrative movement of characters thinking and interacting together. Fourth personhood is expressive of the way sociality and knowledge are co-constituting, and, as such, it is a structure that gives narrative shape to a modality of relation that exceeds the conceptual capacity of the positivist premises of US law, one in some ways embodied by the expansive ontological and relational meaning of manoomin itself. Aubid's invocation of John Squirrel's understanding of manoomin produces a presence unreconcilable to the colonial concepts of witness or testimony and thereby underscores the intrinsic limitation of the colonial law and the colonial present. By identifying this moment as one of obviation, Vizenor signals Aubid's willingness to use the court to sustain Ojibwe narrative and epistemic practices and the court's sense that such practices are unintelligible, or, as in the obviative's etymological sense, are obstructions to the primacy of white supremacist concepts of witness and testimony that subtend US law. In his essay, Vizenor rephrases the court's disavowal of Squirrel as the occasion in which Aubid gathers a set of relations, "a presence," that US law renders absent to preserve the fiction of its authority.

In this sense alone, Vizenor's account identifies the intrinsically extractive logic of colonial law, which produces a concept of a public present (and a present public) that is always a violent reduction of the expansive and living temporal and social potentiality of the people and land it administrates. But the conditions of the case also introduce a second axis of colonial extraction that Vizenor uses as an almost unexplained premise for the elaboration of his theory of cultural sovereignty that he terms *transmotion*. Aubid's testimony in September 1968 was part of a case challenging the regulation of Ojibwe manoomin harvesting on land, adjoining the Leech Lake reservation, that had been ceded to the United States in the Treaty of 1855 and was subsequently named a "Migratory Fowl Refuge" by Franklin D. Roosevelt in 1935—a case that was one of the earliest of a generation of suits brought by Indigenous people asserting treaty-guaranteed rights to hunt, fish, or gather rice on ceded land. Although litigation around Indigenous hunting, fishing, and gathering rights are as old as the treaties in which they were established, beginning in the late 1960s debates about the protection and regulation of manoomin became central to two trajectories of US public policy: (1) the shift from the maliciously assimilative programs of Termination and Relocation to the benevolently assimilative project of a rights-based approach to the administration of Indigenous people and land; and (2) the broader evolution of environmentalism during the rise of corporate power and the simultaneous evisceration of public governance under neoliberalism. The ascendance of rights-based colonial governance and the dismantling of public political structures through which rights protections might be enacted are synchronous political histories that often inflect the practice and regulation of Indigenous interspecies relation, manoomin growing and harvesting in particular. These two trajectories of political history also shape and converge with cultural developments of late modernism broadly speaking, and the narrative and philosophical constructions of dissent, solidarity, identity, and decolonization essential to the rise of Indigenous, Black, and Latinx literature and theory within the US academy and book market.

One aim of this chapter is to unpack the layered logics of colonial power that surround the regulation of Indigenous manoomin growing and harvesting in order to show how frameworks of legal protection, human and natural rights in particular, sustain violences of territorial and political seizure through the formal equivocations of colonial liberalism. The extraction histories of the forms of the public and the person, through which manoomin has been managed, are central to understanding the interrelation of rights and colonialism in the second half of the twentieth century, a convergence I bookmark as *the colonial politics of protection*.[5] On one hand, this is an argument that might seem to overstate the political significance of a plant whose environmental and cultural meaning is regionally produced and contested, and that has thus far endured, especially in comparison to organisms that have been explicitly targeted for extinction by US settlement, colonial assaults on Ojibwe land claims, knowledge systems, food sovereignty, and public health. On the other hand, it is precisely because manoomin is never only a plant—which is to say that its meaning cannot be reduced to the form of the species, but that it has to be understood as a nexus of interdependent ecological, cultural, and political relations—that the question of its well-being exposes the extractive formalisms of colonial protection. Rights produce and manage distributions of interiority insofar as they work by nominating subjects of protection that always bear a formal association with the possessive individual, whether as a person, a class, a quality of experience, someone's idea or action, or a space owned or otherwise notably in/accessible.[6] Because rights structures inevitably interpellate subjects of protection by way of the universalizable but never universally attributed forms of personhood (personhood proper or personhood as an index of property), expressions of colonial protection are always extractive. Rights reduce questions of protection and justice to the administration of forms that have or distribute property. For nationally derivative rights structures, this is a matter of determining whether a form is an acceptable referent of state sovereignty, whereas, for universal rights structures, like the UN Declaration of Human Rights, the question of who or what is rights-bearing is reduced further, to the form of the person, place, or species itself.

In the case of manoomin, each time US law has considered its classification as a protected or unprotected person, species, commodity, space, or culturally significant artifact, the effect has been to legalize and administrate its extraction. However, and not unlike the performance of more-than-present testimony Vizenor describes in "Native Transmotion," manoomin cannot be represented or protected using the formalisms of colonial interiority. Manoomin is nothing less than a living relation in the sense that at every moment or site of its growing, harvesting, and sharing it organizes a convergence of human and other-than-human beings, history, prophecy, and space. Manoomin is not a form, I argue, but a *gathering*—a term that occurs as an aporia in the treaties that accede to the continuity of Indigenous hunting, fishing, and ricing, as in the 1837 White Pine Treaty: "The privilege of hunting, fishing, and gathering the wild rice upon the lands, the rivers and the lakes included in the territory ceded, is guaranteed to the Indians, during the pleasure of the President of the United States."[7] Gathering, even within the meager semantic scaffolding of US law, never only means taking or harvesting because ricing is always expansively social. It is a practice that requires the meeting of and sharing among Indigenous people from different places, generations, bands, and nations. Gathering manoomin is also an Indigenous space, a season, an archive, an aesthetic tradition, at the same time it is a social and an agricultural practice. Beyond the narrowest terms of treaties, because manoomin is not a cultivated crop for Indigenous people but one that moves with living ecosystems along with changing water levels, soil composition, temperature, and human and other-than-human interaction, it is an expression of the nonobjectivity, the ontological and epistemic cooperativity, eventality, and intersystematicity of "the environment." Therefore, even when manoomin is the subject of well-meaning colonial protections—when its harvesting was first regulated in the 1930s, when it was named the state grain of Minnesota in 1977, when sulfate runoff from mines began to be regulated to protect manoomin in the early twenty-first century—its reduction to the ontological and rhetorical formalisms of US law is an act and a precondition for further extraction. Gathering is a more-than-formal performance of Indigenous presence that cannot be reduced—as Aubid and Vizenor point out and as is underscored in the details of the debates around protection that I consider in this chapter—to the terms of the public or the person. Rather than thinking about gathering as an aspect of colonial protection therefore, I conceive of it as the performance of the social, ecological, and political conditions that exceed the necessity of protection. Gathering is decolonial in that it is a demonstration of the possibility of a world in which protection is inessential.

As Vizenor's recounting of Aubid's testimony indicates, this approach to manoomin as a gathering rather than a form is not contradicted when Indigenous people enter the theater of colonial security to advocate for the well-being of manoomin and the array of human and other-than-human worlds to which it is connected. As I write this chapter, manoomin is being named, for the first time in US legal history, as a plaintiff in a suit against the state of Minnesota (*Manoomin et al. v. Minnesota DNR*) for its authorization of the Enbridge 3 Pipeline to be built adjacent to tribal land, with and directly across ricing waters. Even in what Vizenor might call the "pose" of the plaintiff, and even as the other plaintiffs in the case invoke "the Rights of Manoomin," the suit does not depend on a straightforward expansion of US state protection. At the heart of *Manoomin et al.*'s argument is an injunction against the water appropriation permit that the DNR granted to Enbridge and the insistence that manoomin "possesses inherent rights to exist, flourish, regenerate, and evolve, as well as inherent rights to restoration, recovery, and preservation. These rights include, but are not limited to, the right to pure water and freshwater habitat; the right to a healthy climate system and a natural environment free from human-caused global warming impacts and emissions."[8]

Here, the assertion of the rights of manoomin is a narrative and categorical reframing of the question of justice—an invocation of obviation both in the sense that it demands the court assess perspectival capacity of a plaintiff that is a plant and the multitude of social and ecological relations with which it is interdependent, and in the sense that to do so necessitates an obstruction of the infrastructural coherence of US law and petrochemical industry that remakes living things as objects as a function of the transits of power and capital. The rights of manoomin stop a particular gesture of land and water seizure, and they initiate a deconstruction of the fiction of colonial legal totality by using the formal premises of colonialism liberalism—specifically, the always-conditional universalisms rights imply—to claim responsibility to a world extrinsic to colonial interiority and protection. What manoomin asks for, in this suit, is at once a practical injunction against a permit and at the same time the wholesale abolition of the correlated regimes of colonial protection and extraction. In other words, even in the pose of participation in colonial law, the array of social, ecological, and political relations inextricable from manoomin gather well beyond the form of a plaintiff, as a deconstruction and a generativity in excess of the formal horizons of colonial power, that would seek or could be understood to receive the protection.

Rights cannot protect against or in/advertently extend colonial regimes of extraction without recourse to form, including those forms by which manoomin has been interpellated by US law—the public and the person—that structure this chapter's extraction histories. And it is because of the central role form plays in the operation of colonial protection and extraction that Vizenor's work as a theorist and journalist is part of what gathers with manoomin as a social and ecological relation, in court and in the world. A second aim of this chapter is to show that the relentless aformality of Vizenor's writing in general, and his work examining the entanglements of sovereignty and discourse in particular, is itself a trajectory of material relation, an aspect of gathering, rather than an idiosyncrasy of style.[9] By *aformality* I mean two things. First, that Vizenor, whose career as an Ojibwe journalist, writer, and community organizer in Minneapolis was coincident with the rise of the American Indian Movement and Native literary nationalism, steadfastly refused the comfortable correlation of form and power that Native nationalists leverage against colonial governance—a correlation that, as a matter of both Native nationalist political and intellectual history, begins with the articulation of Indigenous sovereignty as autonomous and separate but inevitably facilitates expansions of and incorporation into US power and the academy. Vizenor's writing is notoriously abstract, neologistic, and circular—qualities that risk it seeming disengaged or apolitical in contrast with the polemics of AIM or the positivist approaches of Native nationalist critics. However, I read Vizenor as participating in a performative disavowal of the assumption that formal stability and recognizability is a prerequisite of politics (particularly in his theorization of sovereignty as "transmotion"), an approach that resonates with postnationalist conceptualizations of sovereignty in Indigenous studies, including Cherokee scholar Sean Teuton's work on Indigenous internationalism and Leanne Betasamosake Simpson's theory of sovereignty as "the place where we all live and work together."[10]

Second, I use *aformality* to signal that, particularly as a theorist, Vizenor takes the forms of narrative and politics that generate currency within colonial liberalism as his objects of critique. This aspect of his work also aligns with developments in Indigenous studies that historically succeed the nationalist turn but with which—because of the persistence of disciplinary narratives of generational developmentalism—his work is not often associated. For instance, Vizenor's investment in deconstructing the liberal forms of the public and the person is an older, and actually Indigenous, version of Andrea Smith's argument in "American Studies without America" that Native feminism be defined not by an inevitably anthropological stabilization of Indigeneity and/or gender but by a rigorous critique of US power that might "create the space to reflect on what might be more just forms of governance, not only for Native peoples, but for the rest of the world."[11]

It would be easy to misunderstand the aformality of Vizenor's theoretical writing as an overcorrection against the forms that structure US colonialisms, a giving over to discursivity as a counterpoint to form. But such a reading would reinforce a specious binary between form and formlessness that is itself a legacy of the ascription of vacancy and absence to Indigenous land and life against which colonial personhood, law, and value has been articulated and maintained. Rather, I argue that in essays like "Native Transmotion," Vizenor holds open a space otherwise erased by that binary, a space in which it is possible to intensify a critical proximity to the political histories of colonial forms without reproducing them. To describe a rhetorical position as a "space," in this way, may seem itself an unnecessary abstraction; however, there is a direct trajectory of influence between Vizenor's writing and the material and spatial way manoomin grows and hosts relation that is irreducible to colonial forms. In an essay on Vizenor's writing and ricing, White Earth Ojibwe poet Kim Blaeser describes both as contributing to a "dialogic circle," a mode of "tribal telling [that] always involves a web of connection and continuance."[12] For Blaeser, that way of practicing narrative "'carries' . . . knowledge and builds on it. Just as a fall breeze might sway the rice stalks, a telling wind blows through this spoken *Manidoo-noodin*"—a kind of epistemic choreography she compares to the circularity and aggregation that characterizes Vizenor's writing.[13] Blaeser makes clear that what might be mistaken as Vizenor's stylistic eccentricity or a turn away from everyday practices of tribal knowledge is actually a material commitment that exceeds the descriptive or protective scope of forms including the public and the person.

In the sections that follow, I trace extraction histories of the public and the person as forms of colonial protection, extended to and deconstructed by manoomin gathering. The stakes of these histories include but are also greater than showing that extraction proceeds through protection understood in the terms of conservation and resource access. More specifically, I show that extraction is inherent to the forms with which debates about rights and sovereignty proceed. In and beyond the context of Indigenous communities and the regimes that occupy them, forms like the public and the person are used to reconcile contradictions intrinsic to rights and sovereignty and to equivocate Indigenous political and ecological practices with colonial state and individual interests. In order to think about the histories of these forms outside their own totalizing premises, I return to the constellations of relation inspired by manoomin gathering—that is, to manoomin as an interspecies entanglement, a non-nationalist spatial imaginary, and a food- and knowledge-making practice to which Vizenor's work as a theorist is materially connected. This chapter does not presume that continuities of Indigenous gathering need critical attention of the kind I can offer here, except perhaps to underscore a point that Indigenous communities have consistently made anyway—that gathering is not a relation that colonial forms protect. Beyond this, I show that thinking about manoomin as gathering is a productive challenge to conversations about justice within US literary and environmental studies. Following Vizenor's work in "Native Transmotion," I observe that writing about manoomin invites generative reassessments of the way we talk about the environment, the social and spatial scope of relation, decolonization, and the possibility of justice.

Hearsay Sovereignty

"Native Transmotion," Vizenor's definitive essay on Indigenous sovereignty, begins in a US courtroom, a space, as I have suggested, in which gathering is necessarily reduced to the restrictive terms of citizen, legal canon, and colonial presence. By starting the essay in this space, Vizenor makes two implicit and related points: first, that Indigenous sovereignty is not a claim to colonial redress because US law only has the capacity to misrecognize Indigenous people, land, and knowledge; and second, that sovereignty is less a singular or stable political principle than it is a problem for description. Within US legal structures, what Indigenous sovereignty references—the commingling of self-determination, multidisciplinary knowledge systems, and expansive histories and futures of human and other-than-human relation—is indescribable. In a decolonial sense, sovereignty does not reference an abstract or stable (e.g., constitutional) political framework; it references the continuities of Indigenous life and land of which its articulation and elaboration are always a part. In this sense, sovereignty is a compelling term for Vizenor, especially insofar as its invocation is a chance to show how it is never as normative as it is given to be. Sovereignty marks a site where colonial political discourse fails and Indigenous thought sustains and renews. As Vizenor writes,

> Native sovereignty is sovenance, the immanence of visions, and transmotion in artistic creations. Sovereignty, moreover, is practical, reciprocal, and theoretical, but there is no such word in the *anishinaabe* language . . . the native sense of motion and use of the land in the northern woodlands does not embrace inheritance or tenure of territory. The criteria of transmotion are in the stories of trickster creation, the birch bark documents of the *midewiwin*, song picture, beaded patterns, winter counts, painted hides, ledger art, and other creases of motion.[14]

"Sovenance" is a term Vizenor uses to describe the sociality of Indigenous knowledge and governance structures. A word that layers sovereignty with an obsolete word for remembrance, it suggests that what makes and sustains living systems of relation is precisely that temporal and even ontological complexity that US law cannot bear. It is also what makes sovereignty in an Indigenous context unabstractable, not a description in itself but an occasion for further description. "Sovenance," Vizenor writes, "is that sense of presence in remembrance ... once an obscure noun, the connotation of sovenance is a native presence ... not the romance of an aesthetic absence or victimry."[15] For Vizenor, Aubid's hearsay invocation of John Squirrel is an example of how sovereignty marks the limits of US power and, as an aspect of Indigenous theory, folds back into continuities of material and epistemic production: "Aubid told the judge that there once was a document [that the court would recognize], but the *anishinaabe* always understood their rights in stories, not hearsay. John Squirrel was there in memories, a storied presence, and he could have been heard by the court as a visual trace of a parol agreement."[16]

Sovereignty, for Vizenor and Aubid, is the storied linking of space, time, and relation that creates the possibility for Squirrel to be present in 1968, to be described and to redescribe both the agreement itself (an internationalism the form of the court is designed to forget) and a theory of ecological stewardship in which manoomin would thrive.[17] Neither Vizenor nor Aubid invoke sovereignty as a unilateral or exclusive claim to a resource or territory. Vizenor writes: "Regrettably, the discussions of ... sovereignty ... in a constitutional democracy have been reduced to the metes of territoriality."[18] Aubid, who actually did have a personal claim to Rice Lake, was only in court to argue that he should not have to pay a licensing fee to gather there, not that it was owned by him. This sense of sovereignty as an occasion for the (re)description of generative relations with land is disavowed by colonial rights operating under the rubrics of protection and the public; it also extends a continuity of Indigenous theorizing that can be traced from well before to after the composition of Vizenor's essay.

Notably, in the first major treaty that bears on the question of ricing, neither the United States nor any other single polity is given control over hunting and gathering. Instead, hunting (and all such harvesting practices) is an occasion for the softening, renegotiation, and crossing of boundary lines. Although the United States tried to use this treaty—signed in 1825 at Prairie du Chien—to establish separate and stable territories for Ojibwe and Dakota people under the auspices of peacemaking and with the intention to use the importation of territoriality to eventually erode tribal landholding, the treaty includes an article that states: "It is understood ... that no tribe shall hunt within the acknowledged limits of another without their assent, but it being the sole object of this arrangement to perpetuate a peace among them. ... The Chiefs of all the tribes have expressed a determination, cheerfully to allow a reciprocal right of hunting on the lands of on each other, permission being first asked and obtained, as before provided for."[19] Hunting and ricing are explicitly understood as gathering, as supernational practices both in the sense that negotiation rather than steadfast boundaries was the reigning political premise and in the sense that the United States would not be involved. Further, rather than describing stable or abstract terms of access, the treaty identifies hunting and ricing as the occasion for intertribal (re) description of land and community.

This approach to ricing and to sovereignty in general is echoed in an essay written nearly twenty years after Vizenor's, by Michi Saagiig Nishnaabeg writer Leanne Betasamosake Simpson, "The Place Where We All Live and Work Together: A Gendered Analysis of Sovereignty":

> When Indigenous peoples use the English word *sovereignty* . . . we use it to mean authentic power coming from a generated consensus and a respect for dissent. . . . Borders for indigenous nations are not rigid lines on a map but areas of increased diplomacy, ceremony, and sharing. . . . My understanding of "Kina Gchi Anishinaabeg-ogaming—the place where we all live and work together" . . includes animal nations and plant nations, the water, the air and the soil . . . [and] sacred and spiritual dimensions that transcend time and space. It includes my body, my heart, and my mind.[20]

Across Vizenor's "Native Transmotion," Article 13 of the Treaty of Prairie du Chien, and Simpson's essay, demarcations of sovereignty are sites for gathering and occasions for the elaboration of political, social, and environmental description. Instead of "rigid lines" or the "metes of territoriality" whose interpretation tautologically references a canon it unilaterally authorizes, borders in these texts create new meaning when they are understood as unstable and crossable. Most of all, they are places where sociality accrues and develops—what Simpson calls the "increased diplomacy, ceremony, and sharing," and what I am calling *gathering*.

In stark contrast, the interpretation of sovereignty in US courts depends on and stabilizes abstract forms that simplify political, social, and environmental meaning—forms that contribute to what Lisa Lowe terms the "economy of affirmation and forgetting" that organizes colonial liberalism.[21] In the following section, I offer an extraction history of a legal construction of resource protection (culminating in the framework of "wild rice waters") that uses forms of the public to control the interpretation of sovereignty. I observe that even when courts try to protect tribal usufructuary rights, they do so by defining sovereignty as a condition of political collectively that never implicitly includes but that can be occasionally extended to Indigenous land and lifeways. In these cases, sovereignty defined as a periodically plastic expression of the US public frames Indigenous rights as given and protected by the same logic that protects the right of colonial states and settlers to extract land and resources. I observe that this equivocation—the collateral protection of and from extraction—emanates from the forms the United States uses to articulate the public, forms that these cases regularly cite but never dissect or justify.

Forms of the Public

In the twentieth century, US courts interpreted agreements like the 1837 White Pine Treaty's assurance of continued Anishinaabe manoomin gathering by framing colonial protection of Indigenous land in two ways: as an occasion for the expansion and then as a horizon of colonial power. One genealogy of the first interpretation begins with *U.S. v. 4,450.72 Acres of Land*, a case argued in 1939 in a district court, that asked whether the United States can extend a preserve, adjoining the White Earth Reservation, dedicated to Ojibwe manoomin harvesting by condemning state-owned land. The central question— about land management within US federalism—is inflected by the question of colonial protection, as both parties (the United States and the state of Minnesota) argued that they would preserve exclusive Ojibwe access to ricing, even though neither party included White Earth in their argument and the decision cited no Indigenous people at all. The US plan provided relatively unconditional Ojibwe access to manoomin while the state planned for the land to be used as a public hunting reserve (open to settlers, except during ricing season). In one sense Indigenous sovereignty is not explicitly at stake in this case, which is more immediately about competing visions of land conservation in the aftermath of the Great Depression and during the rise of the federal national land conservation system. For the state, the prospect of controlling access to hunting and ricing was an opportunity to develop an outdoor recreation tourism industry from which it could boost local tax bases, collect licensing fees, and expand its own policing power. For the United States, the preserve mimicked the forms of the national park and the national wildlife refuge which were proliferating during the 1930s and 1940s. In both cases, colonial conservation was depicted as benevolent, progressive, and in the public interest, although it was for both parties an expansion of state control over Indigenous land and lifeways and, as such, an extraction project conducted under the rubric of liberal governance.

The decision in *U.S. v. 4,450.72 Acres of Land* and in its appeal to the Eighth Circuit Court three years later, *State of Minnesota v. United States*, framed tribes as fundamentally dependent on colonial protection and affirmed that the provision of that protection was primarily a federal responsibility. Notably, even as these decisions cite the Marshall Trilogy to justify the status of colonial protection as a federal matter, they do not emphasize the international treaty relation in order to do so, but rather read Marshall as suggesting that protecting tribes is a matter of the public interest, because of tribes' political nonautonomy. In his decision in *U.S. v. 4,450.72 Acres*, Justice Nordbye nowhere cites the sovereign authority of tribes as a function of the treaty relationship, but looks to the constitution to establish tribes as dependents: "In order to regulate commerce completely with the Indians, it was presumably deemed necessary for the Government to assume with them the relationship of guardian and ward."[22] He then concludes, based on the comparative sovereignties of the state of Minnesota and the United States, that the public use in its truest sense is a federal responsibility: "If the public use of both sovereigns is mainly directed to the aid and assistance of the Indians, the Federal government has the exclusive duty to look after its wards, and in carrying out this Federal power, it cannot be restricted by the State."[23] This is a stance affirmed and intensified by Justice Sanborn in his decision in the case's appeal, in which he writes: "It is our conclusion that the guardianship which the United States is required to exercise over the Indians makes the use of lands acquired by it for the purpose of affording them food, occupation, and a place to live, a public use. The problem of providing for the care, protection, and welfare of these dependent tribes is a public problem and one which is necessarily national in its scope and character."[24]

Here, what Sanborn terms "the problem of providing...protection" extends a conclusion central to the Marshall Trilogy, that conceiving of tribes as adjacent to but not included within US federalism creates a possibility of securing the federal government's position as sole guarantor or abrogator of tribal sovereignty. This was a position these cases intensify and link with the formation of conservation networks, during the same decades, like the National Parks System and the National Wildlife refuge system, which, as recent cases involving the Arctic National Wildlife Refuge and the Malheur National Wildlife refuge evince, expose tribes to settler individual and corporate resource extraction under the guise of stable, federal protection. But unlike in Marshall, Nordbye and Sanborn resolve the question of competing federal and state sovereignties by stabilizing the public as a political concept of which the reserve is a formal expression. In this context, the courts' invocation of the public is an occasion to affirm federal sovereignty to define and dispense protection and to erase, or forget, tribal sovereignty altogether. Tribal interests are not public, but they are sites for the expansion of colonial power via the form of the public. Another way to put it is that the court achieved a resolution between competing colonial sovereignties—in these cases, by describing tribes as objects of protection.

The second interpretation of the US power to guarantee Indigenous gathering rights inverted the question of colonial protection. Beginning with *U.S. v. Winans* (1905) but extending through the end of the twentieth century, courts considered whether treaty-guaranteed rights could represent a horizon to the scope of the public. Where the first set of cases asked if the public could expand to protect tribes (who were implicitly positioned as outside the public), *Winans*, *LCO v. Voigt* (1983), *Mille Lacs v. Minnesota* (1999), and an array of still-unresolved environmental policy controversies asked if tribes could actively define their participation in the public. Because this is a question that used treaty provisions like Article 13 of the White Pine Treaty to determine whether tribes could be described as subjects of protection, it is one we can rephrase (adjusting the famous Arendtian formulation "the right to have rights") as a question of whether, in the US public sphere, tribes have the right to reserve.

These cases are prompted by formal restrictions implied by the first interpretation of the US public in that they consider whether Indigenous people have a right to gather outside of the jurisdictional forms of protection provided by the United States—if they, in other words, could gather "off-reservation." In *Winans*, Justice McKenna focused his answer on the intersection of two articles from a 1859 treaty between the United States and the Yakima nation, one that ceded the Yakima "right, title and interest in and to the lands and country occupied by them," and another that established "the exclusive right of taking fish . . . at all the usual and accustomed places, in common with the citizens of the territory . . . together with the privilege of hunting, gathering . . . and pasturing their [livestock] . . . upon open and unclaimed land."[25] In his decision, McKenna framed the latter of these articles as a qualification of the former—or, in his words, that "the treaty was not a grant of rights to the Indians, but a grant of right from them—a reservation of those not granted," which includes a right to fish "not exclusive in the Indians . . . but [of which] the Indians were secured in its enjoyment by a special provision of means for its exercise."[26] In this construction, the public is not a source of tribal protection but a form epiphenomenal to it. The public rights settlers invoke to access "natural resources" are articulated in consort with the reservation of tribal rights to gather beyond the boundaries of delimited sovereignty.

In the late twentieth century, and particularly with the rise of state power associated with Termination policy and Public Law 280, *Winans* became a key precedent in cases like *LCO v. Voigt* and *Mille Lacs v. Minnesota* in which Ojibwe communities successfully objected to efforts by state departments of natural resources to restrict or regulate via licensing their fishing and gathering of manoomin. Conventionally these decisions are understood as a victory for advocates of tribal sovereignty in the sense that they recognize tribes' rights to reserve access to what appears within colonial governance as "natural resources" (e.g., public land, water, fish, manoomin). Specifically, *LCO v. Voigt* and *Mille Lacs v. Minnesota* define tribal "usufructuary rights" as requiring a specific congressional intervention to be abrogated, something that the omission of explicitly reserved rights in later treaties, Zachary Taylor's unconstitutional removal order in 1850, and Minnesota statehood all fail to accomplish. Unlike "aboriginal title," treaty-guaranteed usufructuary rights are not intrinsically delimited, and, in that sense, their scope, according to the Seventh Circuit and US Supreme Courts, is analogous to public rights in general.[27]

However, by redescribing Indigenous people as subjects rather than objects of protection and by affirming an expanded sense of the space of protected Indigenous gathering beyond the form of the reserve, these cases prompted new questions about the formal limits of the US public and about what, in both ontological and regulatory terms, the object of colonial protection would now be. The stakes of these questions exceed the specific context of manoomin gathering and even of the United States' ability to recognize Indigenous rights because protection, in this instance, is an extension of the political and ontological logic I call *the colonial distribution of interiority* and the broader colonial cultural investment in extraction that it organizes. Less abstractly: the United States needs to control and provide forms of protection in order to articulate its sense of itself as a public enterprise, and the forms of protection it underwrites need to have spatial and ontological limits in order to seem politically coherent. Absent the spatial and ontological limits implied by the idea that manoomin gathering was reducible to culture or reserve, it was unclear to colonial officials if the state could understand where protection would occur or what would be protected.

This uncertainty about the public form of colonial protection would be dramatized in the aftermath of one of the most influential federal regulatory expansions (encouraged by the civil rights movement, Red Power, and the writer-activist Rachel Carson): the 1972 Clean Water Act. That law was implemented in Minnesota the following year, with an additional water quality standard designed to protect manoomin from toxification caused by sulfate runoff from mining and wastewater treatment operations.[28] Prior to the *LCO* and *Mille Lacs* cases, the addition of this classification would have impacted the way that the Minnesota Pollution Control Agency (MPCA) and the Minnesota Department of Natural Resources (MDNR) protected settler cultivation and harvesting of manoomin in public lakes and rivers—a practice that has been administrated by the state since 1929.[29] However, with the federal protection of the right for Indigenous people to gather "off-reservation" affirmed by *LCO* and *Mille Lacs*, the classification of where manoomin protection would occur and what resources would need to be protected in order to protect manoomin was no longer a matter of state discretion alone.

These became portentous questions for the state in part because of the special qualities that distinguish manoomin as a plant and a food relation within dynamic freshwater and human ecologies. Unlike when it is "cultivated" (i.e., grown as a monoculture in commercial, colonial farms), naturally grown manoomin is a highly sensitive, mobile, and resilient plant, whose germination and reproduction draws on and moves through all aspects of the ecosystems in which it grows. Among the most consequential of the ecosystemic entanglements on which manoomin depends are the strength and variability of water currents, stream and lake depth, and soil composition, as well as the careful harvesting practices that Ojibwe, Dakota, Menominee, and other Indigenous people have developed over millennia. Manoomin seeds in loamy alluvial mud that cannot be either too sandy or calcic.[30] It is "fragile" in the sense that it does not grow well with chemicals or with unusual shifts in the depth or quality of the water—for instance, shifts caused by damming, runoff, or industrial water seizure. On the other hand, it is a plant that requires certain kinds of disturbances—the aerating movement of animals through its beds, or the encouragement of seed dispersion by Indigenous harvesters—to thrive. Manoomin is ornately interconnected with its ecosystem, from the birds, insects, temperature, and air quality that drive its wind pollination to the hydrological systems (below and above ground) that grow and move manoomin around the streams, shallows, and lake edges of the Great Lakes region. For these reasons, manoomin can grow in almost any of the nontoxic freshwater ecosystems in Minnesota, a fact that meant that the combination of the Clean Water Act provisions and the decisions in *LCO* and *Mille Lacs* created significant challenges for the state's environmental regulatory agencies. In order to guarantee Indigenous access to manoomin, not only would they theoretically have to keep sulfate levels in *all* public waters below 10 mg/l, they would also have to protect all aspects of the ecosystems with which manoomin is connected. Put differently: when, in the aftermath of the rights-era decisions affirming tribal sovereignty, US law made entities like manoomin the objects of protection, rather than tribes, they inadvertently prompted a crisis in the formal conception of the colonial public. Manoomin does not obey the arbitrary territoriality or the special or land use classifications with which colonial protection (always premised on claims to political universality) is normally delimited.

In order to resolve the crisis produced by the combination of new environmental laws and long-standing tribal usufructuary rights, the MPCA classified a new protected form: "wild rice waters." Beginning in 1997, the state identified 124 public lakes and streams as "wild rice waters" that could be monitored for water quality and for ensured access to Indigenous gatherers, although the state neither identified clear mechanisms to establish that monitoring nor did it organize an effective consultation process with which to gain consensus about waters that would or would not be classified "wild rice waters." As tribes working under the organization the 1854 Treaty Authority trenchantly pointed out, the MPCA standards are both arbitrary and entirely dependent on static, colonial territorial and agricultural metrics.[31] In contrast, the 1854 Treaty Authority argued: "In our view, if a lake or river supports any wild rice, it is a wild rice water. We do not see any other way to define it.... Any wild rice is important and worth protecting.... Wild rice is a variable resource across years, and it takes multiple years (and perhaps even a historic look) to understand the potential density and acreage of wild rice in a given water."[32]

"Wild rice waters" is a reformalization of the colonial public as a theater for protection. As a spatial and regulatory classification, it seeks to resolve a contradiction intrinsic to the project of colonial protection: that the formalisms through which colonial governments express ostensible benevolence are inextricable from the extraction. The 1854 Treaty Authority's response exposes the persistence of this contradiction when they state that manoomin is a part of healthy freshwater ecosystems everywhere in the Great Lakes, and that the task of monitoring and assessing individual waters would require reauthorizing Indigenous claims to land and tribal archives otherwise disavowed by the state. The predictable outcome of the development of the form "wild rice waters" was that it became a site of disagreement between, on one side, settlements and mines (who lobbied for a reduction of "wild rice waters" and for the elimination of the 10 mg/l sulfate standard) and, on the other, tribes and environmentalists (who argued for more "wild rice waters" and the maintenance and enforcement of the sulfate standard). With the exception that the MDNR increased the number of "wild rice waters" to 1,200, this disagreement and the ensuing proliferation of negotiation about the category led to the stalling of further protective action by the state altogether.[33] Still, the episode yields important insights about the role that form plays in the construction of sovereignty within US colonialisms.

In one sense, the development of "wild rice waters" shows that the United States depends on a relatively stable theory of form in order to express power. Whether the United States wants to seize resources, remove tribes, or protect people and land, it acts through spatial and regulatory forms that simplify relations and restate a hierarchy of power in which tribes' status is permanently unfixed. The forms of the reserve and "wild rice waters," like the forms of the settlement, the state, and the colonial nation, always address questions of ontological, social, and political complexity with self-assurance and simplification—that is, with "affirmation and forgetting" in the more eloquent terms Lowe uses to describe liberal formalisms.[34] In this case, forms of protection, even when they are deployed to benefit tribes, obscure and erase the entanglements and histories of relation of which the existence of manoomin (always more than a species, and more than a condition of a self-evident present) is a part. From trajectories of seasonal movement and collaboration among tribes, to harvesting, preparing and sharing practices, to the superjurisdictionality of water, soil, pollen, and fauna, formal provisions of protection always forget the scope of the relations they purport to guard. At the same time, they replace occasional, flexible, and negotiated political arrangements (like the one referenced in the Treaty of Prairie du Chien, Article 13) by affirming a federalist hierarchy of power in which tribal sovereignty can be variously coded and recoded as dependent, special, or too expansive to be practical.

In another sense, the failures of the colonial public to protect Indigenous people and land also point to the array of creative and critical Indigenous practices that do not depend on liberal theories of form. In the context of US cultures of extraction, questions like what or where manoomin is are impasses that open out beyond the promises of protection. When colonial rights frameworks name subjects, objects, or spatial limits of protection, they also invite the (re)insistence that complex relational entities like manoomin cannot be protected and that they are not public. The relations manoomin indexes are the terms by which we might remember, despite those rights frameworks, that it is possible to organize life and land without protection when we look beyond "the public" (and the rhetoric of access, property, and policing it implies) to describe and enact collectivity. It is precisely this obstructive and creative quality, the sense of relation as a generative impasse, that Vizenor centers in his account of the 1968 manoomin trial. In that case, the court considered the question of how to balance access to public land and water against the promise to protect it. Aubid, as Vizenor observes, responded by demonstrating that the exclusion of Indigenous social and ecological relations was coextensive with the court's promise to protect the public interest. Aubid "created a presence of John Squirrel" (which the court could only recognize as "hearsay") that was "obviative": a relation necessary to, but not agential within, the story about the land Aubid was telling. Vizenor summarizes: "Squirrel was twice the tease of native evidence; the sense of his presence in stories, an actual presence in the memories of others, and an obviative presence as semantic evidence."[35] The multiplicity and complexity of this relation is what I bookmark in this chapter as *gathering*, and it is a relation that, as Vizenor argues, exceeds the formal contingencies of the colonial public: a continuity of "sovenance," a summoning of human and more-than-human presence with memory.

Constitutional Pronouns

The 1998 court decision that Vizenor describes in "Native Transmotion" could not recognize John Squirrel, who was a presence that exceeded the judicial present—a memory, an obviated social condition of Aubid's testimony, a participant in a material relation that includes Indigenous people, land, water, and manoomin. When Squirrel's testimony was excluded because he was not present, the judge avoided answering a more difficult set of questions about the array of social and political relations that were made present when Aubid cited Squirrel. In other words, Squirrel was disavowed as a member of the public perhaps not because he was insufficiently present, but because he was too richly connected, in temporal, social, spatial, and ontological terms, to be understood by the court as a person. In the context of US law, a person is the form of a specific set of reductions: of being to subjectivity, of relation to reproduction, of mutuality to property, of justice to punishment, of responsibility to impunity. The person is a rights-bearing form, a description usually understood to mean that state-guaranteed safety, liberty, and well-being accumulate to it. And because US law is also a guarantor of global capitalism, rights-bearing forms are also those to which capital, title, and inheritance accrue. The history of the disavowal of Indigenous, Black, and other racialized and gendered people from the rights-bearing form of the person is well documented and theorized.[36] Moreover, the terms of that critical tradition are in one sense enough to explain Squirrel's exclusion. In addition to and inextricable from that explanation is the sense that the court, in order to protect itself, also had to forget the material and ecological connection between Squirrel and land, which is to say, between Squirrel and a set of relations more expansive than colonial forms of sovereignty can control or describe. Squirrel was excluded because he was a part of something, a gathering, that it was not expedient and perhaps not possible for the court to reduce to the form of the person.

In other instances, however, the legal reduction of relations to the form or purview of the person has been instrumental to the articulation and expansion of US colonialisms: when, for instance, allotment reclassified Indigenous people as property holders (or sellers, or subjects of foreclosure); when Indigenous people were made soldiers before they could become citizens; when Indigenous people were made citizens; or when Indigenous people became a new postwar labor class. In Minnesota, the colonial reduction to the form or terms of the person has also been aimed at manoomin, beginning in the 1920s, when settlers began to breed and harvest it as an agroindustrial monoculture—a move that has had devastating and heretofore permanent impacts on Ojibwe and Dakota gathering practices.[37] While manoomin was not reclassified by settler agriculturalists as a person per se, it did become a legal and economic subject of personal property, a commodity whose exchange produced the value that could accrue to and be controlled by colonial persons (including corporations) but not by people excluded from personhood. Manoomin's commodification, its interpellation into the legal and economic frameworks of colonial personhood, reached its apotheosis in the last years of the twentieth century when a strain of manoomin was patented by a company called Nor-Cal, and the University of Minnesota completed a two-decade long project of genetically mapping it.[38] Eventually, tribes lobbied the state of Minnesota to intervene, citing the expectation that genetically modified manoomin strains could cross-pollinate and appear within tribal manoomin paddies (transforming non–genetically modified plants and leaving entire tribal manoomin stocks subject to intellectual property suits and corporate seizure), and that the genetic modification of the plant was a violating manipulation of its complex ecosystemic and cultural meaning.[39]

In a letter to university president Mark Yudof, Minnesota Chippewa tribal president Norman Deschampe summarized and situated these concerns in the context of treaty protections:

We object to the exploitation of our wild rice for pecuniary gain. . . . We are of the opinion that the wild rice rights assured by treaty accrue not only to individual grains of rice, but to the very essence of the resource. We were not promised just any wild rice; that promise could be kept by delivering sacks of grain to our members each year. We were promised the rice that grew in the waters of our people, and all the value that rice holds.[40]

Here, Deschampe rejects the reduction of the meaning of manoomin to the terms of personal interest—as only a food, only a crop, only a commodity, or only an expression of a diplomatic fulfillment. Manoomin, he insists, is all of these at once, and it is inseparable from the specific freshwater ecosystems it depends on. It is a source, not a sign, of meaning. Although the state capitulated in this case, promising to protect "natural populations" of manoomin from genetic modification and patenting, the history of the mapping and commodification of manoomin makes clear that personhood and personal interest had become the state's principal frameworks for assessing questions of its protection. This explains how, the same year the Minnesota MPCA installed a new rule designed to protect "wild rice waters" from sulfate runoff, it also issued an environmental impact statement (EIN) for the Enbridge Line 3 Pipeline Replacement Project—an oil pipeline that endangers the most sensitive freshwater ecosystems in the state—without including any provision protecting manoomin from oil spills.[41] Here, the state could make two seemingly contradictory rules because it understands sulfate and oil as discrete elements for environmental consideration, defined by separate ownership, profit, and liability structures. Further, and despite its own evidence to the contrary, manoomin had become, if not a person specifically, an exceptional regulatory problem for the state, one irreducible to either environmental, cultural, or economic precedents and thus defined by the limits and freedoms of personal interest both for corporations and tribes.

In the aftermath of the Enbridge EIN, the White Earth Band directly addressed the paradox of the state's recourse to legal structures of personal interest in the context of manoomin protection. On December 31, 2018, the band codified the "Rights of Manoomin" in a resolution in which the band clearly established its treaty- and international community-recognized political authority and the imminent threat that the pipeline posed to manoomin. In a four-part definition, the resolution describes the rights of manoomin as intrinsically more than personal, and specifically as environmental, social, economic, and legal all at once:

(a) RIGHTS OF MANOOMIN. Manoomin . . . possesses inherent rights to exist, flourish, regenerate, and evolve, as well as inherent rights to restoration, recovery, and preservation. These rights include . . . the right to pure water and freshwater habitat; the right to a healthy climate system . . . the right to be free from patenting; as well as rights to be free from infection, infestation, or drift by any means from genetically engineered organisms.

(b) RIGHTS OF TRIBAL MEMBERS. Tribal members of White Earth band possess the right to harvest manoomin, and protect manoomin seeds, within the White Earth Reservation.

(c) RIGHT OF SOVEREIGNTY. The White Earth Band and its members possess both a collective and individual right of sovereignty . . . includ[ing] the right to be free from ceiling preemption, because this law expands rights-protections . . . above those provided by less-protective state, federal, or international law.

(d) RIGHTS AS SELF-EXECUTING. All rights secured by this law are inherent . . . and shall be enforceable against both private and public actors without further implementing legislation.[42]

Further, the resolution thwarts any sense that the recognition of these rights imply a kind of legal personification of manoomin by naming it, specifically, "a gift": "Whereas, manoomin, or wild rice is considered by the Anishinaabeg people to be a gift from the creator . . . we recognize that to protect manoomin and our people, we must secure their highest protection through the recognition of legal rights for the protection of manoomin."[43]

In the next and last section of this chapter, I parse this declaration more carefully, observing how the band's framing of the rights of manoomin as a gathering and a gift intervene in the question of what or who rights protect, and if legal gestures like this one might be understood as an elaboration of the complex social and ecological relations manoomin indexes. In broad terms, these are questions about how sovereignty inflects the possibilities of survival under the conditions of colonial extraction as well as about how Indigenous narrative and analytical practices exceed and even renew as they chafe against the formalisms of colonial sovereignty.

They are also questions that Vizenor bookmarks in "Native Transmotion" with the phrase "constitutional pronouns," which is his way of referring to the contradictions of naming and presence intrinsic to the textual demonstrations of colonial democracy, "the manners" as he writes, "of state dominance."[44] Citing the Fourteenth Amendment, Vizenor points out that Indigenous people are only named as an absence: "Representatives shall be apportioned among the several States . . . counting the whole number of persons in each state, excluding Indians not taxed."[45] "Excluding Indians not taxed" is an erasure and a displacement from representation that subtends the form of the colonial person. But it is also an exclusion on which the United States depends, an exclusion coincident with the horizon of constitutional interiority that draws on, as it administrates, the life and land it disavows. Vizenor goes on to observe that "the 'We' in 'We, the people of the United States,' is not the foremost pronoun of native presence," given that Indigenous people would not become citizens until 1924.[46] Nonetheless, the obvious instability and insufficiency of that pronoun, the way its exclusiveness points to what it requires but cannot include or describe, is for Vizenor "a source of justice," an aporia that marks the opening between the "mighty promise" that "We, the People," makes and "the *we*, as Natives of this continent, [who] . . . actuate the observance of natural reason and transmotion in this constitutional democracy."[47]

The "constitutional pronoun" is not a site for the reform or fulfillment of colonial representation, just as, I argue, the "Rights of Manoomin" is not an appeal to protection under the terms of colonial personhood. Rather, Vizenor names the site of an opening and an unreconcilable multiplicity, a splitting or refraction of "we" against "the people" that lays bare an instability inherent to the exclusive universalism of colonial democracy and to the linguistic form of the person as pronoun. Pronouns are perhaps as close as English gets to a kind of obviation. They are names "standing in place of a noun" and, as such, are gestures of comparison that reduplicate and point out, but never describe, what is lost in the formalization of equivalence.[48] Pronouns are haunted by the fullness and specificity of the relations they stand in place of, particularly when they become occasions to doubt the reliability of colonial formalisms, as Vizenor and Aubid do, rather than to reinvest in fantasies of equality or universality via more inclusive formal exclusions backed by colonialism. Vizenor's phrase "constitutional pronouns" points out that democratic formalizations of personhood are more than comparable, they are co-constituting. Therefore, to ask how to name manoomin in the syntax of colonial protection or even simply to ask what kind of pronoun "a gift" is become ways to use the utter limitation of colonial forms and declarations of universality to open toward modalities of living in which protection no longer makes sense as a principal modality of governance.

Rights-Bearing Conditions

In the tradition of US and European thinking about rights, the person is typically understood as the form that principally bears them. Bearing, in this case, means holding or having, as a condition of being a person. However, as is understood by anyone suspicious of the promises of colonial liberalism (as a result of experience and/or attention to history), the idea that personhood is actually a matter of being—that is, that the form of the person is politically unconditional—is naive. Personhood is always an effect of its exclusions, even in the context of universal human rights, as Hannah Arendt observes in *The Origin of Totalitarianism* and bookmarks with her famous phrase "the right to have rights."[49] Bearing, as in holding, rights is always a condition of their being borne, as in given or delivered, by a system of political recognition, what Arendt calls "belonging." The way *rights-bearing* works as both an adjective and an expression of political transitivity underscores the fact that, within imperial democracy, the person is not an ontological category but a form designed to move within its distributions of interiority. The promise of the unconditionality of rights is most convincing to those who are permitted to move between being a rights-bearing subject as a condition of their humanity (i.e., on the condition that their humanity is never doubted) and being delivered rights as a condition of belonging to what Arendt calls an "organized community" (i.e., on the condition of their humanity being measured against the absence of someone else's). That the promise of unconditional rights is always conditional, that it is always an effect of political economy, also evokes a third sense of bearing, as suffering: both as the suffering of those denied the transit between having and being given (as) rights, and as what becomes internalized and reproduced by those for whom that transit becomes a convincing ideological program.

As Vizenor points out, Indigenous people living within and against the fictions of the United States need look no further than the first word of the constitution's preamble to mark the particular conditionality of rights expressed through the form of the person. What, then, does it mean that White Earth invoked a rights framework to protect manoomin in 2018? And how should we interpret a declaration of rights—otherwise generically congruent with the democratic protection of personhood—of a subject described as "a gift"? To address these questions, I read the "Rights of Manoomin" alongside Vizenor's own engagement with democratic rights frameworks in the constitution he drafted for the White Earth Band as well as Jacques Derrida's analyses of the gift as a deconstruction of sovereignty. This constellation of texts throws into relief the way Indigenous writing renews as it frictions against colonial formalisms. Thus, rather than conceptualize the difference between White Earth and US interpretations of sovereignty, rights, and personhood as political or epistemic separatism, I read that difference as the product of generative critique and the sustenance of Anishinaabe intellectual traditions. As they interpret both colonial sovereignty and their own inherent sovereignty, White Earth members, including Vizenor, elaborate the relational systems that link knowledge and ecology; they reveal and intensify the contradictions intrinsic to rights-bearing forms; and they participate in organizing life and land beyond the horizon of protection.

In 2008, White Earth Band chairperson Erma Vizenor began a process of constitutional reform designed to reorganize the band away from the governance structure it adopted through the Indian Reorganization Act (IRA). At the heart of that reform were questions about tribal membership that had been framed in the IRA-era constitution in terms familiar to US constructions of legal personhood: the racialization of kinship, resource accumulation, and presence as a function of property. That constitution made blood quantum the basis for tribal membership, which repeated a genocidal political logic of racial declension and ensured that the tribe's resources were distributed among the smallest possible construction of membership. The constitution linked White Earth with five other Ojibwe communities under the umbrella organization the Minnesota Chippewa Tribe not because those communities were historically cooperating but out of a sense of the geographic proximity of modern reservation spaces. The constitution also imposed a heavily US-influenced, executive-legislative framework on tribal leadership that concentrated power and responsibility in a few people without meaningful ways for members in general to intervene in governance.

To reimagine and dispense with the colonial constructions of person, community, and territory that subtend the IRA-era constitution, Erma Vizenor organized a series of constitutional conventions, attended by elected and at-large delegates, all of whom were White Earth members. She also named Gerald Vizenor (a relative through marriage) the "principal writer" of the constitution that the delegates would invent together. Although Vizenor was significantly influenced by the structure and style of the constitution of Japan, the text he and the constitutional delegates produced is utterly unique. It begins, much in Vizenor's own idiom: "The Anishinaabeg of the White Earth Nation are the successors of a great tradition of continental liberty, a native constitution of families, totemic associations. The Anishinaabeg create stories of natural reason, of courage, loyalty, humor, spiritual inspiration, survivance, reciprocal altruism, and native cultural sovereignty."[50]

Even here, the differences between this constitution's and the US Constitution's descriptions of political constituency are acute. Belonging is a function of generational "success[ion]," kinship, and the Ojibwe social organization of "totems" or clans.[51] Further, as a form of cultural belonging, Ojibwe people are described not as possessors or recipients of sovereignty, but as "creat[ors]" of narrative and political relation. Beyond these beautiful if abstract descriptions of communality, the constitution also made bold revisions to official constructions of the tribe's and its members' sovereignty: the separation of White Earth from the other bands of the Minnesota Chippewa and the establishment of the White Earth Nation; the replacement of blood quantum with lineal descent as the primary basis for determining membership; and the provision of representation to White Earth members living in cities like Minneapolis and St. Paul. These revisions represented a courageous expansion of the tribe's concept of itself in demographic and geographic terms. Not only would far more people with documentable family connections to the tribe become White Earth members, the scope of its living constituency would no longer be restricted to the bounds of its reservation or to a confederation of Ojibwe reservations in northern Minnesota. This expansion was also structured by the creation of separate councils for youth, elders, and community members in general, each of which were vested with specific responsibilities to sustain tribal lifeways, including the care of "the whole of the land . . . water, wild rice . . . and any other environmental estates . . . located within the White Earth Reservation" and the "the creation and formation of associations, events and activities that demonstrate, teach and encourage respect, love, bravery, humility, wisdom, honest, and truth for citizens."[52]

The constitution was ratified in 2009, and, although it offered clear mechanisms for White Earth to organize against the most profound demographic and environmental threats to the tribe, it was eventually withdrawn, and Erma Vizenor was forced to relinquish her chairpersonship. The expansion and new distribution of membership worried or threatened too many White Earth citizens for whom the existing framework offered stable, if precarious, access to land and resources. However, the drafting and ratification of the document itself is significant for the ways it critiques and reorganizes beyond the protocols of constitutional personhood and colonial protection. The 2009 constitution opens the construction of membership to include the array of relational forms and spatial concepts of home through which White

Earth people have lived with and against colonial occupation, including relationships with land, water, and manoomin. It is also a text almost completely absent any constitutional pronouns. Each chapter and article names constructions of collectivity with specificity and intention, usually "The Anishinaabeg" or the "The White Earth Nation." Further, Vizenor seems to not only disavow but almost mock (or, in his terms, "tease") the form of the person specifically. The articles of the chapter that delineates rights and duties of membership alternate between descriptions of responsibilities of "the people" (e.g., "The people shall not be denied the fundamental human rights of citizenship in the White Earth Nation") and descriptions of infringements "no person" will endure (e.g., "No person shall be denied or deprived life or liberty"). In the 2009 constitution there is no form between "the people" and "no person"—the present person is obviated. It is a text that performs a generative theorization against and beyond, thus demonstrating the unnecessity of, colonial mandates of individuated, racialized, and property-holding personhood.

Although there is only one mention of manoomin in the 2009 constitution, and while I am not aware that Gerald Vizenor made any contribution to the drafting or conception of the "Rights of Manoomin," the two texts are philosophically linked. The "Rights of Manoomin" extends a critical logic of the 2009 constitution that antagonizes US sovereignty from within its own formalisms. The premise of IRA-era tribal governance is, as an extension of Marshall's theory of domestic dependency, that tribes are politically (quasi-) external to but formally internal to and mimetic of US constitutional democracy. This is a construction of political relation that has rewarded tribes for embracing some of the most violent expressions of US power, including its carcerality, its misogyny and anti-Blackness, and its replacement of political organizing with capitalism. Thus, theories of tribal sovereignty that rename inherited or imposed hegemonic political structures as separatist simply reiterate a fiction of tribal political externality that is itself seminal to colonial sovereignty while, at the same time, they leave unchallenged the alignment of tribal and US governance that occurs and reproduces through form. In some ways, both the 2009 constitution and the "Rights of Manoomin" do repeat this pattern—for instance, in the decision to name the new White Earth polity the "White Earth Nation." But in other ways both texts also target the formalisms that animate and reproduce colonial power. As I have argued, the 2009 constitution did so by obviating colonial personhood. The "Rights of Manoomin" declaration does so in a number of ways, including through the acknowledgment of the rights of an entity that it describes as "a gift from the Creator," "a staple in the diets of native people for generations," "a central element of culture, heritage, and history," and "an integral part of the wetland ecosystems and natural communities of our traditional lands."[53] I observe that, unlike many "rights of nature" formulations that extend legal protections that derive from the liberal forms of the rights-bearing person or public, the "Rights of Manoomin" is an aporia. To name the rights of "a gift" intensifies a contradiction intrinsic to and disguised by positivist theories of sovereignty. It is an opening out of the unraveling of colonial political form toward the description of relations unregulated and unprotectable by the United States.

To make this point, I draw on language that Derrida develops in two texts on sovereignty and its deconstruction. The first, *Rogues: Two Essays on Reason* (2005) demonstrates how the formal logic of person organizes sovereignty and marks a contradiction between sovereignty and democracy. "Sovereign self-determination," Derrida writes, is "the one-self that gives itself its own law"—what he calls "ipseity," or "the power that *gives itself* its own law, its self-representation, the sovereign and reappropriating gathering of self in the simultaneity of an assemblage or assembly."[54] Here, sovereignty is not identical to a stable form of national or personal selfhood but a formalization of self-sameness out of and under the terms of universal political and onto-logical possibility: it is a "re-turn upon the self."[55] The central contradiction sovereignty indexes is its reproduction of forms of self-similitude in the name of what Derrida calls the "unconditionality" of its power and its political promises. In *Rogues*, he asks if sovereignty's conditional unconditionality can be a site for deconstructing its recourse to the self-same from inside its own logic: to deconstruct "sovereignty in the name of unconditionality" and to be able to "know better what 'democracy' will have been *able* to signify, what it *ought*, in truth, to have meant."[56] To turn sovereignty's unconditionality against itself is to pursue an "impossible" theory of power that "would not be simply negative," but, rather, an "interruption" out of the formal econo-mies of personhood toward "this inconceivable and unknowable thing, a freedom that would not long be the power of the subject, a freedom without autonomy."[57]

Derrida cites two such "figures of unconditionality without sovereignty": "unconditional hospitality" and "the gift."[58] Importantly, these are not stable, emancipatory forms that exist external to sovereignty, but are "figures" (i.e., ap-pearances, apparitions, perhaps even obviations) that express an unbearable intensification of sovereignty's contradictions. The gift, as he writes in *Given Time*, is not separate from economy but "that which interrupts economy" because it "must not circulate."[59] It is "aneconomic" in the sense that it "keeps a relation of foreignness to the circle," rather than being inherent external or foreign to economic circulation.[60] The gift occurs within economic and grammatical distributions of interiority and thus also interrupts the grammars that express and link forms like the person, polity, and resource. That grammar is the "[condition] of possibility of the gift (that 'one' gives some 'thing' to some 'one other') [that] designate[s] simultaneously the conditions of the impossibility of the gift" insofar as participation in an unconditional exchange destabilizes every way (perceptual, economic, or political) that one and another could be described as discrete.[61]

When, in the "Rights of Manoomin," White Earth grants the rights of "a gift," they join a critical practice I have bookmarked in Vizenor's work as *aformality* and that Derrida might describe as a turning of the unconditionality that subtends sovereignty against the rights-bearing conditions of colonial form. The rights of manoomin are an interruption specific to the extractive operations of genetic mapping, patenting, and commodification and of the Enbridge 3 Pipeline Replacement Project. But they are also an interruption that intervenes broadly in the reproduction of colonial political economy via the logic of sovereignty and the forms of the person and nation. Within US law, the rights of manoomin are (in a Derridean sense) impossible not only because they would interfere with extractive colonialism but also because protection occurs according to political and ontological distributions of interiority in which the gift occurs as an unbearable contradiction of ipseity and foreignness. As the declaration clearly states, what it requires to ensure the well-being of manoomin and to be dedicated to its "inherent rights to exist, flourish, regenerate, and evolve" requires nothing less than the guarantee of "pure water and freshwater habitat; the right to a healthy climate system and a natural environment free from human-caused global warming impacts and emissions; the right to be free from patenting; as well as rights to be free from infection, infestation, or drift by any means from genetically engineered organisms, trans-genetic risk seed, or other seeds that have been developed using methods other than traditional plant breeding."[62]

To provide the conditions for the relations the declaration describes would be to commit to an unconditionality the United States as a form and self-authorizing administrator of liberal formalisms could not bear. But as the declaration intricately details, and as I have argued in this chapter, to enact or even to imagine or write about that unconditionality is far from an abstract or utopic project, even in the context of unrelenting colonial extraction. The particular ways manoomin grows, sustains, calls together, remembers, and anticipates people and land is itself a framework for practicing living without colonial protection or the promise of rights-bearing forms. To prompt or engage with the rights of manoomin, then, is to leverage and interrupt sovereignty toward an "impossible that would not be simply negative" and, moreover, an impossible that is always—among texts, people, land, and water—a modality of gathering beyond colonial governance.

Epilogue

Horizon Lines

I have argued that where colonial infrastructures promise belonging, peace, immunity, and protection, what is being disguised is extraction. Where colonial infrastructures offer experiences of social or affective coherence, life and land are being redistributed. This is an account not so much of what US colonialisms make, but how they are made and how they recur. I began this book by observing that this argument creates an archival problem in the sense that the historical and disciplinary forms that situate it are expressions of the same extractive operation; thus the book does not deliver a coherent, cultural historical framework—like an Indigenous literary history of the Twin Cities—of its own. In tracing new constellations, or extraction histories, of colonial policy, cultural history, and Indigenous organizing, I have not closed archival gaps but, rather, have asked if, in holding them open, we can invite new relations among texts, people, and land that do not rely on inevitably extractive forms, including conventional forms of archive.

As I suggested in the introduction, the stakes of this project, of writing against extraction, are different depending on how readers and cultural producers are positioned by colonial infrastructures. For me, and for other people ostensibly protected by whiteness and settlement, those stakes are primarily deconstructive. In other words, I am interested in offering a language with which to describe and deconstruct the vacancy of the colonial forms that promise social and political coherence. However, even the work of description in this context can seem like an impossibility in the sense that I am proposing we address and then dismantle forms that organize everyday life without the promise of new ones to replace them—something I foregrounded by observing the impossibility of language with which to narrate simple and seemingly necessary things like where or who I am from, until colonialism itself is dismantled. Unlike the normative sociality secured by those forms, "impossible" as Derrida notes, "is not nothing. It is even that which happens, which comes, by definition."[1] The work of redescribing, without promise, the gaps that colonial infrastructures make and in which we live, is how what is impossible—which is to say, the possibility of nonextractive relations—might yet still come.

For Indigenous readers and cultural producers, it is not exactly for me to say what the histories of writing against extraction mean or make possible. In this book, however, I have centered the ambivalence of this word *against* as a space and as an acknowledgment of the fact that identifying—or even organizing—new cultural histories around proximity to colonial extraction does not have to be homogenizing. Suggesting that writing against, as in opposing, extraction is necessary for all people to stop colonial violence does not imply an equivocation of the differential proximities to colonialism produced by extractive infrastructures and by the ways, for instance, Indigenous cultural practices have defied and exceeded those infrastructures. In other words, the Indigenous intellectual histories I track in this book are not "lessons," as Kyle Powys Whyte (Potawatomi), Chris Caldwell (Menominee), and Marie Schaefer (Anishinaabe) put it, "for 'all humanity.'"[2] Nor is it the case that my framing of those histories in terms of modernism suggests an alignment with US or European cultural canons. *Against* in this sense signals the question and the urgency of organizing life, land, and thought in ways that do not equivocate experiences of proximity to colonialism, but that do suggest that organizing with difference is possible, and that it makes it possible to expose the tenuousness and vulnerability of colonial power—the ways its breakdowns and failures can become the condition for as of yet unimagined ways of living.

The concepts that this book tracks as expressing colonial cultural and political coherence, as infrastructures that extract to create fictions of belonging, are also sites of breakdown in a recurrent colonial order that is necessarily infrastructural. One continuity among Warren's, Erdrich's, Treuer's, and Vizenor's writing is that they turn toward those sites and, with them, amplify the ambivalence of *against*, that is of the difficult and intimate work of thinking in proximity and opposition to extraction. In each chapter, I have observed how their methods of writing against extraction consistently generate modes of collaboration and political commitments that colonial infrastructures cannot redistribute and thus cannot bear: Warren's autoethnographic interpretation; Erdrich's theory of return as recovery with loss; Treuer's imagination of superjurisdictional location; Vizenor's participation in a trans-species, trans-motive, unprotected gathering. That these writers participate in remaking life and land at sites of colonial breakdown is not a coincidence. Although what I call *US colonialisms* marks an elaborate and shifting array of systems designed to classify and redistribute almost anything under the rubric of interiority, and despite the way the United States obsessively confuses expansion with productivity, colonialism does not have a theory for making the material and social relations we might otherwise describe as land. Making somatic and social relations is what colonial infrastructures fail both to do and to manage, and thus the history of that work is a history of holding out against—that is, pressing (both as analysis and opposition) and thus interrupting colonialism's incessant demand for reproduction.

While I have been writing this book, colonial reproduction is once again in the throes of crisis, what we are often given to call (in consummately equivocating and dehistoricizing terms) *the climate crisis*. In ordinary political discourse, this crisis is the theater for a debate about how to prevent the failure of those infrastructures that have made the United States seem coherent through the global administration of violence and suffering, and whether there is still time to reform those infrastructures such that they might continue to operate but pollute less. To frame the climate crisis in these terms is not to imply that the inevitability of its unfolding will be emancipatory, because, of course, the paroxysms of failing colonial infrastructures are themselves distributable and will be predictably directed toward people and land already marked as objects of extraction. However, it is also a mistake to allow the conditions of colonial infrastructural breakdown that we call *the climate crisis* to be interpreted within the binaries of political and ontological interiority that set it in motion in the first place. The texts that I have read in this book directly attend to the conditions of production of the infrastructures whose systemic breakdown is the contemporary climate crisis. While these texts do not offer lessons for all humanity about how to avert that crisis, they do articulate a shared political insistence and model a method for proliferating material and social meaning when and where colonial infrastructures break down. Where US officials point to those breakdowns as the limit of social and political meaning (in light of which the only possibility of rescue means rescuing colonial infrastructures), these texts elaborate the im/possibility of steadfastly thinking against extraction.

Beyond the Edge of the World

For George Morrison, the elaboration of impossible meaning has a specific shape: the horizon line. It is an element in almost all of his work. Sometimes, as in his collages, the horizon is stark, marking the lower edge of the work's top quadrant; at other times, it is almost indiscernible or is unusually positioned at the bottom of or askance a canvas. Morrison often suggested that the inspiration for this element was the actual horizon line he observed regularly over Gitchi-Gami/Lake Superior, both in his youth and his last years living on the Grand Portage reservation. Despite growing up next to the lake, the horizon line did not become a preoccupation in his work until slightly later in his life, when he moved away, first to Minneapolis and then to New York.

One way to interpret his horizon lines, then, in a biographical context, is as a form for memory, of return through memory, or of the possibility of remaking an aspect of social and somatic relation (i.e., land) against the limits of geography. However, remembering here could not imply a single temporal direction, as it seems clear that what, or the way, Morrison was remembering with the horizon was not only a looking back but also a posture of looking and imagining out or away from. "From the horizon," he wrote, "you go beyond the edge of the world to the sky, and beyond that, to the unknown. I always imagine, in a certain surrealist way, that I am there. I like to imagine it is real."[3] Here, "imagine" conveys a double sense of looking, at once back and away, and suggests that that ambivalence bears a specific relation to reality—that "imagine" is a particular kind of transitivity, a "way that I am there." At the same time, by eliding the "that" that would make "that it is real" a noun clause qualifying "I like to imagine," Morrison emphasizes the ineluctable distinction between imagination and reality; he remembers, that is, that what the horizon is or means is convergent but not coextensive with imagination. Finally, Morrison proposes that the directionality indicated by "beyond the edge of the world" can be both something to think back to and out from, because unlike a purely imaginative form, it is always at the same time a materiality, something "there" in the world and in his art.

In the last years of his life, Morrison returned to work in his studio overlooking Lake Superior. After suffering a heart attack and being diagnosed with Castleman's disease, he moved from the Twin Cities to Grand Portage and gave his full attention to the horizon line. As a feature of the sky and the lake, Morrison describes the horizon as a perceptual event, comparable to

SURREALIST LANDSCAPE WITH FIGURES — FROTTAGE TECHNIQUE — MINNEAPOLIS — 1·22·82

E.1. George Morrison, *Surrealist Landscape with Figures*, 1982, ink on paper, 11⅛ × 8⅜ in. Collection of the Weisman Art Museum at the University of Minnesota, Minneapolis. Gift of Briand Mesaba Morrison, 1993.23.3. Reprinted with permission from Briand Mesaba Morrison.

the changing expression of the lake's motion, texture, and mood: "Dramatic things happen in the sky, with clouds and color. A rough spot appears on the water way off in the distance, or very, very rough water starts toward shore, or a streak of light illuminates the horizon."[4] This convergence of sky and water is not formally stable: "It becomes the horizon at a given time of day, probably sunrise or sunset.... It's the same with anything in nature—light hitting a rock, then bouncing against the water. The shimmer of nature is coming through."[5] As an aspect of art-making, the horizon is where elements transform through but do not become each other, a quality he names in terms of semantic surplus: "enigma," "magic," or, here, "ambiguity" and "mystery": "I am fascinated with ambiguity, change of mood and color, the sense of sound and movement above and below the horizon line. Therein lies some of the mystery of paintings: the transmutation, through choosing and manipulating the pigment, that becomes the substance of art."[6]

For genres, discourses, and political formations conditioned by colonial power, the horizon as a demarcation of limit can be understood to "neutralize," as Derrida puts it, the potentiality of transformation. Conceived as a marker of the recurrence of a teleology or as a point of inflection between what Derrida calls the "unforeseen" and "foreseeing," the "horizon of an idea" is a kind of epistemic infrastructure, a way of distributing meaning away from potentiality to abstraction.[7] However, as in the quotation above, this is a sense Morrison carefully avoids by refusing to collapse the distinction between the materiality and discursivity of the horizon. For Morrison, the horizon is not a limit or an ontological recursion to teleology—in Derrida's terms, what is to become (*avenir*) and what it is to become (*devenir*)—but instead what Derrida calls "a horizon without horizon."[8] The horizon is what is always there anyway but that changes, and changes into and through, art. "The literal idea of space in a painting," as Morrison cogently puts it.[9]

Morrison turned back to, and out from the horizon, when he became terminally ill—that is, when the coherence and continuity of his world became catastrophically uncertain. Unlike the other texts I read in this book, for Morrison, at this moment, it was not an act of policy or the recurrent violence of colonial jurisdiction that precipitated crisis but the perhaps more prosaic form of subjectivity itself, the "horizontal ideality" of its ending, and the fact that that ending implied the end of his art-making.[10] During this last period of his life, he kept painting landscapes with horizon lines, but he also returned to methods that implicated the materiality of his media more complexly than his paintings did; methods including rubbing and frottage in which the history and substance of wood, and his own wood collages themselves, became elemental to composition. But like his paintings, these works extend a methodological interest in working at and beyond the edge where perceptual and interpretive forms falter but remain nonetheless real or material. Read alongside the other texts I consider in this book, Morrison's rubbings underline a simple but important point: that the formations and concepts that organize the colonial world are not just aspects of policy, discipline, or the fortifications of settlement. Those infrastructures and their apparent limits are everywhere, even in everyday materials like scraps of wood and paper—even, for Morrison, in his own art. "Everywhere there is a horizon" as Derrida puts it, to be considered and to be pressed beyond failure through methods of intensifying proximity.[11]

Against the Horizon

Morrison's rubbings can be interpreted as a return to his wood collage practice. Especially in his larger wood-rubbing pieces, the ambivalent invocation of landscape is clear and familiar. So, too, is tension that holds the work between juxtaposing valences: on the one hand, the force of the substantive similarity of the wood held tenuously out by interstitial gaps and, on the other, the sense of scalar breakdown, as the works read down from the genre of landscape to individual pieces of lumber and down further to the prehistories of those forms as once living elements of now unreferenceable forests. The rubbings are also returns to collage as a matter of compositional practice. They are remediations of the collages that he began making in 1965 but are so in such a way that translates the medial, historical, and proximal distance between themselves and those initial collages through an interest in the aesthetics of attenuation: the way the qualities of color, depth, and weight so elemental to the collages are indicated but lost, indicated as lost, or as imperfectly recollected. That Morrison described some of his rubbings as "wood impressions" conveys something of the melancholy mixing of familiarity and estrangement that was an effect of this decision to return to, but not re-create, the practice that marked the ascendance of his career decades earlier. Here "impression" means the technical sense of being produced by pressure or pressing as well as the waning sociality of a fleeting encounter. In both cases, it indicates an interest in externality as the condition of production, and even proliferation, of meaning, and that at the point he began working on his rubbings, his own life and career had become new thresholds of externality to confront and interpret.

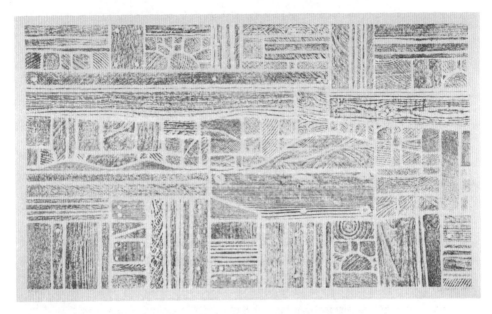

E.2. George Morrison, *Rubbing Print (black)*, 1987, lithograph, 25¾ × 41¾ in. Collection of the Weisman Art Museum at the University of Minnesota, Minneapolis. Gift of Frances and George Reid, 1999.3.36. Reprinted with permission from Briand Mesaba Morrison.

If Morrison's rubbings are a return to collage, return does not imply the resolution or even the stable relation of the two practices. Returning to the problem of landscape, to the catastrophic binary of subject and resource, and to the inexorable fact of his own career and life having nearly passed, Morrison intensified the thresholds of externality that the wood collages suggest. Rubbing the wood fragments under paper charges and proliferates those already latent externalities. The surface of the wood, against crayon or charcoal, pressure and paper, deepens the contrast of the grain lines, nearly to the point of producing a grid or a profusion of grids. The gaps, which in the collages are spaces for suspension, saturate and multiply. They invade and open the wood itself, exposing weaknesses, knots, and the places where the wood had been driven with nails. In so doing, the dispersion of space through the wood aligns the evidence of physical manipulation with human and material histories barely clinging to memory.

As a compositional practice, rubbing is an intensification of the deconstructive and generative quality of being and writing against that I have considered in each of this book's chapters. It is a practice of archive- and art-making that does not obey colonial mandates for administrable and permanent reproduction, the aggregation of value, or social repression. Another way Morrison described rubbing was "frottage," a term that Keguro Macharia uses to think about Afro-diasporic cultural and political archives. For Macharia, frottage is a concept that does not attempt to fill out or redeem fragments or gaps but, rather, transforms them into "grounds for speculation . . . tak[ing] seriously the work speculation does in enlarging our apprehension of the world and our possibilities for being in the world."[12] Here, frottage as a method for reading and making theory about diaspora is capacious: it attends to "a multiplicity of sense-apprehensions," including "the frictions and irritations and translations and mistranslations, the moments when blackness coalesces through pleasure and play and also by resistance to antiblackness."[13] "More than simply proximity," Macharia writes, frottage "is the active and dynamic ways blackness is produced and contested and celebrated and lamented as a shared object."[14]

What I call *Indigenous modernism* in this book references the practices of living and art-making that, like Morrison's rubbings, expose, chafe, and multiply at the thresholds of colonial order. Where extractive infrastructures redistribute Indigenous life and land, the artists I have considered nurture "grounds for speculation." Their practices for doing so require proximity with colonial forms that respond to, remake, but cannot withstand—let alone redress—crisis. As such they are practices (like what Macharia and Morrison call "frottage") that do not retreat from the intensities of experience of living with and through catastrophic change and loss. They are practices that vex and friction the edges of colonial power, that stall or interrupt, and that venture new multiplicities of meaning against the hollow promises of coherence (belonging, peace, immunity, and protection) its infrastructures make.

Notes

Prologue

1. Morrison and Galt, *Turning the Feather Around*, 125?-27.

2. The Grand Portage Band is one of six Ojibwe communities joined together, as a result of the 1934 Indian New Deal, as the Minnesota Chippewa Tribe. Throughout this book, I will use tribal specific names (Ojibwe/ Anishinaabe or Dakota) when possible, and I will use the terms *Native* or *Indigenous* interchangeably when referring to multiple or non-tribally specific issues.

3. Rushing and Makholm, *Modern Spirit*, 43-44.

4. David Martinez tracks and intervenes in the critical debate around both external ascriptions and Morrison's own relationship to Indigeneity in Martinez, "This Is (Not) Indian Painting," 25-51.

5. Morrison and Gault, *Turning the Feather Around*, 135.

6. On the often overlooked history of grassroots Indigenous education in the Twin Cities, see Davis, *Survival Schools*.

7. See Two Pines Resource Group, "Native American Context Statement."

8. Founders of General Mills like Cadwallader C. Washburn rose to economic and political prominence as a direct result of trading and deforesting seized Indigenous land, see Kelsey, "C. C. Washburn," 38-50. Honeywell, a technology and military weapons company, is the most prolific corporate producer of Superfund sites. Center for Public Integrity, "Honeywell International Inc.," accessed September 29, 2022, https://web.archive.org/web/20070605190324, http://www.publicintegrity.org/superfund/Company.aspx?act=12976. Prudential made early profits from race-differentiated insurance policies, financializing the legal dispossession of Black life; see Heen, "Ending Jim Crow Life Insurance Rates."

9. Morrison and Galt, *Turning the Feather Around*, 142.

10. Morrison and Galt, *Turning the Feather Around*, 142.

11. Morrison and Galt, *Turning the Feather Around*, 125, 146.

12. Morrison and Galt, *Turning the Feather Around*, 142.

13. Morrison and Galt, *Turning the Feather Around*, 146.

14. Mitchell, "Imperial Landscape," 10.

15. Hudson, *Half Century of Minneapolis*, 36.

16. Larson, *White Pine Industry in Minnesota*, 56.

17. *Bulletin of the Minneapolis Institute of Arts*, 118.

18. Coulthard, *Red Skins, White Masks*, 9; O'Brien, *Firsting and Lasting*.

19. Barker, "For Whom Sovereignty Matters," 17.

20. *Cherokee Nation v. Georgia*, 30 US 1 (1831).

21. Wolfe, "Settler Colonialism," 388.

22. Jodi Melamed terms this kind of political investment "liberal multiculturalism"—a logic by which institutions or polities respond to antiracist and decolonial insurgencies through the "containing and managing of social movements' deployment of culture by turning it into aesthetics, identity, recognition, and representation." For Melamed, art is a key site of this political containment and management that depends on stabilizing the racial identity of artists, reinterpreting their work as transparently representative of racialized experience, and redefining the political value of art interpretation as "testify[ing] to . . . the race-differentiated history and present of the American experience, multiculturally developed" (*Represent and Destroy*, xix–xx, 36).

23. Lawrence Halprin, the architect of the Nicollet Mall renovation, quoted in Aschman, "Nicollet Mall," 8.

24. In 2018, 3M settled a lawsuit filed by the state of Minnesota accusing the company of producing cancer-causing perfluorochemicals for $850 million (Minnesota 3M PFC Settlement, https://3msettlement.state.mn.us). Honeywell has been linked to three groundwater-contaminating Superfund sites in the Twin Cities area in addition to a Superfund site on Lake Superior about which it settled a lawsuit brought by the state of Minnesota and other polities, including the Grand Portage Band of Lake Superior Chippewa for $8.2 million (St. Louis River/Duluth Intake Tar Site, https://www.pca.state.mn.us/waste/st-louis-river-interlakeduluth-tar-site).

25. See Wynter, "Unsettling the Coloniality of Being."

26. See Fairbanks, *Days of Rondo*.

27. Gottfried, Verges, Melo, Vezner, and Rathbun, "After Weekend Violence," Twin Cities, July 11, 2016, https://www.twincities.com/2016/07/09/amid-racial-strife-hundreds-seek-answers-in-protests-church-service.

Introduction

1. Moten and Harney, *Undercommons*, 17.

2. Melamed, *Represent and Destroy*, 9.

3. For more on the politics of poverty and racial capitalism, see Goldstein, *Poverty in Common*.

4. Melamed, *Represent and Destroy*, 93.

5. Morrison and Galt, *Turning the Feather Around*, 153–54.

6. Davis, *Survival Schools*.

7. Here and in the title of this introduction, I take the phrasing from Goldstein, "Where the Nation Takes Place," 833–61.

8. While this introduction is principally concerned with the ambivalent and charged relation sustained by the texts I read in this book with NAIS, modernism, American studies, colonialism studies, literary studies, and the environmental humanities, the fact that I read works typically interpreted as visual art (i.e., in the context of art history) in the preface, introduction, and epilogue while each of the main chapters examine works of literature, may also prompt questions about the book's investment in the methodological distinction between visual and literary analysis. Ultimately, this is a distinction I intentionally blur for two, related reasons. First, the extraction histories I offer do to not position these texts as objects of analysis; rather, they use the texts as theoretically generative apparatuses in order to target the concepts (removal, the domestic, ruin, and rights) that make colonial worlds seem real and coherent. Second, reading texts toward the exposure of the conditions of production of colonial worlds extends a methodological fluidity that scholars of Indigenous visual and literary texts have long asserted—what Apache art historian Nancy Mithlo describes as the work of "translation between epistemologies" (*Knowing Native Arts*, 36) and an aspect of what Mishuana Goeman describes as "unsettling colonial visual and narrative geographies" ("Disrupting a Settler-Colonial Grammar," 243). For disciplines like art history and literary studies, whose own emergence and histories have in many ways depended on the objectification and interpretive (en)closure of Indigenous texts, investments in methodological propriety reproduce epistemological distributions of interiority—a habit that critically inventive texts like Birgit Brander Rasmussen's *Queequeg's Coffin* powerfully challenges. Rasmussen's attention to superalphabetic Indigenous textual production (including texts made in and with wood), intervenes in the critical habit of reproducing an Indigenous text as an "object—and abject—of inquiry" that has long been central to colonial cultural analysis (3). Rasmussen also evocatively cites Louise Erdrich on this question, who, in her *Books and Islands in Ojibwe Country* (5), points out the intimate etymological relation in Ojibwemowin between the word for "book" (*mazina'igan*) and the word for "rock painting" (*mazinapikinagan*).

9. Derrida, *Archive Fever*, 2.

10. My phrasing "mendacity of settlement" echoes Frank B. Wilderson III's account of the scripts of racializing pathology that obscure actual structures of power: "The grammar of antagonism breaks in on the mendacity of conflict" (*Red, White, and Black*, 11). Wilderson's relation to the question of the politics of archival concealment that I am engaging here is also geographically specific. In his memoir *Incognegro*, his account of growing up in Minneapolis is animated by the specific tension between the palpability and obscurity of violence and power there. "Minneapolis," he writes, "*It's not the end of the world but you can see it from there*" (101). Regarding the phenomenology of archival power, what Derrida calls the "topo-nomology" of the archive is the way its emplacement is also a way to regulate its own disclosure, the way the "scene of domiciliation becomes at once visible and invisible." The archive takes place not to create an "institutional passage from the private to the public . . . from the secret to the nonsecret," but rather "to shelter itself and, sheltered, to conceal itself" (Derrida, *Archive Fever*, 3).

11. Lowe, *Intimacies of Four Continents*.

12. Incommensurability as a decolonial methodology that exceeds the rubrics of global comparison is theorized by Tuck and Yang, "Decolonization Is Not a Metaphor," 31.

13. Coulthard and Simpson, "Grounded Normativity," 254.

14. Williams, *Country and the City*, 9. Williams does not use the term *extraction*, but he gets very close when he writes: "I have been arguing that capitalism, as a mode of production, is the basic process of most of what we know as the history of country and city. Its abstracted economic drives, its fundamental priorities in social relations, its criteria of growth and of profit and loss, have over several centuries altered our country and created our kinds of city. In its final forms of imperialism it has altered our world" (302).

15. When I first conceived it, this book *was* going to be an Indigenous literary history of the Twin Cities. This was an important project to me because I understood that the scope of Indigenous writing in the Twin Cities was such that accounting for it would press the limits of nationalist or cosmopolitan analytics with which we usually interpret Indigenous writing and the cultural life of US cities. Because cities are not national forms, understanding urban Indigenous cultural production through positivist and recognition-based rubrics like sovereignty means treating cities as places where Indigenous people live and make art, but not as places that make art Indigenous. At the same time, understanding urban Indigenous art-making via frameworks like cosmopolitanism prioritizes political and economic systems (globalization, capitalism, migration) that abstract the material and social specificities of the land with which places like the Twin Cities are made. To write an Indigenous literary history of the Twin Cities, then, would be a chance to show how the city could be a salient framework through which to understand the politics of

Indigenous art, and how the history of urban Indigenous cultural production is linked to the specific material and political conditions through which US colonialism and struggles for decolonization unfold. But the book became something else. In part it became a study of the impossibility of this project, an examination of how literary history as methodology would necessarily reduce and therefore fail to express the volatile relationships central to the story of Indigenous art and these cities: between art and Indigeneity and the city form; between Indigenous, Black, and diasporic people in the Twin Cities and the concept of Indigeneity; between theories of colonialism and the always unstable commingling of power and violence; between the categories of literary and visual art and the array of Indigenous social, ecological, and metaphysical practices that are neither separate nor reducible to the categories "literary and visual art"; and, most of all, between all of these things and the land where and through which they constitute ordinary life under occupation.

16. Warrior, *Tribal Secrets*, 4. Throughout this book, I use the terms *Ojibwe* and *Anishinaabe* interchangeably, despite the words having distinct histories, political valences, and specific linguistic meaning.

17. Warrior, *Tribal Secrets*, 6.

18. Lyons, *X-Marks*.

19. Lyons, *X-Marks*, 2.

20. Morrison and Galt, *Turning the Feather Around*, 154.

21. Trouillot, *Silencing the Past*, 25.

22. Trouillot, *Silencing the Past*, 28.

23. Wynter, "Unsettling the Coloniality of Being," 281; Jackson, *Becoming Human*, 3.

24. On the "productivity" of settler expansion, see Wolfe, "Settler Colonialism"; Coulthard, *Red Skin, White Masks*, 11; and Said, *Culture and Imperialism*, 93.

25. Whether colonial power unfolds principally via the interpellation of the human/body or via the land has become a central disagreement between Black and settler colonialism studies; between, for instance, Patrick Wolfe's argument that land is the central target of both anti-Indigenous and anti-Black colonial violence ("Settler Colonialism," 392), and Jared Sexton's trenchant counterargument that this approach sustains occlusion of the originary ontological negation of anti-Blackness ("Vel of Slavery").

26. Povinelli, *Geontologies*, 4.

27. Haraway, *Staying with the Trouble*, 1–4; Bennett, *Vibrant Matter*, xv; Povinelli, *Geontologies*, 16.

28. What Bennett calls the "vague, aporetic, or unstable images and impressions" through which humans engage the "out-side" shares with Haraway's commitment to "staying with the trouble" an investment in a critical immersion in unfolding processes of both becoming and knowing. This open—or, in

Bennett's terms, "naïve"—approach stands in contrast to methods that stabilize a conceptual common denominator (e.g., energy) or a rigid ascription of anti-conceptualism (e.g., object-oriented ontology/speculative materialism). See Szeman and Boyer, *Energy Humanities*; and Harman, "Well-Wrought Broken Hammer," 183–203.

29. As she puts it: "The new materialists may take the intellectual intervention that grounds the vital-materialist creed as something new in the world. But the fundamental insights are not new to everyone. They are ideas that, not so roughly translated, undergird what we can call an indigenous metaphysic: that matter is lively. We Dakota might say 'alive'" (TallBear, "Beyond the Life/Not-Life Binary," 198–99).

30. Harman, "Well-Wrought Broken Hammer," 195–99.

31. Huettl, "Treaty Stories," 216.

32. Huettl refers to Edward Benton-Banai's *The Mishomis Book* when she notes that "from an Ojibwe perspective, ethnogenesis occurred within aadizookanag" ("Treaty Stories," 40).

33. Wolfe, "Settler Colonialism," 388.

34. Wolfe, "Settler Colonialism," 388.

35. O'Brien, "Tracing," 251.

36. Williams, *Culture and Society*, xiv.

37. Byrd, *Transit of Empire*, xiii.

38. Marx, *Capital*, 165.

39. Mill, *Collected Works*, 18:225.

40. Mill, *Collected Works*, 9:564.

41. Mill, *Collected Works*, 9:566.

42. Lowe, *Intimacies*, 106.

43. Lowe, *Intimacies*, 39, 108.

44. Black, *Global Interior*, 5, 13.

45. Black, *Global Interior*, 8.

46. Jodi Byrd identifies that volatility as the "cacophony" of representation, claims, and power created by the collusion of liberal humanism and colonialism: the affective and epistemic din that "misdirect[s] and cloud[s] attention from the underlying structures of settler colonialism that made the United States possible." This formal inclination toward confusion that enacts and normalizes forgetting is also a disciplinary operation. What Manu Vimalassery, Juliana Hu Pegues, and Alyosha Goldstein call "colonial unknowing" indexes the "epistemological orientation" around ignorance that animates disciplinary formations that obscure constitutive histories of, for example, power and violence, which are actually irreducible to singular concepts of domination (e.g., settler colonialism). Vimalassery, Pegues, and Goldstein model a powerfully deconstructive approach to the problem of using colonial forms to understand colonialism by exposing the chaotic and contradictory systematics that underlie supposedly stable,

finished, and clarifying disciplinary forms. In even more explicitly material terms, Coulthard revises the classic Marxian account of the colonial origin of capital's central forms (what Marx calls "primitive accumulation") via a concept of "dispossession." Where the historical and geojurisdictional singularity of primitive accumulation proposes an originary relation between colonialism and capital, Coulthard argues that that relation is recurrent and jurisgenerative, that "dispossession, not proletarianization, has been the dominant background structure shaping the character of the historical relationship between Indigenous peoples and the Canadian state." Byrd, *Transit of Empire*, 53–54; Vimalassery, Pegues, and Goldstein, "Colonial Unknowing," 1042–54; Coulthard, *Red Skin, White Masks*, 13.

47. Goeman, *Mark My Words*, 15.

48. Goeman, *Mark My Words*, 30, 39.

49. This is an idea directly informed by Arvin, "Analytics of Indigeneity."

50. Here, with the phrase *expansively conceived*, I am alluding specifically to theories of modernism that seek to contravene exclusive approaches to modernist periodization, geography, or canon through disciplinary incorporation. The new modernist studies, for instance, which Rebecca Walkowitz and Douglas Mao describe in terms of temporal, spatial, and cultural class "expansions" ("New Modernist Studies," 737–78) and Laura Doyle and Laura Winkiel's theory of "geomodernisms," which globalizes Western cultural geographic frameworks for defining modernism (*Geomodernisms*, 2005).

51. In order to express the impact that noncanonical or non-Western writers have on global modernisms, postcolonial frameworks that describe hybridization, provincialization, or indigenization reinvest in US and European anthropological assessments cultural exchange and overstabilize colonial cultural and political formations. One way to conceptualize this effect is through Eve Tuck and K. Wayne Yang's phrase "colonial equivocation," which describes the way colonial comparative frameworks flatten differences among racialized and colonized people and between those people and settlers themselves ("Decolonization Is Not a Metaphor," 17–18). This is an approach directly applied to Morrison's work, for instance, by the curators of the National Museum of the American Indian's inaugurating exhibition "Native Modernism: The Art of George Morrison and Allan Houser." The catalog for that exhibition includes a defining essay by W. Jackson Rushing III, who celebrated the artists as innovating an "indigenous [modernism]" that "combined certain ideas, techniques, and visual strategies of European and American modern art with an acute awareness of homeland—place, weather, myth, and ritual" ("Modern Spirits," 53).

52. Scholars of Indigenous and American history including Jean O'Brien and Philip Deloria argue that this dynamic is constitutive to American modernity. O'Brien uses the terms "firsting and lasting" and the broader framework "Indians can never be modern" to conceptualize this dynamic (*Firsting and Lasting*, xxi).

Deloria looks to colonial simulations of Indigeneity as gestures evocative of the political demand "either to destroy Indians or to assimilate them into a white American World" (*Playing Indian*, 4).

53. The temporal and political contradictions posed to totalizing conceptions of European modernity by theories of subalternity are not (contra the fundamentally deconstructive and decolonial disposition that describes Indigenous modernism), in Dipesh Chakrabarty's words, about "rejecting or discarding European thought," but rather about how "this thought . . . may be renewed from and for the margins" (*Provincializing Europe*, 16). Similarly, theories of minor literary traditions preserve a governing sense of cultural interiority "within" which thinkers like Gilles Deleuze and Félix Guattari imagine the emergence of "the revolutionary" literature of "deterritorialization" (*Kafka*, 18).

54. Lyons, "X-Marks," 21.

55. Foucault, "What Is Enlightenment," 41.

56. Morrison and Gault, *Turning the Feather Around*, 151.

57. Morrison and Gault, *Turning the Feather Around*, 152.

58. Simpson, *Mohawk Interruptus*, 105.

59. Quoted in Vizenor, "George Morrison," 656.

60. Weaver, Womack, and Warrior, *Nationalism*, 40–41.

61. Weaver, Womack, and Warrior, *Nationalism*, 40.

62. Cook-Lynn, "Who Stole Native American Studies?," 9, 11.

63. See Alfred, "Sovereignty"; and Morris, "International Law and Politics"; and, for a powerful and clarifying overview of theories of sovereignty in Indigenous studies, see Barker, "For Whom Sovereignty Matters."

64. The iteration of Afro-pessimism anchored by Frank B. Wilderson III and Jared Sexton, for instance, frames calls for and the conception of Indigenous sovereignty as the threshold that distinguishes Indigenous people from Black people as a function of their possible achievement of political subjectivity within a fundamentally anti-Black world. Wilderson writes that "the Indian subject's positionality . . . fortifies and extends the interlocutory life of America as a coherent (albeit genocidal) idea, because treaties are . . . brokered between two groups presumed to possess the same kind of historical currency: sovereignty" ("Gramsci's Black Marx," 236). Sexton links Indigenous political investments in sovereignty with not only anti-Blackness but also Indigenous studies as a whole, whose project he reduces to liberal aspirations for "resistance" or "resurgence" and to the "critical knowledge of settler colonialism" ("Vel of Slavery," 592). As Iyko Day writes in her meticulous reading of Wilderson's and Sexton's critique of sovereignty, their principal intervention is to use a severely essentialized concept of sovereignty to reiterate an underlying precept of Afro-pessimism—that is, to establish "the very specificity and singularity . . . of black critical theory's capacity to understand race" ("Being or Nothingness," 112). In order to establish sovereignty as a primal indication Indigeneity's anti-Blackness, land, personhood,

and Indigeneity itself are all rendered as closed and discrete, and as conceptual fodder against which anti-Blackness can be established as the "threshold of the political world" (11). However, the fundamental gesture of conceptual closure, discretion, and hierarchization on which this argument depends is a repetition of the epistemic operation of the colonial political logic that sovereignty itself subtends. In order to establish Blackness as the singular and defining exception to the coherent political world, Wilderson and Sexton need to evacuate the generative indiscretion and irresolution of land, being, art, and relation, and, further, of Indigeneity and Blackness in the same way colonial power needs to, in order to establish subjectivity, territory, and resources as its constituent positions.

65. In that decision, Justice Taney's infamous definition of legal personhood—in which Black people were named "a class of persons . . . not recognized as a portion of the people," and as "rejected from those who formed the sovereignty of the States"—hinged on the political meaning of Dred and Harriet Scott's being moved into Illinois and Wisconsin Territory, and enslavement at Fort Snelling between 1836 and 1837. Taney's decision displaced competing interpretations of the way free territory conveyed freedom by producing a concept of personhood in which Black people "occupied," in Saidiya Hartman's words, "the doubtful position of being free but without the basic rights of citizenship" (Hartman, *Scenes of Subjection*, 174).

66. Agamben, *Homo Sacer*, 166.

67. Waziyatawin, *Justice*, 22.

68. King, *Black Shoals*, 3.

69. Quoted in Vizenor, "George Morrison," 656.

70. Simpson, "Place Where We All Live," 19.

71. On "conquest" as an alternative formulation for understanding the genocidal and anti-Black operation of US colonialisms, see King, *Black Shoals*, 201.

72. Trouillot, *Silencing the Past*, 29.

73. On settler moves to innocence, see Tuck and Yang, *Decolonization*; on the figure of the "critical academic," see Moten and Harney, *Undercommons*, 28.

74. Whyte, Caldwell, and Schaefer, "Indigenous Lessons about Sustainability."

Chapter One. Cultures of Removal

1. O'Brien, *Firsting and Lasting*, 2010.

2. McClintock, *Imperial Leather*, 16.

3. McClintock, *Imperial Leather*, 36.

4. Schenck, "Introduction," viii.

5. Warren, *History of the Ojibway People*, 7.

6. Warren, *History of the Ojibway People*, 6.

7. Coulthard, *Red Skin, White Masks*, 13–16.

8. Pexa, *Translated Nation*, xi.

9. Pexa writes: "Thióŝpaye conceptualizations of virtue as existing in and deriving from relations of mutual responsibility shaped how assimilation-era Dakhóta authors imagined their place within their own communities, as well as how they wrote themselves as ambivalent yet autonomous, amiable but trenchant critics of the U.S. settler-state" (*Translated Nation*, 4).

10. Pexa, *Translated Nation*, 3.

11. Schenck, *William W. Warren*, 128.

12. Warren, *History of the Ojibway People*, 7.

13. O'Brien, *Firsting and Lasting*, 107, 143.

14. Prucha, *Great Father*, 196.

15. Getches, Wilkinson, and Williams, *Cases and Materials*, 100.

16. Getches, Wilkinson, and Williams, *Cases and Materials*, 127.

17. *Cherokee Nation v. Georgia*, 30 U.S. 1 (1831).

18. For his description of the unequal terms of mutual recognition, Marshall saved some of his most pithy lines—including "When the United State gave peace, did they not also receive it?" and "The U.S. received the Cherokee nation into their favour and protection. The Cherokees acknowledge themselves to be under the protection of the United States and no other power. Protection does not imply the destruction of the protected." Here Marshall insists that the United States depends on a diplomatic relation with the people it is actively displacing in order to preserve the historical continuity of its coherence as an international power. In exchange for "protection," the United States gains a new way to compare its political history with "Great Britain" and "other European powers." *Johnson and Graham's Lessee v. McIntosh*, 21 U.S. 543 (1823).

19. *Worcester v. Georgia*, 31 U.S. 515 (1832).

20. During his lifetime, Marshall enslaved between 150 and 250 people, owned several plantations, and, despite having presided over a multitude of freedom cases, never once ruled in favor of an enslaved person.

21. The unreliability of Marshall's protection of tribes is blithely summarized by one of justices historically most antagonistic to tribal sovereignty, Antonin Scalia, in the 2001 case *Nevada v. Hicks*: "Our cases make clear that the Indians' right to make their own laws and be governed by them does not exclude all state regulatory authority on the reservation. State sovereignty does not end at a reservation's border. Though tribes are often referred to as 'sovereign' entities, it was 'long ago' that "the Court departed from Chief Justice Marshall's view that 'the laws of [a State] can have no force' within reservation boundaries." *Nevada v. Hicks*, 533 U.S. 353 (2001).

22. Said, *Culture and Imperialism*, 9.

23. *Worcester v. Georgia*, 31 U.S. 515 (1832).

24. Said, *Culture and Imperialism*, xiii.

25. Case, *Relentless Business of Treaties*, 79.

26. Schenck, "Introduction," xi.

27. Warren, *History of the Ojibway People*, 3.

28. Schoolcraft, *History of the Indians Tribes*, 27–28.

29. Schoolcraft, *History of the Indians Tribes*, vii.

30. Schoolcraft, *History of the Indians Tribes*, 28.

31. Schoolcraft, *History of the Indians Tribes*, vii.

32. Schoolcraft, *History of the Indians Tribes*, xv.

33. Schoolcraft, *History of the Indians Tribes*, 30.

34. Foucault, *Order of Things*, 217.

35. Foucault, *Order of Things*, 218.

36. Foucault, *Order of Things*, 219.

37. Warren, *History of the Ojibway People*, 26.

38. Schenck, *William W. Warren*, 11–18.

39. Warren, *History of the Ojibway People*, 27–28.

40. Warren, *History of the Ojibway People*, 34.

41. Schoolcraft, *History of the Indians Tribes*, vii.

42. *Cherokee Nation v. Georgia*, 30 U.S. 1 (1831).

43. Foucault, *Order of Things*, 17.

44. Foucault, *Order of Things*, 21.

45. Foucault, *Order of Things*, 220.

46. Warren, *History of the Ojibway People*, 31.

47. Warren, *History of the Ojibway People*, 38.

48. *Treaty with the Chippewa*, August 5, 1826, 7 Stat., 290, Articles 3, 4, 8.

49. *Treaty with the Chippewa*, October 4, 1842, 7 Stat., 591.

50. "Sandy Lake Tragedy and Memorial," Great Lakes Indian Fish and Wildlife Commission, accessed October 18, 2021, https://glifwc.org/publications /pdf/SandyLake_Brochure.pdf.

51. Schenck, *William W. Warren*, 123–55.

52. Schenck, *William W. Warren*, 68.

53. Pexa, *Translated Nation*, 104, 106.

54. Simpson, *Mohawk Interruptus*, 177.

55. Pexa, *Translated Nation*, 91.

56. Melas, *All the Difference*, 11, 21.

57. Melas, *All the Difference*, 7.

58. Melas, *All the Difference*, 31. See also Tuck and Yang, "Decolonization Is Not a Metaphor."

59. Melas, *All the Difference*, 32, 38; Derrida, *Politics of Friendship*, 32.

60. Warren, *History of the Ojibway People*, 71.

61. Warren, *History of the Ojibway People*, 74.

62. Warren, *History of the Ojibway People y*, 74.

63. Warren, *History of the Ojibway People*, 141.

Chapter Two. Domestic Affects

1. James Mooney, quoted in Wolfe, "Settler Colonialism," 391–92.

2. This is, to my mind, a significantly underutilized aspects of Wolfe's account of settler colonialism, one that gives useful, descriptive language to the overtly cooperating or permissive relation between settler vigilantes evident in white supremacist marches in places like Charlottesville, Virginia, and Portland, Oregon, and as a regular aspect of daily life in Zionist-occupied Palestine.

3. Wolfe, "Settler Colonialism," 391.

4. Wolfe, "Settler Colonialism," 392.

5. Coulthard, *Red Skins, White Masks*, 13.

6. Moten and Harney, *Undercommons*, 8.

7. The specific sense of the domestic as a theater of political production is drawn from Armstrong, *Desire and Domestic Fiction*.

8. Beth Piatote's crucial and influential study of assimilation-era Indigenous writing uses the term *domestic* to refer to layered and antagonistic categories of social and political life including "Native American domesticity" (Indigenous home life) that exists within the political construction the "tribal-national domestic" (a production of US imperialism specifically articulated via the Marshall Trilogy), which became a "site through which the settler state" produced its own senses of "settler colonial nationalism" (*Domestic Subjects*, 4, 9). The distinction between my approach and Piatote's is subtle in the sense that I am also interested in parsing the complex historical relation between the US production of its own political coherence via extractive assaults on Indigenous polities and social life. The fundamental difference in approaches, therefore, has to do with my interest in exposing and parsing the production of colonial cultural and political formations ultimately reproduced via the absence of actual sociality. The domestic is the category that colonial systems themselves use to describe and historicize this. Furthermore, I do not see an advantage in restricting theorizations of the vital heterogeny, histories, and proliferation of Indigenous kinship, care, and social reproduction by way of an ultimately homogenizing colonial concept like the domestic.

9. See McClintock, *Imperial Leather*; and Kaplan, *Anarchy of Empire*.

10. Lomawaima notes that Indian affairs commissioner Cato Sells made clear that "he felt Indian school graduates could be judged 'competent' in the legal sense" as a result of their interpellation into colonial domesticity, and that this was a "judgement crucial to the successful allotment of land. Dispossession of communal tribal lands, coupled with the creation of small 'Indian homesteads,' supported the rationale of domestic education for Indian women" (*Prairie Light*, 86). A century later, in adoption cases including *Adoptive Couple v. Baby Girl* (2013) and *Brackeen v. Haaland* (2022), settlers and settler courts repeat the same underlying logic that it is only via inclusion in white, colonial domesticity that Indigenous people can be proper subjects of jurisdictionally organized

and distributed rights. Not only do these cases expose the colonial sense that domesticity either as a cultural or jurisdictional category does not apply to Indigenous people or nations, but also the deployment of that framework in defense of tribes and tribal citizens unduly restricts the scope of extractive violence settlers and settler courts intend. To suggest, for instance, that the removal of an Indigenous child from their family/kinship system is a domestic question in the sense that it frames assessments of harm or care through the forms of the child, the custodial couple, or the household reinforces the social vacancy inherent in the concept of the domestic onto Indigenous people, both by normalizing these cultural forms as well as by disavowing the question of whether what is actually at stake is the continuity of those social and material practices (e.g., language, epistemic and metaphysical traditions, and land relations) that constitute a world.

11. On racialization through property, see Harris, "Whiteness as Property"; and TallBear, *Native American DNA*.

12. The children of Indigenous families suddenly forced into resource depravation or wage labor by allotment were often targeted by boarding schools. In other cases, families reluctantly sent their children to boarding schools in order to sustain jobs. Not infrequently, as is the case with Fleur in *Four Souls*, Indigenous women raised money by taking jobs as domestic workers in colonial households. For context on gender and labor in the boarding school era, see Lomawaima, "Domesticity in the Federal Indian Schools."

13. Although Erdrich's mother's family is primarily connected with Turtle Mountain land, Erdrich herself grew up on the Sisseton (Dakota) reservation.

14. See, for instance, Ransom, *Afterlives of Modernism*; Huhndorf, "Mapping the Future"; and Furlan, *Indigenous Cities*, 2017.

15. Erdrich, *Four Souls*, 12.

16. *Cherokee Nation v. Georgia*.

17. As Getches, Wilkinson, and Williams put it, Marshall defines Cherokee sovereignty in the context of a case that the state of Georgia cannot challenge because the court's decision was to deny the injunction requested by the tribe (*Cases and Materials*, 134).

18. Rancière, *Dissensus*, 71.

19. Rancière, *Dissensus*, 144.

20. Fletcher, "Tribal Consent," 54.

21. For instance, in *U.S. v. Kagama*, Justice Miller summarizes this circuitous and self-authorizing logic: "The power of the General Government over these remnants of a race once powerful, now weak and diminished in numbers, is necessary to their protection. . . . It must exist in that government, because it never has existed anywhere else because the theatre of its exercise is within the geographical limits of the United States, because it has never been denied, and because it alone can enforce its laws on all the tribes."

22. Amnesty International, *Maze of Injustice*, 27–52.

23. Rehnquist writes: "We are not unaware of the prevalence of non-Indian crime on today's reservations which the tribes forcefully argue requires the ability to try non-Indians. But these are considerations for Congress" (*Oliphant v. Suquamish*).

24. According to the National Congress of American Indians, 55 percent of Indigenous women experience domestic violence, and in 90 percent of those cases is the perpetrator nontribal (National Congress of the American Indian, VAWA, 3). Here and going forward in this chapter, I describe gendered violence against Indigenous people as targeting both women and gender nonconforming people, despite the fact that Erdrich's novels do not explicitly name its main characters as being nonbinary. Here I hope both to challenge the colonial gender binary that would exclude the ways violence against Indigenous women and gender nonconforming people are both orchestrated by patriarchy and refuse to erase or conflate violence committed against Indigenous nonconforming people. Erdrich's interest in these questions, across her oeuvre, is clear, and even within *Tracks* and *Four Souls* the instability of Fleur's gender performance can be understood in relation or response to the range of gendered expressions of colonial demands on her body, her land, and the social relations she sustains.

25. Siegel, "Rule of Love," 2139, 2161.

26. Siegel, "Rule of Love," 2190.

27. Siegel, "Rule of Love," 2170.

28. Pleck, "Wife Beating in Nineteenth-Century America," 198.

29. Siegel, "Rule of Love," 2199.

30. Siegel, "Rule of Love," 2200.

31. This exception was amended in 2021 such that tribes now have limited freedom to prosecute nontribal perpetrators who commit "crimes of domestic violence, dating violence, obstruction of justice, sexual violence, sex trafficking, stalking, and assault of a law enforcement or corrections officer" (H.R. 1620, 117th Cong.).

32. I am suggesting that Black and Indigenous social relations (unadministrated by colonial social orders) are made to be jurisgenerative by way of the imposition of the domestic as an ostensibly cultural framework. This echoes an argument Hortense Spillers makes about the domestic in the context of enslavement: "'Gendering' takes place within the confines of the domestic. . . . Domesticity appears to gain its power by way of a common origin of cultural fictions that are grounded in the specificity of proper names . . . which, in turn, situates those persons it 'covers' in a particular place" ("Mama's Baby, Papa's Maybe," 72).

33. Byrd, *Transit of Empire*, xiii.

34. Under the Kinkaid Act, settlers in Nebraska could acquire 640-acre homesteads; see Hibbard, *History of the Public Land Policies*, 392.

35. Codified in the Timber Culture Act of 1873.

36. Hibberd, *History of the Public Land Policies*, 411–23.

37. Lee and Ahtone, "Land Grab Universities."

38. For instance, the history of Diné hogans built on allotments out of radioactive uranium tailings by settler mining companies and governments under the terms of social remediation that exposed Diné women—who, prior to the installation of the Indian Reorganization Act tribal constitutional system and the mining economy, would not necessarily have been associated with the domestic—to constant radiation and, as a result of which, lung and thyroid cancers. See Voyles, *Wastelanding*.

39. Although reservations existed well before the Indian Appropriations Act, insofar as the act marked the end of treaty-making, it codified tribes' territorial status as formally internal to the governance structure of the United States (even as the basic distinction between tribes and other US polities, as established in treaties, were understood to remain "the law of the land"). The reservation at this point became the only territorial formation through which the United States conceived of Indigenous sovereignty.

40. See Spence, *Dispossessing Wilderness*.

41. One of the early founders and advocates of the US National Park system was Frederick Billings, owner of the Northern Pacific Railroad, who understood that the parks would become permanent destinations for transit and hospitality infrastructures; see Spence, *Dispossessing Wilderness*, 36.

42. As the Board of Indian Commissioners put it in 1869, "The white man has been the chief obstacle in the way of Indian civilization.... The policy of collecting the Indian tribes upon small reservations contiguous to each other, and within the limits of a large reservation, eventually to become a State of the Union ... seems to be the best that can be devised" (Getches, Wilkinson, and Williams, *Cases and Materials*, 176–77).

43. Lippert, *Sanctuary, Sovereignty, Sacrifice*.

44. Spence, *Dispossessing Wilderness*, 25–40.

45. As Wexler points out, it is essential to think of these constraints as generic in the sense that they are structural and communal processes that produce political aphasias that appear individuated: "Sentimentalization ... expands within the group to make individual awareness unlikely, just as if our whole society, without comment, blithely encouraged our children to play 'concentration camp,' or 'gas chamber,' or indeed 'cowboys and indians.'... in the quest twilight streets after dinner, with Native Americans and Holocaust survivors alongside our fond selves as witnesses" (*Tender Violence*, 116, 125).

46. Erdrich, *Tracks*, 8.

47. Erdrich, *Tracks*, 8.

48. Erdrich, *Tracks*, 9.

49. Erdrich, *Tracks*, 220.

50. Erdrich, *Tracks*, 220.

51. Erdrich, *Four Souls*, 210.

52. Erdrich, *Four Souls*, 6–7, 9.

53. Erdrich, *Four Souls*, 31–42.

54. Freud, "Uncanny," 237.

55. Freud, "Uncanny," 260.

56. Erdrich, *Four Souls*, 15, 24.

57. Romero, *Home Fronts*, 41; Kaplan, *Anarchy of Empire*, 27.

58. Freud, "Uncanny," 258.

59. Moscufo, "For These Indigenous Artists 'Land Back' Is Both a Political Message and a Fundraising Opportunity," *Forbes*, September 29, 2020, https://www.forbes.com/sites/michelamoscufo/2020/09/29/for-these-indigenous-artists-land-back-is-both-a-political-message-and-a-fundraising-opportunity/?sh=5747daf26c9c.

60. Derrida, *Specters of Marx*, 9.

61. Derrida, *Specters of Marx*, 33.

62. Spivak, "Ghostwriting," 70. Interestingly, Spivak articulates this elaboration of hauntology with reference to tribal practices of decolonization, specifically the Ghost Dance, which she erroneously calls a "Sioux effort," but that might be more accurately described as a counterinsurgency inspired by the Paiute leader Wovoka and most famously practiced by Lakota people in the last decade of the nineteenth century. Spivak's reading of the Ghost Dance, which she describes as an alignment with the subaltern studies investment in "texts produced from the other side," is actually a reading of the white anthropologist James Mooney's reading of the Ghost Dance and involves no formal or political account from the perspective of a tribal practitioner or theorist. Thus, oddly, as Spivak celebrates Ghost Dancers for deciding "to be haunted by the ancestors rather than treat them as objects of ritual worship," her analysis refetishizes tribal insurgent thought and practice as an object of theory. Using the Ghost Dance as her pivot away from Derrida, her "inspiration . . . from elsewhere," is not particularly malicious, but is interesting for what it reveals about how US and European literary and cultural theory in general (including projects within subaltern and postcolonial studies) often finds itself haunted by tribal continuities of thought and practice—much in the same way colonial discourses of the domestic, of rights, of social justice, do—precisely because, in order to be revolutionary, theory has to return to land (or have land return through it), a project whose superdimensionality of time and ontology makes it impossible for even critical epistemic frameworks derived from the European enlightenment to do alone.

63. Spivak, "Ghostwriting," 71.

64. Justice Ginsburg's opinion in the 2005 Supreme Court case *City of Sherrill v. Oneida Indian Nation of New York* famously memorializes this perspective. While the court found that the tribe did retain a viable sovereign claim over the land

occupied by the colonial settlement, Sherrill, Ginsburg decided: "Given the longstanding, distinctly non-Indian character of the area and its inhabitants, the regulatory authority constantly exercised by New York State and its counties and towns, and the Oneidas' long delay in seeking judicial relief against parties other than the United States, we hold that the Tribe cannot unilaterally revive its ancient sovereignty, in whole or in part, over the parcels at issue." Here, the specter of tribal autonomy haunts and reveals the essential limits of the domestic as a political framework (its jurisdictionalization of time, its racializing and nationalizing effect ["non-Indian character of the area"], and its displacement of dependency ["the Tribe cannot unilaterally revive its ancient sovereignty"]). However, and perhaps evocatively of Armstrong's argument about the production of white female power via the domestic, Ginsburg successfully represses the ghosts of tribal land claims not only because she asserts the tribe's claim (and the tribe itself) to be ancient, but because she understands that their "disruptive remedy" would establish a precedent that would throw all US property holding into question.

65. Spivak, "Ghostwriting," 71.
66. Erdrich, *Four Souls*, 127.
67. Erdrich, *Four Souls*, 48.
68. Erdrich, *Four Souls*, 50.
69. Erdrich, *Four Souls*, 47.
70. Gordon, *Ghostly Matters*, 182.
71. Erdrich, *Four Souls*, 207.

Chapter Three. The Ruins of Settlement

1. Dawson, *Extreme Cities*, 9.
2. As a rethinking of the co-constitution of race and space, Dawson's work extends environmental justice frameworks like those established in Bullard, *Dumping in Dixie*, Bullard and Wright, *Race, Place, and Environmental Justice after Hurricane Katrina*, and Taylor, *Toxic Communities*. Dawson's approach is also heavily informed by postcolonial urbanism scholars working at the intersection of environmental studies—for instance, Pulido, "Rethinking Environmental Racism," and Roy, *City Requiem: Gender and the Politics of Poverty* and her coedited volume with Ong, *Worlding Cities*. Finally, his work draws on Marxist frameworks of neoliberalism and creative destruction that organizes works including Harvey, *Condition of Postmodernity* and "Neoliberalism and Creative Destruction"; and, more recently, Highsmith, *Demolition Means Progress*.
3. Dawson, *Extreme Cities*, 7, 276.
4. Using explicitly racializing language, historians have classically depicted post-allotment reservation life as squalid and depressed ("Social life for Chippewas . . . consisted of drinking beer, hunting wild game, and asking

for government doles in the winter months") and post-"urbanization" life as fundamentally alienating ("the hard realities of urban life soon destroyed Indian hopes for a successful livelihood . . . relocation . . . was a threatening cultural shock")—for instance, Philp, "Stride toward Freedom"; and Fixico, *Termination and Relocation*, 139. Proponents of relocation also operated under the premises that cities were categorically extricable from Indigenous land and people and that histories of Indigenous urban life could be equivocated with those of other racially marked populations. In some ways these premises live on even in contemporary assessments of relocation, for instance, those that center concepts of Indigenous adaptation to urban life—for instance, Blackhawk, "We Can Carry on From Here"; Miller, *Indians on the Move*. The implicit or explicit distinction between urbanity and Indigeneity is clearly contradicted by the long histories of Indigenous city-building and cosmopolitanism stretching back millennia in the Americas. Not only does this categorical separation overlook cities like Tenochtitlan, Cahokia, and Chaco and smaller or seasonal cosmopolitan forms like ceremony sites and hunting and gathering camps, but it also elides the fact that, in the Twin Cities, for instance, settlers cities are almost always built over existing Indigenous settlements.

5. Star, "Ethnography of Infrastructure," 382.

6. Here, I nod to Baker's use of the term *deformation* (Baker, *Harlem Renaissance*, xvi).

7. Gikandi, *Maps of Englishness*, 161.

8. For Rancière, "the distribution of the sensible reveals who can have a share in what is common to the community based on what they do and on the time and space in which this activity is performed." Modernism participates in the distribution of material and cultural knowledge primarily, for Rancière, not as a break but a regularization and occlusion of the politics of knowledge: "Aesthetic modernity conceals—without conceptualizing it in the least—the singularity of a particular regime of arts . . . [the] specific type of connection between ways of producing works of art . . . forms of visibility that disclose them, and ways of conceptualizing the former and the latter" (Rancière, *Politics of Aesthetics*, 12, 30).

9. Huhndorf (Yup'ik), *Mapping the Americas*; Teuton (Cherokee), "Cities of Refuge."

10. Ramirez (Ho-Chunk), *Native Hubs*, 12.

11. Goeman, *Mark My Words*, 136.

12. Goeman, *Mark My Words*, 137.

13. Warrior, *People and the Word*, 6.

14. Forgetting, in this context, also occurs through recategorization—that is, through the renaming of other ways of having shelter and belonging under new terms, like *homeless*. On the sociological iteration and disciplinary productivity of this effect, see Willse, *Value of Homelessness*.

15. Treuer, *Hiawatha*, 43.

16. Treuer, *Hiawatha*, 55.

17. Scott, *Seeing Like a State*, 1–52.

18. The no-numbered house is demolished by a crew that ultimately has to ask Simon to help them. This moment of self-demolition warrants analysis beyond the scope of this chapter, particularly insofar as it echoes the self-demolition of Black and Indigenous neighborhoods by crews hired as part of the installation of the interstate highway system after 1956, and also as it echoes contemporary self-demolition mandates Palestinians are forced to participate in (see Frère, "House Demolitions").

19. Treuer, *Hiawatha*, 59.

20. Masco, "Survival Is Your Business," 362.

21. *Berman v. Parker*, 348 U.S. 26 (1954).

22. Nixon, *Slow Violence*, 2.

23. Stoler, *Duress*, 350–51.

24. Stoler, *Duress*, 350.

25. Stoler, *Duress*, 351.

26. See Harvey, "Neoliberalism as Creative Destruction." Scholars often identify Marx's *Grundrisse* as the source for the idea of "creative destruction," specifically where Marx writes: "The growing incompatibility between the productive development of society and its hitherto existing relations of production expresses itself in bitter contradictions, crises, spasms. The violent destruction of capital not by relations external to it, but rather as a condition of its self-preservation" (793).

27. Weizman, *Forensic Architecture*, 58.

28. Nemser, *Infrastructures of Race*, 5.

29. Nemser, *Infrastructures of Race*, 5.

30. Gilmore, "Race and Globalization," 261.

31. Ammon, *Bulldozer*, 80.

32. Ammon, *Bulldozer*, 37.

33. Ammon, *Bulldozer*, 185.

34. Nowhere is this historical continuity of the empty spaces clearance left behind more jarringly named than in the large plot of undeveloped land in St. Louis, cleared during urban renewal, known vernacularly as "Hiroshima Flats" (Ammon, *Bulldozer*, 221).

35. Governor's Human Rights Commission, *Minnesota's Indian Citizens*.

36. Barker, "For Whom Sovereignty Matters."

37. South Minneapolis Residential Soil Contamination, accessed June 1, 2021, https://cumulis.epa.gov/supercpad/SiteProfiles/index.cfm?fuseaction=second .cleanup&id=0509136.

38. See Philp, "Stride toward Freedom"; "Dillon S. Myer."

39. See Masco, *Nuclear Borderlands*; and Carson, *Silent Spring*.

40. Black, Indigenous, and other racialized populations have lived amid world-ending social and ecological harm since 1441, but contemporary discourses

typically locate the beginning of climate crisis at moments when those trajectories of harm finally extend to white people, even as the urgency of those moments is often narrated in universalizing terms. On the date 1441, see King, *Black Shoals*; on coloniality and the Anthropocene, see Zoe Todd, "Indigenizing the Anthropocene"; and, for an example of the climate crisis as an occasion to universalization, see Chakrabarty, "Climate of History."

41. Dillon Myer, quoted in Drinnon, *Keeper of the Concentration Camps*, 29.

42. Drinnon, *Keeper of the Concentration Camps*, 55.

43. This is a term Kenneth Jackson uses specifically in the context of the Greenbelt Town Program, based in part on British planner Ebenezer Howard's "New Town Movement." In the Twin Cities, the most iconic materialization of this approach—which is animated by logics of racial concentration and clearance as whiteness—is Riverside Plaza, a skyscraper that is now one of the centers of the Somali population in the cities. Jackson, *Crabgrass Frontier*, 194.

44. Jackson, *Crabgrass Frontier*, 249.

45. "State Superfund Site Summaries," Minnesota Pollution Control Agency, accessed October 29, 2021, https://www.pca.state.mn.us/waste/state-superfund -site-summaries.

46. Wolfe, "Settler Colonialism."

47. Treuer, *Hiawatha*, 17.

48. Stoler, *Duress*, 313.

49. Treuer, *Hiawatha*, 113.

50. Treuer, *Hiawatha*, 114.

51. Treuer, *Hiawatha*, 228.

52. Treuer, *Hiawatha*, 233–35.

53. Scott, *Domination and the Arts of Resistance*, 183.

54. Scott, *Domination and the Arts of Resistance*, 196.

55. Treuer, *Hiawatha*, 86.

56. Treuer, *Hiawatha*, 166.

57. Treuer, *Hiawatha*, 73.

58. Eulogy for John Elliot Tappan, delivered by Thomas Gallagher, May 11, 1957, Hennepin County Bar Association District Court, Minneapolis, Minnesota. The history of Target's suburbanization after 1956 includes the replacement of local food and health care access in Indigenous and Black neighborhoods in the Twin Cities with huge and highly surveillant box stores, a process that some use the framework of the production of "food deserts" to describe. For me, the development of these stores advances the neoliberal, carceral, and biopolitical logics inherent to the colonial formalism I am calling *clearance*. By this logic, I read the "looting" and burning of the Target store (and others like it) in South Minneapolis during the uprisings following the murder of George Floyd as a potent gesture of decolonial anti-clearance.

59. An aesthetic definitively described by Fredric Jameson, writing about the Wells Fargo Court in Los Angeles: "This great sheet of windows, with its gravity-defying two-dimensionality, momentarily transforms the solid ground on which we stand into the contents of a stereopticon, pasteboard shapes profiling themselves here and there around us. The visual effect is the same from all sides: as fateful as the great monolith in Stanley Kubrick's *2001* which confronts its viewers like an enigmatic destiny, a call to evolutionary mutation" (Jameson, *Postmodernism*, 12–13).

60. Treuer, *Hiawatha*, 130.

61. Treuer, *Hiawatha*, 130.

62. Treuer, *Hiawatha*, 130.

63. Treuer, *Hiawatha*, 87.

64. Scott, *Seeing Like a State*, 193.

65. Scott, *Seeing Like a State*, 190.

Chapter Four. The Right to Gather

1. Vizenor, "Native Transmotion," 168.

2. Vizenor, "Native Transmotion," 169.

3. Rand Valentine, "Verbal Artistry," 82. Where other languages organize nouns into categories of gender, Ojibwemowin's basic nominal classifications are "animate persons" and "inanimate persons."

4. Valentine, "Verbal Artistry," 82.

5. The colonial politics of protection that I also used in Hooley, "Sanctuary."

6. See McPherson, *Political Theory of Possessive Individualism*; Moyn, *Not Enough*; and Lowe, *Intimacies*.

7. Treaty with the Chippewa, 7 Stat., 536, July 29, 1837.

8. *Manoomin et al. vs. Minnesota DNR Commissioner Strommen et al. Complaint for Injunctive and Declaratory Relief*, White Earth Band of Ojibwe Tribal Court (2021).

9. On Vizenor's style see Blaeser, *Oral Tradition*; Blair, "Text as Trickster"; and Hume, "Metaphysics."

10. Teuton, "Internationalism and the American Indian Scholar"; Simpson, "Place Where We All Live."

11. Smith, "American Studies without America," 312.

12. Blaeser, "Wild Rice Rights, 250, 240.

13. Blaeser, "Wild Rice Rights," 240.

14. Vizenor, "Native Transmotion," 178.

15. Vizenor, *Fugitive Poses*, 15.

16. Vizenor, "Native Transmotion," 168.

17. The term "storied," here echoes Goeman, "Land as Life," 72.

18. Vizenor, "Native Transmotion," 182.

19. Treaty with the Sioux, etc., 7 Stat., 272, August 19, 1825, Article 13.

20. Simpson, "Place Where We All Live," 19.

21. Lowe, *Intimacies*, 39.

22. *U.S. v. 4,450.72 Acres of Land*, 27 F. Supp. 167 (D. Minn. 1939).

23. *U.S. v. 4,450.72 Acres of Land*, 27 F. Supp. 167 (D. Minn. 1939).

24. *State of Minnesota v. United States*, 125 F.2d 636 (8th Cir. 1942).

25. *U.S. v. Winans*, 198 U.S. 371 (1905).

26. *U.S. v. Winans*, 198 U.S. 371 (1905).

27. *LCO v. Voigt* cites *United States v. Santa Fe Railroad*, 314 U.S. 339 (1941) to define "aboriginal title" to access to land implicitly extinguished by the creation of a reservation. Here, the court repeats a premise, which appears throughout US Federal Indian Law, that actual ramifications of agreements the United States made would be simply too significant for the United States to tolerate—an argument made in cases specifically bearing on manoomin gathering, as in *State v. Keezer*, 292 N.W.2d 714 (Minn. 1980), which rejected the interpretation of the Treaty of Greeneville as granting Indigenous sovereignty within the entirety of the Northwest Territory, and in cases with broad and devastating consequences like *City of Sherrill v. Oneida Indian Nation of N.Y.*, 544 U.S. 197 (2005), in which Justice Ginsburg disavowed treaty-granted sovereignty by concluding that honoring the terms of a 1795 treaty was "impractic[al]." In *Mille Lacs v. Minnesota*, the majority distinguishes the rights reserved in the White Pine Treaty from those in the treaty referenced in *Ward v. Race Horse*, 163 U.S. 504 (1896), which "contemplated that the rights would continue only so long as the hunting grounds remained unoccupied and owned by the United States."

28. Minn. R. 7050.0224, subp. 2.

29. Minnesota Statues 84.091.

30. Vennum, *Wild Rice*, 13.

31. The 1854 Treaty Authority summarizes the arbitrariness of these metrics: "The MPCA is proposing to base the definition of a wild rice water on the food energy needs of a duck pair for two months. The proposed criteria includes a natural bed of wild rice of at least 0.25 acres in an area with a stem density of at least 8 stems per square meter, or 0.5 acres in an area with a stem density of at least 4 stems per square meter." See 1854 Treaty Authority, "Re: Draft Technical Support Document: Refinements to Minnesota's Sulfate Water Quality Standard to Protect Wild Rice," September 6, 2016.

32. 1854 Treaty Authority, "Refinements," accessed October 1, 2022, https://www.1854treatyauthority.org/management.html

33. Chief Administrative Law Judge's Order on Review of Rules Under Minn. Stat. 14.16, subd. 2, and Minn. R. 1400.2240, subp. 5.

34. Lowe, *Intimacies*, 39.

35. Vizenor, "Native Transmotion," 169.

36. See, especially, Hartman, *Scenes of Subjection*; Wynter, "Unsettling the Coloniality of Being"; and Allewaert, *Ariel's Ecology*.

37. LaDuke, *Recovering the Sacred*; Child, *My Grandmother's Knocking Sticks*.

38. These proceedings were enabled by the growth of US agribusiness in the legal sphere. Policy like the Plant Patent Act (1930) and cases like *Diamond v. Chakrabarty* (447 U.S. 303, 1980) ontologically and economically reclassified plants that had been created by colonial scientists and corporations as human creations and therefore subject to colonial ownership and litigation processes. See Bouayad, "Wild Rice Protectors"; and Raster and Hill, "Dispute over Wild Rice."

39. In 2007 the state passed a law increasing restrictions on genetic modification and following a MDNR report (*Natural Wild Rice in Minnesota: A Wild Rice Study Document Submitted to the Minnesota Legislature by the Minnesota Department of Natural Resources*, February 15, 2008) the state, the University of Minnesota, and tribes created a memorandum of agreement limiting the further genetic research and patenting of manoomin (*Wild Rice Whiter Paper*). See Bouayad, "Wild Rice Protectors," 34.

40. Quoted in LaDuke, *Recovering the Sacred*, 179.

41. "White Earth Band of Ojibwe's responses to the Draft Environmental Impact Statement," July 9, 2017.

42. White Earth Band of Chippewa Indians, Resolution No. 001-19-009.

43. White Earth Band of Chippewa Indians, Resolution No. 001-19-009.

44. Vizenor, "Native Transmotion," 187.

45. US Constitution, Fourteenth Amendment; cited in Vizenor, "Native Transmotion," 187.

46. Vizenor, "Native Transmotion," 197.

47. Vizenor, "Native Transmotion," 199.

48. Online Etymology Dictionary, s.v. "pronoun," accessed October 31, 2021, https://www.etymonline.com/word/pronoun#etymonline_v_2674.

49. Arendt, *Origins of Totalitarianism*, 296.

50. Vizenor and Doerfler, *White Earth Nation*, 63.

51. *Totem* is a corruption of the Ojibwemowin word for "clan," which in fact requires a prefix clarifying the relation it describes. In other words, there is not a word for "clan" as an abstraction, but rather a proliferation of word forms describing, for instance, "my clan" (*nindoodem*), "your clan" (*gidoodem*).

52. Vizenor and Doerfler, *White Earth Nation*, 69.

53. White Earth Band of Chippewa Indians, Resolution No. 001-19-009.

54. White Earth Band of Chippewa Indians, Resolution No. 001-19-009.

55. Derrida, *Rogues*, 13.

56. Derrida, *Rogues*, 142, 17.

57. Derrida, *Rogues*, 152.

58. Derrida, *Rogues*, 149.

59. Derrida, *Given Time*, 7.

60. Derrida, *Given Time*, 7.

61. Derrida, *Given Time*, 7.

62. White Earth Band of Chippewa Indians, Resolution No. 001-19-009.

Epilogue

1. Derrida, *Rogues*, 172.
2. Whyte, Caldwell, and Schaefer, "Indigenous Lessons about Sustainability."
3. Morrison and Gault, *Turning the Feather Around*, 192.
4. Morrison and Gault, *Turning the Feather Around*, 168.
5. Morrison and Gault, *Turning the Feather Around*, 170.
6. Morrison and Gault, *Turning the Feather Around*, 174–75, 170–71.
7. Derrida, *Rogues*, 143.
8. Derrida, *Rogues*, 143, 11.
9. Morrison and Gault, *Turning the Feather Around*, 192.
10. Derrida, *Rogues*, 144.
11. Derrida, *Rogues*, 143.
12. Macharia, *Frottage*, 14.
13. Macharia, *Frottage*, 14.
14. Macharia, *Frottage*, 17.

Bibliography

Adoptive Couple v. Baby Girl. 570 U.S. 637 (2013).

Agamben, Giorgio. *Homo Sacer: Sovereign Power and Bare Life.* Translated by Daniel Heller-Roazen. Stanford, CA: Stanford University Press, 1998.

Alfred, Taiaike. "Sovereignty." In *Sovereignty Matters: Locations of Contestation and Possibility in Indigenous Struggles for Self-Determination,* edited by Joanne Barker, 33–50. Lincoln: University of Nebraska Press, 2005.

Allewaert, Monique. *Ariel's Ecology: Plantations, Personhood, and Colonialism in the American Tropics.* Minneapolis: University of Minnesota Press, 2013.

Ammon, Francesca. *Bulldozer: Demolition and Clearance of the Postwar Landscape.* New Haven, CT: Yale University Press, 2016.

Amnesty International. *Maze of Injustice: The Failure to Protect Indigenous Women from Sexual Violence in the USA.* New York: Amnesty International, 2006.

Arendt, Hannah. *Origins of Totalitarianism.* New York: Harcourt, 1973.

Armstrong, Nancy. *Desire and Domestic Fiction: A Political History of the Novel.* Oxford: Oxford University Press, 1990.

Arvin, Maile. "Analytics of Indigeneity." In *Native Studies Keywords,* edited by Stephanie Nohelani Teves, Andrea Smith, and Michelle Raheja, 119–29. Tucson: University of Arizona Press, 2015.

Aschman, Frederick T. "Nicollet Mall: Civic Cooperation to Preserve Downtown's Vitality." *Planner's Notebook* 1, no. 6 (September 1971): 1–8.

Baker, Houston A., Jr. *Modernism and the Harlem Renaissance.* Chicago: University of Chicago Press, 1989.

Barker, Joanne. "For Whom Sovereignty Matters." In *Sovereignty Matters: Locations of Contestation and Possibility in Indigenous Struggles for Self-Determination,* edited by Joanne Barker, 1–32. Lincoln: University of Nebraska Press, 2005.

Bennett, Jane. *Vibrant Matter: A Political Ecology of Things*. Durham, NC: Duke University Press, 2010.

Benton-Benai, Edward. *The Mishomis Book: The Voice of the Ojibway*. Minneapolis: University of Minnesota Press, 2010.

Berman v. Parker. 348 U.S. 26 (1954).

Black, Megan. *The Global Interior*. Cambridge, MA: Harvard University Press, 2018.

Blackhawk, Ned. "We Can Carry On from Here: The Relocation of American Indians to Los Angeles." *Wicazo Sa Review* 11, no. 2 (Autumn 1995): 16–30.

Blaeser, Kimberly. "Wild Rice Rights: Gerald Vizenor and an Affiliation of Story." In *Centering Anishinaabeg Studies: Understanding the World through Stories*, edited by Jill Doerfler, Niigaanwewidam James Sinclair, and Heidi Kiiwetinepinesiik Stark, 237–57. East Lansing: Michigan State University Press, 2013.

Blaeser, Kimberly. *Writing in the Oral Tradition*. Norman: University of Oklahoma Press, 1996.

Blair, Elizabeth. "Text as Trickster: Postmodern Language Games in Gerald Vizenor's *Bearheart*." *MELUS* 20, no. 4 (December 1995): 75–90.

Bouayad, Aurelien. "Wild Rice Protectors: An Ojibwe Odyssey." *Environmental Law Review* 22, no. 1 (2020): 25–42.

Bullard, Robert. *Dumping in Dixie: Race, Class, and Environmental Quality*. New York: Routledge, 2009.

Bullard, Robert, and Beverly Wright. *Race, Place, and Environmental Justice after Hurricane Katrina*. New York: Routledge, 2009.

Byrd, Jodi. *The Transit of Empire: Indigenous Critiques of Colonialism*. Minneapolis: University of Minnesota Press, 2011.

Carson, Rachel. *Silent Spring*. Boston: Houghton Mifflin, 1962.

Case, Martin. *The Relentless Business of Treaties: How Indigenous Land Became U.S. Property*. St. Paul: Minnesota Historical Society, 2018.

Center for Public Integrity. "Honeywell International Inc." Accessed September 29, 2022. https://web.archive.org/web/20070605190324/http://www.publicintegrity.org/superfund/Company.aspx?act=12976.

Chakrabarty, Dipesh. "The Climate of History: Four Theses." *Critical Inquiry* 35, no. 2 (Winter 2009): 197–222.

Chakrabarty, Dipesh. *Provincializing Europe: Postcolonial Thought and Historical Difference*. Princeton, NJ: Princeton University Press, 2000.

Cherokee Nation v. Georgia. 30 U.S. 1 (1831).

Chief Administrative Law Judge's Order on Review of Rules under Minn. Stat. 14.16, subd. 2, and Minn. R. 1400.2240, subp. 5.

Child, Brenda. *My Grandmother's Knocking Sticks*. St. Paul: Minnesota Historical Society, 2014.

City of Sherrill v. Oneida Indian Nation of N.Y. 544 U.S. 197 (2005).

Cook-Lynn, Elizabeth. "Who Stole Native American Studies?" *Wicazo Sa Review* 12, no. 1 (Spring 1997): 9–28.

Coulthard, Glen. *Red Skins, White Masks: Rejecting the Colonial Politics of Recognition.* Minneapolis: University of Minnesota Press, 2009.

Coulthard, Glen, and Leanne Betasamosake Simpson. "Grounded Normativity/ Place-Based Solidarity." *American Quarterly* 68, no. 2 (June 2016): 249–55.

Davis, Julie L. *Survival Schools: The American Indian Movement and Community Education in the Twin Cities.* Minneapolis: University of Minnesota Press, 2013.

Dawson, Ashley. *Extreme Cities: The Peril and Promise of Urban Life in the Age of Climate Change.* London: Verso, 2017.

Day, Iyko. "Being or Nothingness: Indigeneity, Antiblackness, and Settler Colonial Critique." *Critical Ethnic Studies* 1, no. 2 (Fall 2015): 102–21.

Deleuze, Gilles, and Félix Guattari. *Kafka: Toward a Minor Literature.* Minneapolis: University of Minnesota Press, 1986.

Deloria, Philip J. *Playing Indian.* New Haven, CT: Yale University Press, 1998.

Derrida, Jacques. *Archive Fever: A Freudian Impression.* Chicago: University of Chicago Press, 1998.

Derrida, Jacques. *Given Time: I. Counterfeit Money.* Translated by Peggy Kamuf. Chicago: University of Chicago Press, 1992.

Derrida, Jacques. *The Politics of Friendship.* Translated by George Collins. London: Verso, 1997.

Derrida, Jacques. *Rogues: Two Essays on Reason.* Stanford, CA: Stanford University Press, 2005.

Derrida, Jacques. *Specters of Marx: The State of the Debt, the Work of Mourning, and the New International.* New York: Routledge, 2006.

Diamond v. Chakrabarty. 447 U.S. 303 (1980).

Doyle, Laura, and Laura Winkiel. *Geomodernisms: Race, Modernism, Modernity.* Bloomington: Indiana University Press, 2005.

Drinnon, Richard. *Keeper of the Concentration Camps: Dillon S. Myer and American Racism.* Berkeley: University of California Press, 1989.

1854 Treaty Authority. "Re: Draft Technical Support Document: Refinements to Minnesota's Sulfate Water Quality Standard to Protect Wild Rice." September 6, 2016.

1854 Treaty Authority. "Refinements." Accessed October 1, 2022. https://www.1854treatyauthority.org/management.html

Erdrich, Louise. *Books and Islands in Ojibwe Country: Traveling through the Land of My Ancestors.* New York: Harper Perennial, 2014.

Erdrich, Louise. *Four Souls.* New York: HarperCollins, 2004.

Erdrich, Louise. *Tracks.* New York: Harper Perennial, 2004.

Fairbanks, Evelyn. *The Days of Rondo.* St. Paul: Minnesota Historical Society, 1990.

Fixico, Donald. *Termination and Relocation: Federal Indian Policy, 1945–1960.* Albuquerque: University of New Mexico Press, 1990.

Fletcher, Mathew L. M. "Tribal Consent." *Stanford Journal of Civil Rights and Civil Liberties* 8 (2012): 45. https://papers.ssrn.com/sol3/papers.cfm?abstract_id =1932331.

Foucault, Michel. *The Order of Things: An Archeology of the Human Sciences.* New York: Vintage, 1994.

Foucault, Michel. "What Is Enlightenment?" In *The Foucault Reader*, edited by Paul Rabinow, 32–51. New York: Penguin, 2020.

Frère, Antoine. "House Demolitions and Forced Evictions in Silwan: Israel's Transfer of Palestinians from Jerusalem." *Al Haq*, August 26, 2020. https:// www.alhaq.org/cached_uploads/download/2021/08/17/silwan-webversion-1 -page-view-1629184473.pdf.

Freud, Sigmund. *The Complete Psychological Works of Sigmund Freud, Vol. 17: An Infantile Neurosis and Other Works.* Translated by J. Strachey. London: Vintage, 2001.

Furlan, Laura. *Indigenous Cities: Urban Indian Fiction and the Histories of Relocation.* Lincoln: University of Nebraska Press, 2017.

Getches, David, Charles F. Wilkinson, and Robert A. Williams Jr. *Cases and Materials on Federal Indian Law.* 5th ed. St. Paul, MN: Thompson West, 2005.

Gikandi, Simon. *Maps of Englishness: Writing Identity in the Culture of Colonialism.* New York: Columbia University Press, 1996.

Gilmore, Ruth Wilson. "Race and Globalization." In *Geographies of Global Change: Remapping the World*, 2nd ed., edited by R. J. Johnston, Peter J. Taylor, and Michael J. Watts, 261–74. Malden, MA: Wiley Blackwell, 2002.

Goeman, Mishuana. "Disrupting a Settler-Colonial Grammar of Place: The Visual Memoir of Hulleah Tsinhnahjinnie." In *Theorizing Native Studies*, edited by Audra Simpson and Andrea Smith, 235–65. Durham, NC: Duke University Press, 2014.

Goeman, Mishuana. "Land as Life: Unsettling the Logics of Containment." In *Native Studies Keywords*, edited by Stephanie Nohelani Teves, Andrea Smith, and Michelle Raheja, 71–89. Tucson: University of Arizona Press, 2015.

Goeman, Mishuana. *Mark My Words: Native Women Mapping Our Nations.* Minneapolis: University of Minnesota Press, 2013.

Goldstein, Alyosha. *Poverty in Common: The Politics of Community Action during the American Century.* Durham, NC: Duke University Press, 2012.

Goldstein, Alyosha. "Where the Nation Takes Place: Proprietary Regimes, Antistatism, and U.S. Settler Colonialism." *South Atlantic Quarterly* 107, no. 4 (Fall 2008): 833–61.

Gordon, Avery. *Ghostly Matters: Haunting and the Sociological Imagination.* Minneapolis: University of Minnesota Press, 2008.

Gottfried, Mara H., Josh Verges, Frederick Melo, Tad Vezner, and Andy Rathbun. "After Weekend Violence, Philando Castile's Family Calls for Calm." *Twin Cities Pioneer Press*, July 11, 2016. https://www.twincities.com/2016/07/09 /amid-racial-strife-hundreds-seek-answers-in-protests-church-service.

Governor's Human Rights Commission. *Minnesota's Indian Citizens (Yesterday and Today)*. St. Paul: State of Minnesota, 1965.

Haaland v. Brackeen. *Oyez*. Accessed December 25, 2022. https://www.oyez.org /cases/2022/21-376.

Haraway, Donna J. *Staying with the Trouble: Making Kin in the Chthulucene*. Durham, NC: Duke University Press, 2016.

Harman, Graham. "The Well-Wrought Broken Hammer: Object-Oriented Literary Criticism." *New Literary History* 43, no. 2 (2012): 183–203.

Harris, Cheryl. "Whiteness as Property." *Harvard Law Review* 106, no. 8 (June 1993): 1707–91.

Hartman, Saidiya. *Scenes of Subjection: Terror, Slavery, and Self-Making in Nineteenth Century America*. Oxford: Oxford University Press, 1997.

Harvey, David. *The Condition of Postmodernity*. Malden, MA: Wiley Blackwell, 1991.

Harvey, David. "Neoliberalism and Creative Destruction." *Annals of the American Academy of Political and Social Science* 610 (March 2007): 22–44.

Heen, Mary L. "Ending Jim Crow Life Insurance Rates." *Northwestern Journal of Law and Social Policy* 4, no. 2 (2009): 360–99.

Hibbard, Benjamin Horace. *A History of the Public Land Policies*. New York: Macmillan, 1924.

Highsmith, Andrew R. *Demolition Means Progress: Flint Michigan and the Fate of the American Metropolis*. Chicago: University of Chicago Press, 2015.

Hooley, Matt. "Sanctuary: Literature and the Colonial Politics of Protection." In *The Cambridge Companion to American Literature and the Environment*, edited by Sarah Ensor and Susan Scott Parrish, 189–203. Cambridge: Cambridge University Press, 2022.

Hudson, Horace B. *A Half Century of Minneapolis*. Minneapolis: Hudson, 1908.

Huettl, Margaret. "Treaty Stories: Reclaiming the Unbroken History of Lac Courte Oreilles Ojibwe Sovereignty." *Ethnohistory* 68, no. 2 (April, 2021): 215–36.

Huhndorf, Shari. *Mapping the Americas: The Transnational Politics of Contemporary Native Culture*. Ithaca, NY: Cornell University Press, 2009.

Huhndorf, Shari. "Mapping the Future: Indigenous Feminism." In *The Cambridge History of Native American Literature*, edited by Melanie Taylor, 365–78. Cambridge: Cambridge University Press, 2020.

Hume, Kathryn. "Gerald Vizenor's Metaphysics." *Contemporary Literature* 48, no. 4 (Winter 2007): 580–612.

Jackson, Kenneth T. *Crabgrass Frontier: The Suburbanization of the United States*. Oxford: Oxford University Press, 1989.

Jackson, Zakiyyah Iman. *Becoming Human: Matter and Meaning in an Antiblack World*. New York: New York University Press, 2020.

Jameson, Fredric. *Postmodernism, or, The Culture of Late Capitalism*. Durham, NC: Duke University Press, 1997.

Johnson and Graham's Lessee v. McIntosh. 21 U.S. 543 (1823).

Kaplan, Amy. *The Anarchy of Empire in the Making of U.S. Culture*. Cambridge, MA: Harvard University Press, 2005.

Kelsey, Albert V. B. (Kerck). "C. C. Washburn: The Evolution of a Flour Baron." *Wisconsin Magazine of History* 88, no. 4 (2005): 38–51.

King, Tiffany Lethabo. *The Black Shoals: Offshore Formations of Black and Native Studies*. Durham, NC: Duke University Press, 2020.

Lac Courte Oreilles Band of Lake Superior Chippewa Indians v. Voigt. 700 F.2d 341 (Seventh Cir. 1983).

LaDuke, Winona. *Recovering the Sacred: The Power of Naming and Claiming*. Cambridge, MA: South End, 2005.

Larson, Agnes Mathilda. *The White Pine Industry in Minnesota: A History*. Minneapolis: University of Minnesota Press, 2007.

Lee, Robert, and Tristan Ahtone. "Land Grab Universities." *High Country News*, March 30, 2020. https://www.hcn.org/issues/52.4/indigenous-affairs-education-land-grab-universities.

Lippert, Robert. *Sanctuary, Sovereignty, Sacrifice: Canadian Sanctuary Incidents, Power, and Law*. Vancouver: University of British Columbia Press, 2006.

Lomawaima, K. Tsianina. "Domesticity in the Federal Indian Schools: The Power of Authority over Mind and Body." *American Ethnologist* 20, no. 2 (May 1993): 227–40.

Lomawaima, K. Tsianina. *They Called It Prairie Light: The Story of Chilocco Indian School*. Lincoln: University of Nebraska Press, 1995.

Lowe, Lisa. *The Intimacies of Four Continents*. Durham, NC: Duke University Press, 2015.

Lyons, Scott. *X-Marks: Native Signatures of Assent*. Minneapolis: University of Minnesota Press, 2010.

Macharia, Keguro. *Frottage: Frictions of Intimacy across the Black Diaspora*. New York: New York University Press, 2019.

Manoomin et al. vs. Minnesota DNR Commissioner Strommen et al Complaint for Injunctive and Declaratory Relief. White Earth Band of Ojibwe Tribal Court, 2021.

Martinez, David. "This Is (Not) Indian Painting: George Morrison, Minnesota, and His Return to a Land He Never Really Left." *American Indian Quarterly* 39, no. 1 (Winter 2015): 25–51.

Marx, Karl. *Capital: A Critique of Political Economy, Vol. 1*. New York: Penguin Classics, 1992.

Marx, Karl. *Grundrisse: Foundations of the Critique of Political Economy*. New York: Penguin, 1993.

Masco, Joseph. *The Nuclear Borderlands: The Manhattan Project in Post–Cold War New Mexico*. Princeton, NJ: Princeton University Press, 2006.

Masco, Joseph. "Survival Is Your Business: Engineering Ruins and Affect in Nuclear America." *Cultural Anthropology* 23, no. 2 (May 2008): 361–98.

McClintock, Anne. *Imperial Leather: Race, Gender, and Sexuality in the Colonial Contest*. New York: Routledge, 1995.

McPherson, C. B. *The Political Theory of Possessive Individualism: Hobbes to Locke*. Oxford: Oxford University Press, 2011.

Melamed, Jodi. *Represent and Destroy: Rationalizing Violence in the New Racial Capitalism*. Minneapolis: University of Minnesota Press, 2011.

Melas, Natalie. *All the Difference in the World: Postcoloniality and the Ends of Comparison*. Stanford, CA: Stanford University Press, 2006.

Mill, John Stuart. *The Collected Works of John Stuart Mill*. Vols. 9 and 18. Edited by J. M. Robson. Toronto: University Toronto Press; London: Routledge and Kegan Paul, 1963–91.

Mille Lacs v. Minnesota. 526 U.S. 172 (1999).

Miller, Douglas K. *Indians on the Move: Native American Mobility and Urbanization in the Twentieth Century*. Chapel Hill: University of North Carolina Press, 2019.

Minneapolis Society of Fine Arts. *Bulletin of the Minneapolis Institute of Arts* 3, no. 10 (October 1914).

Minnesota Pollution Control Agency. "State Superfund Site Summaries." Accessed October 29, 2021. https://www.pca.state.mn.us/waste/state-superfund-site-summaries.

Mitchell, W. J. T. "Imperial Landscape." In *Landscape and Power*, edited by W. J. T Mitchell, 5–34. Chicago: University of Chicago Press, 2002.

Mithlo, Nancy Marie. *Knowing Native Arts*. Lincoln: University of Nebraska Press, 2016.

Morris, Glenn T. "International Law and Politics: Toward a Right to Self-Determination for Indigenous Peoples." In *The State of Native America: Genocide, Colonization, and Resistance*, edited by M. Annette Jaimes, 23–37. Boston: South End, 1992.

Morrison, George, and Margot Fortunato Galt. *Turning the Feather Around*. St. Paul: Minnesota Historical Society, 1998.

Moscufo, Michela. "For These Indigenous Artists 'Land Back' Is Both a Political Message and a Fundraising Opportunity." *Forbes*. September 29, 2020. https://www.forbes.com/sites/michelamoscufo/2020/09/29/for-these-indigenous-artists-land-back-is-both-a-political-message-and-a-fundraising-opportunity/?sh=5747daf26c9c.

Moten, Fred, and Stefano Harney. *The Undercommons: Fugitive Planning and Black Study*. New York: Minor Compositions, 2013.

Moyn, Samuel. *Not Enough: Human Rights in an Unequal World*. Cambridge, MA: Belknap Press of Harvard University Press, 2019.

National Congress of the American Indian. *VAWA 2013's Special Domestic Violence Criminal Jurisdiction Five-Year Report*. March 20, 2018.

Nemser, Dan. *Infrastructures of Race: Concentration and Biopolitics in Colonial Mexico*. Austin: University of Texas Press, 2017.

Nevada v. Hicks. 533 U.S. 353 (2001).

Nixon, Rob. *Slow Violence and the Environmentalism of the Poor*. Cambridge, MA: Harvard University Press, 2011.

O'Brien, Jean M. *Firsting and Lasting: Writing Indians Out of Existence in New England*. Minneapolis: University of Minnesota Press, 2010.

O'Brien, Jean M. "Tracing Settler Colonialism's Eliminatory Logic in *Traces of History*." *American Quarterly* 69, no. 2 (June 2017): 249–55.

Pexa, Christopher. *Translated Nation: Rewriting the Dakhóta Oyáte*. Minneapolis: University of Minnesota Press, 2019.

Philp, Kenneth R. "Dillon S. Myer and the Advent of Termination: 1950–1953." *Western Historical Quarterly* 19, no. 1 (January 1988): 37–59.

Philp, Kenneth R. "Stride toward Freedom: The Relocation of Indians to Cities, 1952–1960." *Western Historical Quarterly* 16, no. 2 (April 1985): 182–83.

Piatote, Beth. *Domestic Subjects: Gender, Citizenship, and Law in Native American Literature*. New Haven, CT: Yale University Press, 2013.

Pleck, Elizabeth. "Wife Beating in Nineteenth-Century America." In *Household Constitution and Family Relationships*, edited by Nancy Cotter, 189–203. Berlin: De Gruyter, 1992.

Povinelli, Elizabeth. *Geontologies: A Requiem to Late Liberalism*. Durham, NC: Duke University Press, 2016.

Prucha, Francis Paul. *The Great Father: The United States Government and the American Indians*. Lincoln: University of Nebraska Press, 1986.

Pulido, Laura. "Rethinking Environmental Racism: White Privilege and Urban Development in Southern California." *Annals of the Association of American Geographers* 90, no. 1 (March 2000): 12–40.

Ramirez, Renya. *Native Hubs: Culture, Community, and Belonging in Silicon Valley and Beyond*. Durham, NC: Duke University Press, 2007.

Rancière, Jacques. *Dissensus: On Politics and Aesthetics*. Edited and translated by Steven Corcoran. New York: Bloomsbury Academic, 2015.

Rancière, Jacques. *The Politics of Aesthetics: The Distribution of the Sensible*. Translated by Gabriel Rockhill. New York: Continuum, 2000.

Ransom, John Carlos. *Afterlives of Modernism: Liberalism, Transnationalism, and Political Critique*. Hanover, NH: Dartmouth College Press, 2011.

Rasmussen, Birgit Brander. *Queequeg's Coffin: Indigenous Literacies and Early American Literature*. Durham, NC: Duke University Press, 2012.

Raster, Amanda, and Christina Gish Hill. "The Dispute over Wild Rice: An Investigation of Treaty Agreements and Ojibwe Food Sovereignty." *Agriculture and Human Values* 34, no. 2 (2016): 267–81.

Romero, Lora. *Home Fronts: Domesticity and Its Critics in the Antebellum United States*. Durham, NC: Duke University Press, 1997.

Roy, Anaya. *City Requiem: Gender and the Politics of Poverty*. Minneapolis: University of Minnesota Press, 2002.

Roy, Anaya, and Aihwa Ong. *Worlding Cities: Asian Experiments and the Art of Being Global*. Malden, MA: Wiley Blackwell, 2011.

Rushing, W. Jackson, III. "Modern Spirits: The Legacy of Allan Houser and George Morrison." In *Essays on Native Modernism: Complexity and Contradiction in American Indian Art*, 53–68. Washington, DC: National Museum of the American Indian, 2006.

Rushing, W. Jackson, III, and Kristin Makholm. *Modern Spirit: The Art of George Morrison*. Norman: University of Oklahoma Press, 2013.

Said, Edward. *Culture and Imperialism*. New York: Vintage, 1994.

"Sandy Lake Tragedy and Memorial." Great Lakes Indian Fish and Wildlife Commission. Accessed October 18, 2021. https://glifwc.org/publications/pdf/SandyLake_Brochure.pdf.

Schenck, Theresa. "Introduction." In William Whipple Warren, *History of the Ojibway People*, 2nd ed., edited by Theresa Schenck, vii–xxiv. St. Paul: Minnesota Historical Society, 2009.

Schenck, Theresa. *William W. Warren: The Life and Times of an Ojibwe Leader*. Lincoln: University of Nebraska Press, 2007.

Schoolcraft, Henry Rowe. *History of the Indians Tribes of the United States: Their Present Condition and Prospects, and a Sketch of Their Ancient Status*. Philadelphia: J. B. Lippincott, 1857.

Scott, James C. *Domination and the Arts of Resistance: Hidden Transcripts*. New Haven, CT: Yale University Press, 1990.

Scott, James C. *Seeing Like a State: How Certain Schemes to Improve the Human Condition Have Failed*. New Haven, CT: Yale University Press, 1998.

Sexton, Jared. "The Vel of Slavery: Tracking the Figure of the Unsovereign." *Critical Sociology* 42, nos. 4–5 (2014): 583–97.

Siegel, Reva B. "'The Rule of Love': Wife Beating as Prerogative and Privacy." *Yale Law Journal* (June 1996): 2117–207.

Simpson, Audra. *Mohawk Interruptus: Political Life across the Borders of Settler States*. Durham, NC: Duke University Press, 2014.

Simpson, Leanne Betasamosake. "The Place Where We All Live and Work Together: A Gendered Analysis of 'Sovereignty.'" In *Native Studies Keywords*, edited by Stephanie Nohelani Teves, Andrea Smith, and Michelle Raheja, 18–24. Tucson: University of Arizona Press, 2015.

Smith, Andrea. "American Studies without America: Native Feminisms and the Nation-State." *American Quarterly* 6, no. 2 (2008): 309–15.

South Minneapolis Residential Soil Contamination. *United States Environmental Protection Agency*. Accessed June 1, 2021. https://cumulis.epa.gov/supercpad/SiteProfiles/index.cfm?fuseaction=second.cleanup&id=0509136.

Spence, Mark David. *Dispossessing Wilderness: Indian Removal and the Making of the National Parks*. Oxford: Oxford University Press, 2000.

Spillers, Hortense. "Mama's Baby, Papa's Maybe: An American Grammar Book." *Diacritics* 17, no. 2 (Summer 1987): 64–81.

Spivak, Gayatri. "Ghostwriting." *Diacritics* 25, no. 2 (Summer 1995): 64–84.

Star, Susan Leigh. "The Ethnography of Infrastructure." *American Behavioral Scientist* 43, no. 3 (November–December 1999): 377–91.

State of Minnesota v. Keezer. 292 N.W.2d 714 (Minn. 1980).

State of Minnesota v. United States. 125 F.2d 636 (Eighth Cir. 1942).

Stoler, Ann Laura. *Duress: Imperial Durabilities in Our Times*. Durham, NC: Duke University Press, 2013.

Szeman, Imre, and Dominic Boyer, eds. *Energy Humanities: An Anthology*. Baltimore, MD: Johns Hopkins University Press, 2015.

TallBear, Kim. "Beyond the Life/Not-Life Binary: A Feminist-Indigenous Reading of Cryopreservation, Interspecies Thinking, and the New Materialisms." In *Cryopolitics: Frozen Life in a Melting World*, edited by Joanna Radin and Emma Kowal, 198–99. Cambridge, MA: MIT Press, 2017.

TallBear, Kim. *Native American DNA: Tribal Belonging and the Fall Promise of Genetic Science*. Minneapolis: University of Minnesota Press, 2013.

Taylor, Dorceta E. *Toxic Communities: Environmental Racism, Industrial Pollution, and Residential Mobility*. New York: New York University Press, 2014.

Teuton, Sean. "Cities of Refuge: Indigenous Cosmopolitan Writers and the International Imaginary." *American Literary History* 25, no. 1 (Spring 2013): 33–53.

Teuton, Sean. "Internationalism and the American Indian Scholar: Native Studies and the Challenge of Pan-Indigenism." In *Identity Politics Reconsidered*, edited by Linda Martín Alcoff, Michael Hames-García, Satya P. Mohanty, and Paula M. L. Moya, 264–28. New York: Palgrave Macmillan, 2006.

Todd, Zoe. "Indigenizing the Anthropocene." In *Art in the Anthropocene: Encounters among Aesthetics, Politics, Environments, and Epistemologies*, edited by Heather Davis and Etienne Turpin, 241–54. London: Open Humanities, 2014.

Treaty with the Chippewa. 7 Stat., 290, August 5, 1826.

Treaty with the Chippewa. 7 Stat., 536, July 29, 1837.

Treaty with the Sioux, etc. 7 Stat., 272, Article 13, August 19, 1825.

Treuer, David. *The Hiawatha*. New York: Picador, 1999.

Trouillot, Michel-Rolph. *Silencing the Past: Power and the Production of History*. Boston: Beacon, 1995.

Tuck, Eve, and K. Wayne Yang. "Decolonization Is Not a Metaphor." *Decolonization: Indigeneity, Education & Society* 1, no. 1 (2012): 1–40.

Two Pines Resource Group. "Native American Context Statement and Reconnaissance Level Survey Supplement." Prepared for the City of Minneapolis Department of Community Planning & Economic Development, July 2016.

U.S. v. 4,450.72 Acres of Land. 27 F. Supp. 167 (D. Minn. 1939).

U.S. v. Kagama. 118 U.S. 375, 6 S. Ct. 1109, 30 L. Ed. 228.

U.S. v. Santa Fe Railroad. 314 U.S. 339 (1941).

U.S. v. Winans. 198 U.S. 371 (1905).

Valentine, Rand. "Verbal Artistry of 'Sun and Moon.'" *Oshkaabewis Native Journal* 4, no. 1 (Spring 1997): 63-120.

Vennum, Thomas, Jr. *Wild Rice and the Ojibway People*. St. Paul: Minnesota Historical Society, 1988.

Vimalassery, Manu, Juliana Hu Pegues, and Alyosha Goldstein. "Colonial Unknowing and Relations of Study." *Theory and Event* 20, no. 4 (2017): 1042-54.

Vizenor, Gerald. *Fugitive Poses: Native American Scenes of Absence and Presence*. Lincoln: University of Nebraska Press, 1998.

Vizenor, Gerald. "George Morrison: Anishinaabe Expressionist Artist." *American Indian Quarterly* 30, nos. 3-4 (2006): 646-60.

Vizenor, Gerald. "Native Transmotion." In *Fugitive Poses: Native American Scenes of Absence and Presence*, 145-66. Lincoln: University of Nebraska Press, 1998.

Vizenor, Gerald, and Jill Doerfler. *The White Earth Nation: Ratification of a Native Democratic Constitution*. Lincoln: University of Nebraska Press, 2012.

Voyles, Traci Brynne. *Wastelanding: Legacies of Uranium in Navajo Country*. Minneapolis: University of Minnesota Press, 2015.

Walkowitz, Rebecca, and Douglas Mao. "The New Modernist Studies." *PMLA* 123, no. 3 (May 2008): 737-48.

Warren, William Whipple. *History of the Ojibway People*, 2nd ed. Edited by Theresa Schenck. St. Paul: Minnesota Historical Society, 2009.

Warrior, Robert. *People and the Word: Reading Native Nonfiction*. Minneapolis: University of Minnesota Press, 2005.

Warrior, Robert. *Tribal Secrets: Vine Deloria, John Joseph Mathews, and the Recovery of American Indian Intellectual Traditions*. Minneapolis: University of Minnesota Press, 1994.

Ward v. Race Horse. 163 U.S. 504 (1896).

Waziyatawin. *What Does Justice Look Like? The Struggle for Liberation in Dakota Homeland*. St. Paul, MN: Living Justice Press, 2008.

Weaver, Jace, Craig Womack, and Robert Warrior. *American Indian Literary Nationalism*. Albuquerque: University of New Mexico Press, 2006.

Weizman, Eyal. *Forensic Architecture: Violence at the Threshold of Detectability*. New York: Zone Books, 2017.

Wexler, Laura. *Tender Violence: Domestic Visions in an Age of U.S. Imperialism*. Chapel Hill: University of North Carolina Press, 2000.

White Earth Band of Chippewa Indians. Resolution No. 001-19-009, 2018.

Whyte, Kyle, Chris Caldwell, and Marie Schaefer. "Indigenous Lessons about Sustainability Are Not Just for 'All Humanity.'" In *Sustainability: Approaches to Environmental Justice and Social Power*, edited by Julie Sze, 149-79. New York: New York University Press, 2018.

Wilderson, Frank B., III. "Gramsci's Black Marx: Whither the Slave in Civil Society?" *Social Identities* 9, no. 2 (2003): 225–40.

Wilderson, Frank B., III. *Incognegro: A Memoir of Exile and Apartheid*. Durham, NC: Duke University Press, 2015.

Wilderson, Frank B., III. *Red, White, and Black: Cinema and the Structure of U.S. Antagonisms*. Durham, NC: Duke University Press, 2010.

Williams, Raymond. *The Country and the City*. New York: Oxford University Press, 1973.

Williams, Raymond. *Culture and Society: 1750–1950*. Garden City, NY: Anchor, 1960.

Willse, Craig. *The Value of Homelessness: Managing Surplus Life in the United States*. Minneapolis: University of Minnesota Press, 2015.

Wolfe, Patrick. "Settler Colonialism and the Elimination of the Native." *Journal of Genocide Research* 8, no. 4 (December 2006): 387–409.

Worcester v. Georgia. 31 U.S. 515 (1832).

Wynter, Sylvia. "Unsettling the Coloniality of Being/Power/Truth/Freedom: Towards the Human, After Man, Its Overrepresentation—An Argument." *CR: The New Centennial Review* 3, no. 3 (Fall 2003): 257–337.

Index